Advance Praise for *Pro-Child Politics*

"A strange thing happens when you examine every cultural, economic, and national issue through the lens of child protection. You end up with conservatism. But not rigid or academic conservatism. Conservatism that speaks about who we are for, not what we are against. *Pro-Child Politics* is not only good for kids, but smart policy."

—Mollie Hemmingway, Editor-in-chief at
the *Federalist*

"We have utterly forsaken children in every area of life which is why my wife and I have dedicated our lives to ending policies that harm children. Our nation will crumble completely if we don't make this the fight of our lives. *Pro-Child Politics* lays out the pro-active case of the what, when, and who of child defense. The answers? Engaging every area of politics, every pillar of culture and defending every segment of childhood innocence."

—Robby Starbuck, Director of
The War on Children

T0283113

"Katy Faust is doing God's work, leading a movement that puts children first, where they belong. *Pro-Child Politics* offers a blueprint for success for any political party that understands that happy healthy children are the key to a successful society. If you really want to change the world, prioritize the welfare of children over the desires of adults."

—Miranda Devine, *New York Post* columnist

"There is no issue more vital to a nation than the moral, emotional, and spiritual wellbeing of its children. Civilizations rise and fall on the formation of future generations. And as the contributors of *Pro-Child Politics* show, the policy decisions the United States made yesterday is wreaking terrible costs on the children of today. But it is possible to turn back and restore America's bright future prospects through politics that protect the most vulnerable citizens among us—our kids. This book not only explains how children are victimized when we get politics wrong, but how elevating children can make things right again—for all our sakes."

—Megan Basham, Daily Wire Culture Reporter and Author of *Shepherds for Sale*

"Jesus makes it known in the gospel of Matthew that not only are we to protect children, we are to become like children in their innocence, goodness, and wonder. *Pro-Child Politics* addresses the fundamental dual flaws in modern society—our failure to both defend and identify with the needs of children. As adults, we quickly become self-interested, and politicians are no different, often taking care of their own best interests before those they are meant to represent, particularly those who cannot advocate for themselves. *Pro-Child Politics* offers a different perspective, a better perspective, putting the children first. A world that looks at politics through the lens of a child would not have closed schools or churches during the covid lockdown, would not be encouraging the surgical mutilation and chemical castration of children suffering gender dysphoria, and would not be enabling mass immigration which victimizes both native and immigrant children.

"A pro-child politics is a better politics."

—Fr Calvin Robinson, Priest and Broadcaster

"You don't have to look far to realize our world has been turned wrong side out and this upheaval exacts the greatest toll on our children. We need guidance so that we that know better, and can do better. *Pro-Child Politics* is a compilation of compelling and expert voices that call us back to sanity and away from the cultural mire threatening to overwhelm our children and grandchildren. You are going to want a copy for every concerned friend you know."

—Lisa Bevere, *New York Times*
Bestselling Author

"This is a vitally important resource to understand the most critical and fundamental issue of our time: the rights of the defenseless children among us. In a day when parental rights are eroded by and abdicated to the state, it is incumbent upon every adult to stand firm for children's rights. *Pro-Child Politics* equips the only people talking—adults— to represent the genuine interests of children on every major political issue. If we really want to be a moral and upright society, we have to take this seriously."

—Jenna Ellis, American Family Association

Also by Katy Faust

*Raising Conservative Kids in a Woke City: Teaching Historical,
Economic, and Biological Truth in a World of Lies with Stacy Manning*

*Them Before Us: Why We Need a Global Children's
Rights Movement with Stacy Manning*

PRO-CHILD POLITICS

**WHY EVERY CULTURAL, ECONOMIC, AND NATIONAL
ISSUE IS A MATTER OF JUSTICE FOR CHILDREN**

PRO-CHILD POLITICS

WHY EVERY CULTURAL, ECONOMIC, AND NATIONAL ISSUE IS A MATTER OF JUSTICE FOR CHILDREN

EDITED BY KATY FAUST

Post Hill
PRESS

A POST HILL PRESS BOOK
ISBN: 979-8-88845-708-5
ISBN (eBook): 979-8-88845-709-2

Pro-Child Politics:
Why Every Cultural, Economic, and National Issue Is a Matter of Justice for Children
© 2024 by Katy Faust
All Rights Reserved

Cover design by Christian Watson

All book proceeds will go to Them Before Us, a 501c3 nonprofit.

Post Hill Press
New York • Nashville
posthillpress.com

Published in the United States of America
1 2 3 4 5 6 7 8 9 10

"Do it for the children."
They say it, we're doing it.

TABLE OF CONTENTS

ECONOMIC

NATIONAL

INTRODUCTION

Kids come last.

In matters of culture and politics, the well-being of children never tops the list.

This lack of child prioritization was on full display during the COVID lockdowns. We knew early on that the virus wasn't a threat to most children, and that kids were not major vectors of COVID-19 transmission.[1] We nevertheless sacrificed children's physical, mental, and emotional health in the name of "stopping the spread." The results were as predictable as they were avoidable. Shutting down youth sports, removing basketball hoops from public parks, and filling skate parks with sand in the name of "social distancing" has contributed to skyrocketing rates of child obesity.[2] Some kids, especially the poor and marginalized, may never recover their educational losses after yearslong school closures. Our youngest children, deprived of normal human interaction due to masking and distancing during critical stages of development, battle speech and language delays. Despite evidence that screen-addicted children were struggling to engage with the real world, we forced them into "online learning," aka screen-required "education" for eight hours a day. The increased screen time during lockdowns has yet to drop.[3] The already sky-high rates of depression and suicide climbed further. Rates of overdose, self-harm, substance use, and claims for depression and anxiety disorders[4] rose precipitously[5] amid state-enforced peer isolation.

How could we visit such devastation on our children? The ugly answer is because it served adults.

Teachers claimed their students were potentially deadly and refused to teach in-person to "[protect] their health or even [their] lives."[6] Unions[7] that lobbied for extended school closures[8] received much more money and much less accountability for their actions.[9] Public-service announcements instructed kids to stay home, not because it was good for *them*, but because it was good for Grandma.[10] Journalist David Leonhardt[11] succinctly described our pandemic response: "more harm to children in exchange for less harm to adults." In short, we made kids sacrifice on our behalf.

If only COVID lockdowns were the singular example of adults putting their interests before the needs of children. Parents regularly sacrifice for their children and put them first, as natural bonds often dictate. But beyond the home, there's really no area in our society broadly, whether politics, culture, or economics, where we prioritize what is best for children. For example,

- Forcing our children and grandchildren to pay for our mismanaged, superficial spending projects in the form of crushing *taxes* and *debt*
- *Environmental* policy that elevates the value of dead trees over living children
- Distorting the most fundamental aspects of children's identities, whether *race, gender, masculinity, femininity,* or *religious convictions,* to advance ever-changing ideological narratives
- Destroying the *family* bond a child has to his mother or father in service to an adult who desires a child

- *Economic policies* that favor foreign businesses and foreign governments above children's living standards
- Violation of children's right to *life* at the hands of the baby-making and baby-taking industries
- Unserious *immigration* and *foreign policy* that result in a weaker, less secure country for future generations
- An *educational system* that elevates adult employment over student achievement
- Favoring adult access to *digital technology* and *pornography* above child development and child protection
- "Green" *energy* subsidization that makes poor children poorer
- Deluded *policing* policies that put children's lives and safety at risk
- Robbing children's opportunities and innocence to advance corporate environmental, social and governance *(ESG)* scores

When we prioritize adult desires and agendas, we force children to shoulder a load that we adults are unwilling to bear. When adults refuse to do hard things, we transfer the responsibility to our children and grandchildren, allowing their problems to multiply exponentially. Preference for our immediate comfort has made it much harder for the next generation to deal with debt, national security, open borders, economics untethered to fiscal reality, distorted human identity, and invasive technologies. By shirking the responsibility of addressing the problems when they were smaller, we adults become the perpetrators of grave intergenerational injustice.

Children are the only demographic that would accept such a "you pay the lifelong price for my irresponsibility and misbehavior" trade. Anyone else would put up a fight and decry the injustice. A demographic with a voice would remove the powerful from office, open investigations, and sue you for dereliction of duty.

But kids can't fight back. They can't defend their own rights, hire lawyers, lobby, submit amicus briefs, go on strike, or vote. Children depend entirely on the advocacy of adults. And the current crop of adults has refused to stand up for them. We've failed to perform our most fundamental duty of protecting the weak. The result is insecure, confused, broken children, and an insecure, confused, broken nation.

The question we address in this book is, "What if we put children first?"

What exactly would it look like to put them (the children) before us (the adults)? How could our society improve if we considered their rights, needs, and well-being before our own? I daresay that we would have secure, healthy, thriving children, and by extension a secure, healthy, thriving nation as well.

I have been actively advocating for the rights of children above adult desires since 2018. My nonprofit, Them Before Us, is dedicated to defending each child's right to his or her mother and father. But the reality is, children are being victimized in domains far beyond the family.

The tagline for *Pro-Child Politics* is "Why every cultural, economic, and national issue is a matter of justice for children." "Justice" is classically defined as "giving others what they are due." But these days, we are far from *giving* children what they are due, what they deserve. Rather, we are *taking* from children. Taking, or more accurately *stealing*, their identity, their security, their potential, their opportunities, their health, their resources, their innocence, their money, their future, their families, and sometimes even their lives.

In every area of politics, we are committing *injustice* against children. We adults—the strong—are committing a generational crime against the weak: children. It's high time to apply the *them* before *us* perspective to every cultural, economic, and national issue.

I alone cannot tell you how to do that. I may be an authority on marriage, modern families, reproductive technologies, adoption and surrogacy, but I'm no expert on policing, religious liberty, ESG, national security, or energy. The good news is, I know the people who are. And you are about to know them as well.

The contributors in this book are authorities on their issues. You will be treated to the chairman of Promise Keeper's take on masculinity. The founder of Moms for Liberty will detail the pitfalls of the US education system. The architect of the nearly forty-year-old Taxpayer Protection Pledge explains how high taxes hurt families and children. The man who has become a walking billboard declaring "children cannot consent to puberty blockers" will explain the dangers of the transgender movement. A veteran of the law firm renowned for defending religious liberty before the Supreme Court will explain why our first freedom is a matter of justice for children. These authors are experts *and* groundbreakers in their respective fields.

Each contributor has masterfully distilled immense topics into one chapter. Each chapter transforms often complex issues into something understandable, tangible and actionable. They share stories of real-life children who've been harmed because we've failed to focus on these perpetual issues with a child-centric gaze. The authors highlight the most damaging counternarratives of their subject and explain how those lies harm kids; they then identify the truth and detail how those truths protect kids. They finish with real-world examples of how to change hearts and laws in favor of children.

This book not only offers a child-centric understanding of all these critical topics, it tells you who you can trust when you need more information. You may find you need more than three thousand words to understand what's happening in the realm of environmental policy. If so, you can check out the American Conservation

Coalition, whose president penned our environment chapter. If you're hungry for more information about femininity, there's good news! Peachy Keenan wrote a whole book about it. If you want more details on how to protect kids from online pornography, the American Principles Project, for which Jon Schweppe is policy director, has everything you need to know.

There probably isn't another title at Amazon or on your shelf that covers both race and foreign policy, both masculinity and energy, both border security and digital technology. You can't come up with nineteen more diverse topics than the ones you will find in the following pages. But each chapter has one overarching truth: when we believe the political lies, children are victimized.

Pro-child politics require every adult to prioritize the rights and well-being of children above their self-interest. This means thinking beyond the effect of ideas and policy on the GDP, adult emotional fulfillment, or DEI scores. Our first question on every topic should be "What about the child?" How will this bill or cultural trend or international agreement advance children's interests, needs, and rights? And if the answer is "It won't," then we must stand against it.

In every area of politics, someone is going to have to sacrifice. For years, we have insisted that children sacrifice for adults. That has to change. It's time to put them before us.

CULTURAL

ABBY JOHNSON

It was dark most of the time. Warm. He was happy there. He had only been alive for thirteen weeks. He could feel his heart beating, and he had just learned how to swallow. His mother's name was Sarah. She knew about him. Well, she didn't know he was a boy, but she knew he was there.

His mother had plans and he was not part of them. She was in college. She wanted to be a doctor. She had a vacation planned with her friends. She just did not want him right now. It wasn't a good time. She made her choice. She called the clinic and made the appointment.

When his mother walked in on that Saturday, she was wearing sweatpants and a sweatshirt. The receptionist on the phone had told her to wear something comfortable. They called Sarah's name and the baby's world got brighter under the harsh examining room lights. He felt her lie down as she leaned back on the hard but padded table.

He heard someone walk in. He heard whirring.

Suddenly, it was not warm anymore. His heart was beating faster and faster. He didn't feel happy anymore. Was this fear? Is that what he was feeling? Everything was so new to him. He only knew happiness. The surrounding softness was broken. He tried to move away. A new sensation. Pain. He felt something poking his body. Now, nothingness. His body was twisting and turning like clothes in a washing machine. Piece by piece, his body was torn out of his mother's womb.

I never touched that baby, knew his name, or said a word to him. But I watched him die, live, via ultrasound.

At the time, I was the clinic director at Planned Parenthood, the country's largest abortion provider. But watching that child recoil and try to escape the abortion doctor's baby vacuum made me question all of the lies we've been told about life.

▬ BIG LIES ABOUT LIFE

Lie #1: We Don't Know When Life Begins.

"The embryo is clearly prehuman," writes Leonard Peikoff for the pro-choice Ayn Rand Institute. "Only the mystical notions of religious dogma treat this clump of cells as constituting a person."[1]

"[L]ife begins at conception" is a religious, not scientific, concept" writes Dr. Richard J. Paulson for the American Society of Reproductive Medicine. "We, who dedicate our lives to helping patients achieve pregnancies and build their families, know that we do *not* create life in the laboratory. We do not witness a human death when an embryo fails to survive cryopreservation. We observe the continuous nature of human life, with fertilization representing only one key step…"[2]

"It's just a clump of cells. If you get it early enough it doesn't even look like a baby."—Planned Parenthood receptionist.[3]

One of the greatest lies of the life debate is the debate over when life actually begins. Not surprisingly, doctors in both the abortion industry and in vitro fertilization (IVF) industry have an interest in obscuring the scientific origins of life. Why is that? Leonard Peikoff, quoted above, tells us why.

"[A]bortion rights advocates keep hiding behind the phrase 'a woman's right to choose.' Does she have the right to choose murder? That's what abortion would be, if the fetus were a person. The status of the embryo in the first trimester is the basic issue that cannot be sidestepped."

What this self-identified "objectivist" means is that life's beginning is subjective, because pro-abortion advocates *need* to believe that a tiny baby isn't a life to uphold their political and ethical priors. Those whose business involves the taking of little lives—of which both abortion and IVF are a part—need life to begin at some point *other* than conception. Because if it does, that would hinder their business that, as we will see, consumes hundreds of thousands of little lives annually.

Lie #2: A Child's Right to Life Depends on "Wantedness."

The other part of that lie is reflected in how differently people respond to pregnancy based on whether or not the child is wanted. If wanted, it's a baby deserving of protection. If it's unwanted, it's just a "fetus," which can be discarded. It's a nonsensical position. That's like saying a book lying on your bookshelf isn't a book until you pick it up and read it.

Do you remember when your mom was pregnant with your little brother or sister? Or maybe it was an aunt or a friend of your family that was expecting a baby. Maybe you attended a baby shower where the mom to be was given presents for her baby: a crib, baby clothes, and adorable stuffed animals.

I bet you didn't go to a "fetus shower," though. No mom who is excited to have her baby calls it a fetus, even though that's the scientific name for a baby growing inside a woman's uterus. A woman who is pregnant and plans to have her baby will always refer to that growing child as a "baby." Why? Well, because that's what it is, of course—it's a growing baby, a unique human being that is just as much of a human as you are, just younger and smaller.

What about babies that are growing in their mother's womb who won't be allowed to make it to birth? They are often referred to as "fetuses" because they are unwanted. Their right to life isn't protected because their parents don't want them.

If you believe this lie, then if children are *unwanted*, you can violate their right to life and force them *out of existence* through abortion. It also means that if a child is *very wanted*, you can violate some child's right to life or right to their mother and father and force them *into existence* through technologies like IVF, sperm and egg donation, and surrogacy.

Lie #3: Abortion Is Wrong, But IVF Is Good.

The lie that "a baby isn't a baby until it's wanted" is the kind of lie that snowballs into countless others, leaving a tragic mess in its wake. Wantedness doesn't determine our value. Our value and our dignity are determined at the moment of our conception. It's a dignity that applies to babies made the old-fashioned way (sex) and babies made the new-fashioned way, through IVF.

IVF means "in vitro fertilization," that is, fertilizing a human egg "in vitro" or in glass. Basically, making babies in a Petri dish. About 2 percent of babies born in the US today are products of IVF. But many more babies created via IVF are never given the chance to be born at all.

How the story is told is that a husband and wife want to have children but cannot seem to conceive a baby. So the husband and wife pay a scientist to make an embryo, aka baby, in a lab with the wife's egg and the husband's sperm. Then they implant the embryo into the biological mother. But not *all* the embryos. The fertility clinic will encourage them to discard the babies who aren't "viable" or don't make the grade or who are the wrong sex. If they aren't discarded, they're donated to research or frozen forever. The result is 92–97 percent of IVF babies will not be born alive.[4] By the numbers, fertility clinics destroy more embryonic life each year than Planned Parenthood.[5]

Lie #4: "My Body, My Choice."

Have you seen pictures in the news of women holding up these signs outside abortion clinics or at protests? The slogan *"My body, my choice"* refers to a woman's decision to have an abortion, which is the intentional killing of her unborn baby by pills or surgery. She believes that she has every right to do so because she should be alk-abouts. Last accessed May 30, 2024. https://www.walkabouts.com able to make decisions about her own body.

It's a talking point repeated by celebrities everywhere.

- "I stand with the women ...everywhere, who have the right to decide what happens to their bodies, as we all do." Ellen DeGeneres
- "Women should say, should do and feel and be exactly what they want. There should be nobody else telling them how to live their life, how to do [s----].... Men should not make women's choices—that's all I have to say." Billie Eilish
- "This whole abortion law thing in America is a mess, I mean you're completely taking away the rights of women and the ownership of the bodies that belong to them." Liam Payne[6]

I agree. Women should certainly be able to make decisions about their bodies. The problem is, when it comes to baby-making or baby-taking, there's more than just the woman's body involved.

Conception—either in vitro or in the flesh—creates a new human being. The baby does rely on his/her mother's body to grow and develop during the first nine months. However, that growing baby has his/her own body. He or she is not a new organ of his or her mother's own body: he/she has their own heart, lungs, legs, arms, head, and hands. If the baby is unwanted, the mother isn't deciding to remove a kidney or her appendix. When she decides to have an abortion, she's not the one dead at the end of the procedure.

It's not her body, but thanks to contemporary law, it is her choice. She should not have that choice. *No one* should have that choice.

HOW THESE LIES HARM CHILDREN

Most human rights abuses rely on dehumanizing a certain people group; think about the "animalistic subhuman" label for Blacks during chattel slavery, or the Holocaust where Jews were regarded as an "illness spreading parasite."[7] Snuffing out the life of the unborn does too. That's why we say "fetus" instead of "baby," why we say "they aren't real children yet" or "life doesn't begin until birth."

These lies have real-world consequences. In 2023, 1,026,690 babies were aborted in the United States.[8] That's like wiping out the entire state of Delaware. When millions of women believe the lie that they are entitled to end their babies' lives, and choose that option, millions of babies die. This lie has resulted in more than sixty million deaths through abortion over the last fifty years.[9] That's almost one-fifth of the population of our country.

Believing lies about life is not only harmful to babies, but harmful to women, both physically and emotionally. The physical risks of abortion include hemorrhage (excessive bleeding), infection, retained parts of the baby left in the woman's womb, sepsis (very serious infection), loss of fertility (the ability to have children), risk of breast cancer, and even death. The emotional consequences include an increased risk of depression, anxiety, and suicide.

But it's not just the abortion industry that is victimizing children. IVF routinely creates many more embryos than the couple would ever implant or raise, about fifteen embryos—each a tiny human being—for every cycle. If the baby is *not* donated to research or thrown out for being the wrong sex or having some kind of defect, most of them will be suspended in frigid orphanages. IVF has resulted in about 1.5 million "surplus" embryos sitting in frozen storage.[10]

Even if that embryo is one of the lucky few who is not frozen or donated to research, they are still at risk. If the IVF baby is found to have a disability, the husband and wife may choose abortion so they don't have a disabled baby. Abortion is even more common if that baby was implanted into someone else's womb—a surrogate. Now you've not only paid the $15,000–$20,000 for IVF but the $100,000 for the use of another woman's body. When someone is playing six figures for a baby, they want exactly what they ordered. Abortion clauses are included in many surrogacy contracts for that very reason.[11]

But it's not just the *life* of the child at risk with IVF. It's their relationship with their own mom and dad as well. Once we figured out how to make babies in laboratories, we weren't limited to using only the husband's and wife's gametes. Now we can use a stranger's sperm or egg to make a baby. In fact, "intended parents" can browse online catalogs to shop for their child's mother or father. They can design a baby based on race, education, hair color, eye color, and filter them just like filtering search results for a shirt they plan to wear to their sister's baby shower. If these children *are* one of the 2 percent to 7 percent who make it through IVF alive, they will grow up being denied a relationship with their biological mother or father.[12]

It's a consumer world. And both the baby-taking industry and the baby-making industry are happy to accommodate. You order a baby and you order the shirt. You are unhappy with the baby; you are unhappy with the shirt. What's the difference?

Obviously, the difference is massive. A baby is a created human being with infinite value. Many such unique lives are ended because they are valued to the extent that they're wanted—like a piece of merchandise. Fertility services, especially surrogacy, encourage this way of thinking by treating children as disposable designer products.

The stakes are very high for babies in their tiniest forms, and each year, lies about life result in the destruction of a heartbreaking number of innocent children.

▉ THE TRUTH ABOUT LIFE

Truth #1: Life Begins at Conception.

When conception happens, that is, when the sperm from the man is joined with a woman's egg, an entirely new human being is created. Scientifically, this is the beginning of life. That's an objective reality made irrefutable by modern ultrasound technology.

When *Roe* was first passed, it was easier to believe that the pregnancy was just an undeveloped blob of cells. Now thanks to ultrasound, we can now see three- and four-dimensional images of babies in their mothers' wombs. We watch those little hands and feet, and see these unborn children suck their thumbs. That's how I learned that life in the womb existed, and that a woman was pregnant with a baby and not just a "clump of tissue" like maybe you've heard people say.

Doctors have even performed surgeries on babies inside of their mother's wombs. There is a famous photo from 1999 by photographer Michael Clancy that showed a twenty-one-week-old baby named Samuel grasping the hand of the surgeon who was attempting to fix his spina bifida in utero.[13] A "clump of tissue" didn't grab the doctor's hand. A living baby did.

The reality is, we do know when life begins—at conception, when the sperm and egg join. It's both miraculous and simple. A new life gets half its DNA from its mother and half from its father. At that moment, a new genetic blueprint appears, sex is determined, blood type is determined, and a new set of fingerprints is designed. Mom + Dad = Baby. Easy, right?

The new person is called an embryo. This is science;[14] it's not someone's opinion. The embryo develops rapidly and is called by different names throughout its development in the womb, but right from conception, it is a new, living human being.

Truth #2: Every Baby—Every Human—Has the Right to Life.

Each of us is unique and unrepeatable. There was never another you in the past and there won't be another you in the future.

It doesn't matter if babies are wanted or unwanted. They all have a right to life. It doesn't matter if they are called babies or fetuses. It doesn't matter if they were conceived at a fertility clinic or in the bedroom. It doesn't matter if they are disabled or fully abled. All children, from the moment they are conceived, have inherent dignity, value, and a right to life, whether they are wanted or not. Every one of them has the right to live and not be killed because of their age (very, very young) or location (in the womb or test tube).

Truth #3: It's Not Her Body; It's the Baby's.

Was baby Samuel just an organ in his mother's body? Absolutely not! He was, and still is, his own person. While the nature of human development required that he be enveloped in his mother's body, his life is distinct from his mother's life. He has his own complete body, which is different from her body. He is a separate human being. In the end, the truth is simple: Abortion and (often) IVF kill innocent human beings. They take away human dignity and snuff out precious lives.

■ HOW THESE TRUTHS PROTECT CHILDREN

As a parent, I will do anything to protect my kids, just as your own parents would do anything to protect you. Remember when you had to sit in a car seat and be buckled in tight? You had a booster seat that I'm sure you loved. You always had to wear your seat belt in the car. Your parents took you to the doctor when you were sick. Your parents made you wear sunscreen to protect you from painful sunburns. I'm positive you can think of a thousand examples of things your parents did in order to protect you. Because that was their job as parents! And if you didn't have that kind of loving parents, I'm sure you can still feel the sting.

Kids of all ages and sizes deserve protection, whether they are brand-new embryos, toddlers, or teenagers. Parents have a solemn obligation to protect our children and to value their lives, even before they are born.

If we truly recognized and valued the dignity and life of every human child at every stage of development, it would mean that whether wanted or unwanted, both mother and father would reorient their life around the baby's right to life. We would empathize with women in unplanned pregnancies, and with women struggling with infertility, but insist that no child's right to life should be violated because of her longings, fears, or priorities. It would be a world where women with unplanned pregnancies are supported by extended families and church communities, even if they were the only parent willing to protect their baby. It would be a culture that says no to the consumerist mentality of the IVF industry and one that would recoil at the very suggestion of freezing "surplus" babies. It would be a nation where every life, disabled, or fully abled, would be welcomed into the world with rejoicing.

Laws need to be fixed. Hearts need to be converted. Families need to be healed.

▮ CHILD PROTECTION IN ACTION

In 2011, Texas passed the twenty-four-hour ultrasound law. It required that all women be shown an ultrasound of their baby by the physician performing their abortion at least twenty-four hours before the abortion.

Because the majority of abortion facilities are not staffed with full-time doctors, this caused a problem for them. There was no doctor there to perform these ultrasounds twenty-four hours beforehand.

This simple law closed down dozens of abortion facilities in the state.

It was also common sense. Of course a woman should have all of the information available to her before she undergoes an invasive medical procedure. An ultrasound is part of her medical chart and should be shown to her.

Two years later in the next legislative session, pro-life forces were able to defund the abortion industry. Our legislature voted to remove state dollars from any entity that provided abortions. This closed down even more facilities. It was an interesting move by the abortion industry. For years, these facilities had claimed that abortion was "only 3 percent" of their business yet losing "only 3 percent" of their budget forced them to close. Clearly, abortions make up a way more than 3 percent of their revenue. And clearly, the lies about trying to "prevent" abortion and being a leader in "family planning" had all been a farce. They were an abortion provider, plain and simple. The passage of this law exposed that truth.

Several years later, pro-lifers were able to pass the Texas Heartbeat Act, which protected babies from the moment a heartbeat could be detected (usually around six weeks). Abortion numbers in Texas plummeted. The abortion industry was on edge. Criminal charges were on the line for any physician who crossed the line.

The same legislative year, Texas passed the Human Life Protection Act, otherwise known as a "trigger ban." The purpose of this law was to ban abortion at the moment of conception in the state of Texas should *Roe* be overturned. We didn't know that was coming right around the corner.

Little by little, pro-life advocates and pro-life legislators worked together to protect our most innocent brothers and sisters. It took time and we are still working.

But we need more than legislation. The law is certainly a teacher, but it is not the only thing needed to change hearts. We are still a long way from making abortion unthinkable, which is the ultimate goal.

Dr. Abby Johnson, CEO and founder of And Then There Were None and ProLove Ministries, author of *Fierce Mercy, Unplanned,* **and** *The Walls Are Talking*

Abby Johnson went to work for Planned Parenthood believing she would be helping women. Working her way up from volunteer to director of one of their facilities, Abby had a surprising change of heart after witnessing a live ultrasound guided abortion procedure. It became clear that abortion did not provide the freedom she had promised so many women in those counseling rooms. Abby left her job in the abortion industry and has been sharing her experiences ever since.

Her story was chronicled in a bestselling book, *Unplanned,* which was later turned into a major motion picture with the same name. She has gone on to write several other books, including *The Walls Are Still Talking* and *Fierce Mercy.*

She is the CEO of two successful prolife nonprofits and hosts her own podcast, *Politely Rude.* One of Abby's ministries, And Then There Were None, has helped almost seven hundred abortion workers leave the abortion industry and come into a saving relationship with Jesus Christ.

MASCULINITY

KEN HARRISON

When I was a Los Angeles police officer, I wanted to be a cold-blooded, hardened gunfighter who took vengeance on the wicked. I grounded my identity in the role, and I thought that's who I was until one of the most horrific cases of my life: a horrific child-abuse situation.

I partnered with a man named James. He was one of my best friends, a huge bodybuilder, and the father of a five-year-old daughter. I wasn't married and had no kids at the time, but I was known as a Christian around the station, which is why our sergeant assigned us this case.

When James and I arrived on the scene, we met a five-year-old girl whom I will never forget. She was wearing a yellow dress with a matching ribbon in her hair: beautiful, smiling, and completely innocent. She was so innocent that there was no hint of hatred or shame or bitterness in her voice when she described her sexual abuse to me in detail—only sadness.

Every week, her father, her uncle, and her father's best friend abused her.

We took her to the hospital for medical treatment and then to her mother, who had left the father a few months earlier. Typically, after establishing that the little girl was safe with her mother, we would leave and refer the case to the child-abuse detectives. But as we were leaving, the mother said, "I'm worried about my son. He's with their father."

The father lived only two miles away, and we rushed to his apartment. We climbed the filthy stairs of a rickety apartment to meet a monster who represented the worst of what men can become. We stood in the dark outside a dilapidated door. I drew my pistol and kicked the door off its hinges.

The father jumped out of bed. He was naked, and so was the toddler in bed with him. I holstered my gun and crossed the room, closing my left fist around his throat and starting to throw a punch with my right. James's massive forearm swept me back from the man as he jammed his Beretta 9mm against the man's temple and started to pull the trigger. He was strong, but he was totally out of control.

From the corner of my eye, I could see the little boy standing on the bed, staring at us.

Just as James was about to shoot, I jammed my finger behind the trigger on his weapon to prevent him from firing it. James screamed and cussed as we fell to the ground. I kept punching him with my free hand as he twisted the gun, trying to free it. At that moment, a lieutenant appeared in the door, shocked to see his officers on the ground fighting over a gun.

Lieutenants normally didn't leave the station, and James's shock at seeing our commanding officer standing over us allowed me to wrest away his gun and slide it across the floor.

We booked the father and returned the boy safely to his mother. We finished our reports, omitting the part about James nearly executing a man. But James looked at me with disgust. "You should have let me kill him," he said. "He'll just hurt more kids." The next day, James asked for a new partner, and he never spoke to me again.

▬ BIG LIES ABOUT MASCULINITY

Lie #1: Masculinity Means Machismo.

I let go of my vigilante mentality that day, but it wasn't easy to do the right thing. As a child, I was taught Christian love and restraint, but growing into adulthood, the message was that being a man meant doling out violent justice as I saw fit.

I had a choice to make and thankfully, my biblical upbringing—that being a man required mercy and loving one's enemies, was stronger than what I'd learned elsewhere. Even this monster of a man deserved a fair trial and a chance at repentance. His wife and kids deserved the chance to face him and begin healing. Those things could not have happened if I had let my friend James kill this man in cold blood.

But I don't blame James. Like me, and like so many other men in the latter half of the twentieth century, he grew up in a world where "real men" drank a lot, suppressed all emotions, and slept with many women. "Real men" didn't spend time with their children unless it was to briefly appease their mother. "Real men" were emotionless and impervious to hurt. "Real men" were macho.

How did we come to think like this? Traditionally, men have occupied roles that hold authority and come with the responsibility to protect and provide for women and children. It's obvious that physical traits like superior strength and high testosterone levels equip men for these jobs.[1] Unfortunately, these natural advantages are not always geared toward providing and protecting. Biologically speaking, men's greater physical power and stronger sex drive also allow some men to exploit women.[2] And the fact that women, not men, get pregnant means that men need not take responsibility when they father children.

For much of history (and still today, in places) this out-of-bounds drive resulted in the practice of polygamy. Christian civilization largely stamped out that custom, choosing instead to harness male strength toward the building, protecting, and leading of families. But during the twentieth century, as the Christian influence on American society weakened, aspects of the old masculinity reemerged.

The idea that men should be protectors and gentlemen became offensive to sexual revolutionaries. They viewed it as a kind of condescension—men, from a place of strength, bending low on behalf of those who can't match it: women and children. They were ridiculed for it. So men began to abandon gentlemanly restraint, but maintained their worst desires.

Legal changes didn't help. No-fault divorce broke down legal guardrails around marriage, and the feminist movement changed cultural expectations of wives and husbands. The advent of the pill "freed" women from needing to be married before sex and removed one more argument against male promiscuity. The protective gentleman was gradually replaced by James Bond, who exhibits lots of masculine power and competence but behaves like a pig toward women.

And then the world was shocked when #MeToo hit the headlines. Men felt entitled to use and abuse women and children as they pleased. It was no longer women and children first off the *Titanic*, but whoever could get to the lifeboat first—and that was the men.

Big changes in the economy played a role, too. The Industrial Revolution separated men and their work from the home, and from their wives and children. Men had always been viewed as providers in some sense, but now providership just looked like a paycheck. Before they had to go off to factories for the day or week, families would work the farm together, or run the store together, with constant connection between husband and wife, parents and kids. An industrial economy meant spending only evenings and weekends (if even those) actually in the household. It's easy to see how physical separation from the home stokes the macho vices, encouraging emotionally distant fatherhood and creating endless opportunities for infidelity.

Lie #2. Masculinity Is Toxic.

Machismo disfigures characteristics that can be harnessed for good if disciplined, such as aggressiveness and physical and emotional toughness. As the destructive effects of this distortion have become evident, many people have drawn the exact wrong conclusion: that *masculinity itself* is toxic.

"Why can't we hate men?" asked a *Washington Post* opinion piece six years back.[3] Writer John Stoltenberg asserted that "talking about 'healthy masculinity' is like talking about 'healthy cancer.'"[4] Macho men despise as weaklings those who regulate their strength for the good of others; the radical reaction to machismo teaches men that weakness is a virtue and demonizes the naturally competitive and aggressive behavior of boys. In too many elementary school classrooms, boys' tendency for challenging, questioning, and demanding proof is stigmatized as disruptive.[5]

Transgender activists give boys a grisly off-ramp to escape "toxic" manhood. Just become a girl. Then you'll no longer be part of the "patriarchy" responsible for keeping women down. Even some people who recognize that men and women are physically different deny gender differences; that is, they deny there's anything that distinguishes them in their social roles. Men's and women's bodies are different, but they are still socially interchangeable. This idea actually follows the logic of transgenderism: that masculinity isn't connected to biological maleness.

■ HOW THESE LIES HARM CHILDREN

Machismo has caused grief to countless children. Its unrestrained aggression has given too many men a pass to verbally and physically abuse their wives and children. The womanizing glorified in the age of *Playboy* magazine wrecked marriages and set wretched examples for sons. Even when the consequences aren't that dramatic, the demand for toughness to the point of invulnerability makes for remote fathers who fail to forge real connections with their sons and daughters.

The modern-day replacement for machismo—the idea that masculinity is "toxic"—is also taking its toll on America's sons. One in four Gen Z men say they have been mistreated or discriminated against because they were male. Nearly half believe that such discrimination happens, and half agree that "These days, society seems to punish men just for acting like men."[6]

This suspicion toward masculinity starts early. In elementary schools nationwide, behavior that comes earlier and more naturally to girls is rewarded: sitting still, attentiveness, working quietly. Behavior that is normal for young boys—fidgeting, rowdiness, asking lots of questions—is discouraged or punished.[7] Although it may be unintentional, classroom dynamics hinder boys, and it shows: male students are held back in school at twice the rate for female students, and get expelled from preschool five times more often.[8]

Even more seriously, boyish behavior is pathologized and medicated. Gerry Garibaldi has described the rise of a special-ed apparatus that diagnoses boys with learning disabilities when they exhibit perfectly typical male behavior. These diagnoses tend to produce apathy and harm self-confidence.[9] Three times as many male students as female students get labeled with ADHD, and 16 percent of boys are receiving ADHD medication.[10]

When my son, Hunter, was four, he had the endless energy and need for competition that many boys have. His preschool teachers insisted we put him on medication. My wife was appalled as his teachers condescendingly characterized his drive and energy as distracting. He needed to be "controlled," and "many of the boys in his class are on medication." Instead of medicating a healthy boy, we enrolled him in karate. Almost immediately, Hunter became a model student. Competition, discipline and room to move were all he needed. Hunter went on to become an all-state and college wrestler and won the outstanding character award at his high school. Hunter didn't need to be medicated; he needed the proper outlets of a competitive boy. He didn't need to be discouraged; he needed to express his energy in the right ways.

The antimasculinity crusade has hurt boys in a more indirect way too: by provoking a toxic backlash. Boys, especially those without a connected dad, need someone, a man, to show and tell them how to be a man. Many are getting sucked into the online "manosphere," where gurus like Andrew Tate urge young men to dominate others, to treat women as toys or slaves, to neglect any children they might father. Ever heard of Bronze Age Pervert (BAP)? He's an online figure with a huge following of young men who are tired of being told they suck just because they're guys. BAP puts forward a kind of neopagan model of heroic manhood that spits on the weak, using masculine strength to exploit and subdue, not protect, women and children.[11] BAP types smear the Christian ethic of manly service to others as a sly deception contrived by women and weak men to tie strong men down and repress their true natures. Modern society hates you, so burn it down! They see the lies about masculinity, and respond by creating an even more callous version of machismo's evils.

The antimasculinity agenda also harms children by implying that fathers are unnecessary. This despite the long-established fact that fatherlessness lies at the root of so many social ills. The story of abuse at the beginning of this chapter was unusual in that most abuses and rapes I encountered on the job did not involve the father. Rather, abuse occurred because there was *no* father. Abusers look for the unprotected. What I saw on the LAPD, what nearly any police officer will report, and what data confirm, is that most child-abuse victims come from fatherless homes.[12] Sometimes it's Mom's live-in boyfriend. Sometimes it's a coach who has offered to be a "father figure." Sometimes it's a kid who got caught up in a gang because he was looking for fatherly love.

When we communicate that real men are optional in the lives of children, fathers leave. And then it's open season for predators.

THE TRUTH ABOUT MASCULINITY

Truth #1: Masculinity Means Strength Under Control.

The biblical book of Proverbs says that "a man without self-control is like a city broken into and left without walls."[13] Strength out of control, in other words, is weakness. Macho men and their "manosphere" spinoffs idolize strength, but they are actually weak because they refuse to regulate their strength. When men let their appetites (whether anger, lust, or pride) rule them, they diminish their power by becoming slaves to those urges. Men who cannot lead themselves aren't capable of leading others.

Of course, you can't control your strength if you don't have any. Contemporary calls to (sometimes literal) self-emasculation are no solution to male misbehavior. We desperately need strong, ambitious, capable, courageous men who can act vigorously for the common good. We especially need those strong men to protect the weak.

Truth #2: Masculinity Means Fatherhood.

This is not to say that you can't be a real man without fathering biological children. But fatherhood does capture something essential to true manhood: using one's strengths and talents to protect, serve, and lead others well. You could almost say that you become a real man once you've taken responsibility for someone other than yourself—whether that's a wife, children, or the neighborhood kid who doesn't have a dad.

Being a man means acting as a father, usually but not exclusively to your own children. It means challenging them to pursue excellence and modeling that excellence in your life. It means cultivating strength and then expending that strength on others' behalf, and leading others in an outward-facing mission. To become a man, a boy needs a father to imitate, a figure who will affirm his growth, rebuke his misdeeds, and teach him skills. Fatherhood carries with it responsibility, authority, and self-sacrifice—things for which every man should prepare himself.

▄ HOW THESE TRUTHS PROTECT CHILDREN

When people call masculinity toxic, they are thinking of strength out of control for the sake of selfish pleasure or domination. They fear eruptions of displaced anger against the weak.

Truly masculine strength under control does not feed into these problems; it's actually their solution. The best defense against aggressive, bad men are aggressive, good men. As political theorist Harvey Mansfield has pointed out, "It was men who destroyed the World Trade Center, and it was also men who rushed in to save people who were trapped."[14] Our society's very existence depends on the willingness of courageous men to die to protect it.

Telling boys the lie that their nature is fundamentally defective kneecaps their manhood. And that means there will be fewer good men to battle against *actually* toxic men. Pathologizing normal behavior undermines male achievement, and no good will come of medicating healthy boys. Raising the kind of men we want to be the fathers and husbands of the future starts with recognizing that boys just don't learn or think or act in the exact same way as girls.

Likewise, when we understand the close relationship between masculinity and fatherhood, children thrive.

Without fathers, they suffer. A child raised without a father in the home is 400 percent more likely to live in poverty and 500 percent more likely to commit suicide.[15] Even more shocking, 80 percent of rapists motivated by anger and 90 percent of runaway and homeless children are from fatherless homes.[16] But there's a positive side to these statistics: children who have a father in the home are much less likely to live in poverty, commit suicide, or become rapists.

Serving as a police officer in a high-crime area of L.A., I saw firsthand the effects of widespread fatherlessness on neighborhoods. I also saw the contrast with those few homes that had present, connected fathers. The difference in the children and home life was staggering. I dealt with the Crips and the Bloods gangs all the time, and I can't recall ever being in the home of a gang member where there was a father present.

■ CHILD PROTECTION IN ACTION

Reviving a healthier masculinity will require telling boys that their maleness isn't a birth defect, and reforming early education accordingly. Some people are already doing this, including a platform called Walkabouts that brings more physical activity into the learning process.[17] Given that boys in particular learn by imitation, reintroducing biographies of great and virtuous men into the school day would inspire many male students.

Groups like Promise Keepers are reintroducing the necessity of older men mentoring and discipling younger men. Younger men need to see authentic masculinity in those who have lived it, and have permission to ask them tough questions. Many grandfathers have made the mistakes that could save young men from heartache and danger, if they only had a trusted relationship and open communication. Promise Keeper gatherings and the Promise Keeper app are helping facilitate those connections.

Even more crucial for child welfare would be the widespread restoration and honoring of fatherhood. We should eliminate all remaining marriage penalties in our welfare system. And we need to roll back no-fault divorce, which often separates children from their fathers.

We should also use policy to revive economic sectors—like manufacturing—where men disproportionately work, which have declined in the last several decades. Families have suffered as a result.

Know what else we need to do? Honor good men.

Governing bodies, religious leaders, advertisers, and individuals ought to publicly honor fatherhood in a way that simply doesn't happen very much right now. It is common for mothers to receive adulation from politicians, entertainers, and the pulpit, and this is entirely fitting. But if we want more men to aspire to present, engaged fatherhood, the same should be done for fathers. Because when men do not flourish, no one does.

Ken Harrison, chairman of Promise Keepers and author of *A Daring Faith in a Cowardly World*

Ken Harrison is the chairman of Promise Keepers and the CEO of Water-Stone, a large Christian foundation that gives away over $3 million per week to Christian causes. Ken is a former Los Angeles police officer, graduate of Marine Corps Officer Candidate School, and former CEO of the largest commercial real estate valuation company in the world.

An author and corporate speaker, Harrison has appeared on many television and radio interviews, including *Fox News*, *The Huckabee Show*, *Blaze TV*, *Fox Nation*, and *The 700 Club*. He is a Colson Fellow and has served on many boards, including Promise Keepers, Fellowship of Christian Athletes, Corban University, Colorado Uplift, and Urban Youth Ministries.

Harrison has authored three books: *A Daring Faith in a Cowardly World*, *The Rise of the Servant Kings—What the Bible Says About Being a Man*, and *Victors and Victims*.

Ken lives in Colorado with his wife, Elliette, and near his three adult children.

FEMININITY

In 2015, new mother Amber Scorah left her three-month-old son Karl at a daycare in Manhattan so she could finally return to work after maternity leave. It was the first day he had been away from her since his birth. Amber went back to the daycare at her lunch break to breastfeed him. She walked in to find her baby turning blue as a staff worker performed CPR incorrectly.

According to the daycare, Karl had been fed and put down for a nap, and sometime later was found blue and not breathing. He died that day at the hospital. A year later, his devastated mother wrote an essay for the *New York Times*, where she said:

> This article isn't about daycare safety. This isn't an indictment of the company I work for; I had one of the better parental leave policies of anyone I know. What this article is about is that my infant died in the care of a stranger, when he should have been with me. Our culture demanded it. A mother should never have no choice but to leave her infant with a stranger at three months old if that decision doesn't feel right to her. Or at six weeks old.

Or three weeks old. I would have stayed home
with Karl longer, but there just didn't seem to be a
way. And I knew well enough that a million other
mothers in America before me had faced the same
choice and had done the same, even earlier than I
had, though it tortured them emotionally, or physically, to do so.[1]

Twelve million infants and small children are left in daycare
each year, all day long, so their mothers can work. Most don't meet
tragic ends like Karl, but many suffer from long-lasting psychological
and behavioral effects associated with early and extended maternal
separation. It turns out that babies are wired to be physically close
to their mothers, and we seem to have forgotten (on purpose) this
elemental biological truth.

Meanwhile, an epidemic of anxiety, depression, and behavioral
issues overwhelms kids. Studies prove that early separation from a
child's mother and hours spent in the care of a "caregiver" who is
not a parent and does not love the child leads to significantly worse
outcomes.[2]

Amber Scorah has no way to know if Karl would have died had
he been home with her. But at a daycare filled with fifteen babies,
it's impossible for each child to receive the same level of attention.
Choking or gasping noises can be lost amid other sounds. Infant daycares are holding pens where your precious newborn is treated like a
factory-farmed ungulate.

▰ BIG LIES ABOUT FEMININITY

Lie #1: Your Career Is More Important Than a Family.

Teenage girls are taught from an early age exactly what society expects
from them: they are to suppress their innate biological impulses and

God-given desires for monogamous love and family in favor of new, more enlightened desires. Feminism teaches girls that having children will repress you, but a boss will give you freedom.

This lie has hatched the plague of the Girl Boss. Young girls are taught they can "be anything" and "rule the world." But they are not reading the fine print, which stipulates that "being anything" will require them to delay motherhood until they must rely on invasive reproductive technology—IVF, egg freezing, even surrogacy—to get pregnant.

If you actually want a family, waiting too long to get started can backfire dramatically. If you do have children and a career, the pressure to immediately abandon the kids to daycare and get back to work can be overwhelming. Your friends will think you're crazy for dreading leaving your baby to go back to work. Your coworkers will think you're a bad person for not coming back. Like it or not, your baby will have to be raised by strangers who don't love them. There's almost no way out of this trap unless you are: 1) Able to live on your husband's income, 2) Already poor and on welfare, or 3) Decide to radically downsize your lifestyle to make it happen. Young women are carefully groomed for the inevitable daycare handoff. They ship the newborn off to some dank basement that smells like Lysol and dirty diapers, and get back to *contributing to the economy*.

It's a deranged and inhuman system, and even the cheapest daycares will wipe out a huge chunk of your salary. Is it any surprise that young women are rejecting motherhood completely? In late empire America, most young women are terrified of the expense and emotional trauma that awaits them when a baby is around four months old and they are forced to endure the all-day separation. It's shocking that anyone is still having children.

Lie #2: Marriage Is Optional for Raising Children.

This lie tells girls that marriage is oppressive. Husbands dim your light. There is an entire book industry devoted to married women dumping their spouses so they can find themselves, sleep with as many people as possible, and finally stop having to focus on someone other than themselves twenty-four hours a day. Feminist author Lyz Lenz published a bestseller this year titled *This American Ex-Wife: How I Ended My Marriage and Started My Life.* She boasts online about how huge numbers of women reach out to tell her that her book inspired them to leave their own husbands and children and start their lives, too. It's a horror story sold as a manifesto of female liberation from the crushing weight…of having a devoted partner who loves you.

There are also single women raising children because they failed to find a suitable partner when they were at their most marriageable, or because they believed the lie that kids don't need fathers. But study after study proves that children raised in single-parent households have worse outcomes.[3] And when you're the only breadwinner, you have no choice but to drop that six-week-old off at daycare; no one else can help pay the bills.

Lie #3: Birth Control Is Harmless.

The third big lie we teach girls is that birth control pills are harmless, and indeed required in order to take part in the glories of sexual exploitation masquerading as sexual exploration. Birth control indoctrination starts when twelve-year-old girls are encouraged not to avoid sex until marriage, but to indulge in it early. The only rules are to try and avoid pregnancy and STDs. Based on current rates of abortion and STDs, women are ignoring these rules as they enjoy all the fruits of the sexual revolution, like super gonorrhea, unplanned pregnancy, herpes, and repeated heartbreak. "Rates of

STDs continue to rise in the United States, with CDC data showing increases year after year."[4]

Young girls are taught *at school* and online that exploring their sexuality early and often with multiple partners of all genders is not only good for them, but it's what a truly enlightened woman does. The only shame is in restricting yourself to one partner, or—horrors—waiting until marriage.

A 2024 teen video series Planned Parenthood posted on YouTube reveals the mainstream message America is sending to teenage girls. In one called "What happens the first time you have sex?" the narrator opens with this: "So you've decided you're ready to have sex for the first time. There's no one way to have sex that's better than another—whatever works for you and your partner, and makes you both feel good, is good sex."[5]

Another video with the same narrator titled "What Is Virginity" includes this banger of a quote: "Virginity is a completely made-up concept. It's a term that was created simply to control and shame people, mainly women."[6]

Government-funded Planned Parenthood helps write and design the sex-ed curriculum for many government-funded K-12 public schools. This is the message girls are getting about sex—and you're paying for it.

■ HOW THESE LIES HARM CHILDREN

Taken together, these three lies have made women's lives—and children's lives—objectively worse. Being a woman used to mean that yes, you could pursue many career options, get an education, and enjoy the same rights as a man, but we all agreed that there was one job *only* women could do, and they really did it best: birth, nurse, and nurture an infant. Now, fur babies replace actual babies. Joy comes not from natural endorphins released while breastfeeding your newborn, but from the artificial chemical release of antidepressants into your bloodstream. Why choose one lifelong loving mate when you can order casual pleasure with strangers delivered to your door via Tinder?

Thanks to our blessed technological progress, all the messy parts of motherhood can now be outsourced and delayed, even forgotten altogether. You can remain free from the burden of your biology—but at what price?

Children raised without fathers, in daycares, by women who rely on birth control and abortion to limit their fertility and dull their maternal instincts are essentially being raised by wolves.

Marriage becoming optional for family formation has visited devastating consequences on kids. Children raised by single mothers, either by choice or by necessity, are at high risk of negative outcomes. The epidemic of fatherlessness, triggered by the breakdown of femininity and the debasement of marriage and men's vital role in society, has been a disaster for children—especially boys.

I wrote about the effect of single motherhood on children in my book:

> The trend of fatherless boys raised by single mothers is not a new one, but it is no longer just a trend—it's a massive cohort. According to the 2020 U.S. Census, 30 percent of all American children grow up without a father at home. Millions of little boys are living in mini-matriarchal societies with no male energy to temper all that estrogen— no one to play catch with them, teach them how to deal with bullies, treat girls, and warn them away from pornography, drugs, and other dangers. Is it any wonder so many boys fail to launch?[7]

Lies around birth control have their own destructive effects. You're not even allowed to suggest that chemical birth control is anything other than a miracle drug—say this on social media and women freak out. But the uncomfortable truth is that these chemicals can trigger depression,[8] weight gain, cardiovascular issues,[9] and severe personality changes, including loss of libido[10] and even any interest in men.[11] Is rampant birth control use triggering the explosion in divorce memoirs?

Chemical birth control has another disastrous physical effect, one that hits young boys especially hard. Artificial female hormones have built up in the environment, thanks to sixty-plus years of chemical birth control in female urine that has been flushed into the water supply.[12] These billions of gallons of estrogen-infused water are used to grow food, feed farm animals, and fill babies' bathtubs. It's an ironic plot twist: if a boy's mother took contraceptive pills to prevent his birth, those same chemicals in the local water supply may render him incapable of having her grandchildren. Little boys are literally swimming in a toxic environmental stew of feminizing chemicals from birth.

Separation for long hours, for years, can negatively affect not just the child but the bond between mother and child, making disobedient and aggressive behavior more likely.[13] You're not allowed to discuss these findings in polite society—how dare you suggest to a mother that she actually *stay home and raise her own child!* You're a "misogynist" who "wants to chain women to the kitchen." Feminists who have gone all-in on careerism do not want anyone to point out that daycare is not, in fact, optimal for small children:

> [M]ore hours per week in child care across the early years of life predicted lower social competence, higher externalizing problems, more adult-child conflict, and more negative peer play... these

negative outcomes remained even after accounting
for the quality of the child care....[14]

Strangers, even nice ones, are no substitute for a loving mother.

These three big lies—career over motherhood, the rejection of marriage, and the pill—are harming children and their mothers in ways too numerous to count.

THE TRUTH ABOUT FEMININITY

The Truth About Being a Woman Is That It's Elemental.

It doesn't need to be taught. It is innate and inborn, baked into the essence of femaleness from the instant of God's creation.

Which is exactly why it requires twelve-plus years of feminist indoctrination and birth control miseducation to burn away this ancient knowledge.

As I wrote in my book:

> Pharmaceuticals and feminism have now turned at least two generations of young women into—I need to choose my words carefully here—extremely affordable concubines. Ninety-nine-cent escorts. Is this what liberation looks like? You may be the one who gets ghosted by guys, but in a cruel plot twist, *you* end up becoming the phantom who never really lived. The inconvenient truth of human fertility is that it fades. Ask any Beverly Hills fertility doctor driving a $400,000 car if women tend to struggle to get pregnant after a certain age. Even the name— birth control—is straight out of a dystopian horror movie. Who is controlling whom?[15]

Not all women need to have children. But too many women are falling prey to a system set up to hurt them and their children.

■ HOW THESE TRUTHS PROTECT CHILDREN

The message to women from feminists is always the same: your children are expendable. Do we really think children don't pick up this message from a mother who leaves them in daycare for all their waking hours and never marries their father? This system chews young families up and spits them out, all so that women can enjoy the "liberation" promised to them.

Children raised in strange daycares or forced to coexist with a rotation of their mother's boyfriends or stepfathers, face the highest risk of neglect, abuse, and even death (read this book's chapter on family for the full frightening picture of these risks). Data backs this up overwhelmingly; the absolute safest environment in which to raise a child is a home with his or her married mother and father. This should be the goal of anyone who aspires to motherhood. The normalization of "alternative" families and the elevation of paid "caregivers" over mothers has debased and diminished the crucial maternal pillar in a child's life.

The fact that infants thrive when in close physical proximity to their biological mothers over any other adult, even including their father, is not a bad thing! Nature designed the baby and the mother to be a perfect pair, each dependent on the other. This is treated as an unfortunate deficiency in female biology when it's one of the most perfect systems God designed. Smart women lean into their femaleness and embrace motherhood with all their might. These are the truly liberated women.

Meanwhile, the women and children who submit to the system of birth control, career, and daycare, are not free; they are unwitting slaves caught in an antiwoman, antichild machine. The only way out is to utterly reject the normalization of early maternal separation at all costs. If you choose to be a mother, you owe your baby the thing he needs most in life, which is his mother.

Children blessed with mothers who understand these truths will reap every advantage. A child born to a married mother willing to sacrifice for her maternal vocation will benefit enormously. Children who are raised in loving homes, with a mother and father, *by their* mother and father, will simply not have to deal with the hardships other children are forced to endure: single parenthood, hours and hours and years and years in daycare, a potentially weakened maternal bond.

We all want the best for our children. Is it really too much to ask that we give our babies what they want and need more than anything else?

▉ CHILD PROTECTION IN ACTION

Convincing young women to lean into motherhood, embrace marriage, reject synthetic hormones, and stay home as long as they can with their babies is tricky. This course entails financial sacrifice, and it's a societal taboo to even hint that motherhood is a more important use of their time than a job, at least in the beginning. But more women are starting to listen to their maternal instincts.

As I recount in my book, I have talked several career girls out of shunting their babies into daycare:

> It's like deprogramming a cult victim. One woman I met, a nurse, cried and told me she was dreading going back to work when her newborn turned twelve weeks old. She didn't know how she was going to do it. A colleague of mine made the mistake of asking me why I had never put a baby in daycare. After calmly explaining that the idea of

leaving my baby for ten hours a day felt like saw-
ing my arm off, that I simply could not physically
do it and would have happily lived in a trailer park
to afford not to for a few years, she nodded. After
having her first child, this coworker resigned. A
year later, she had a second baby. I hope those kids
know Auntie Peachy is the one who saved them
from doing hard time.[16]

Young women, it turns out, are wondering who designed a cruel,
inhuman system that forces them to work full time forever and never
see their kids and put them in daycares they can't even afford. Tik-
Tok overflows with young women rejecting feminist lies, announc-
ing that, actually, they *do* want to get married—and be married until
death do them part.

These girls are learning the benefits of traditional marriage the
hard way—through trial and error. There is even a new, hopeful
trend of young women rejecting birth control after witnessing firsthand what it did to them: rapid weight gain, depression, and anxiety,
triggered by the pill.

The stubborn fact remains that it's almost impossible to support
a family on one income in modern America.

That's why Amber Scorah had to leave baby Karl at the daycare
on that fateful day in 2015. She and her husband lived in New York
for their careers. Perhaps as our cities decay, overrun by insane levels
of crime and violence, people who want to have kids will decide that
maybe they don't need the sort of career that requires them to live in
an expensive urban core. Perhaps more mothers will embrace the joy
of raising their own infants.

Maybe it's okay to have a smaller house and less stuff if this sacrifice lets you give yourself and your baby a priceless gift no one else
can provide and money can't buy: each other.

Peachy Keenan, author of *Domestic Extremist:*
A Practical Guide to Winning the Culture War

Peachy Keenan is the author of *Domestic Extremist: A Practical Guide to Winning the Culture War* (Regnery), contributing editor for *The American Mind* at the Claremont Institute, and a senior contributor to *The Federalist.* Her bylines have appeared in *Newsweek, First Things, Tablet, Washington Examiner,* and *The Blaze.* A convert to Catholicism from secular atheism and liberal feminism, she also identifies as a husbosexual, which means she is only attracted to people who identify as her husband. Mrs. Keenan resides in Southern California, her ancestral homeland, with her family. You can find her on X as @keenanpeachy and on Substack at peachykeenan. substack.com.

FAMILY

KATY FAUST

Nate's parents divorced when he was three. He cried because he went from seeing his dad every day to every other weekend. His two homes were so different—drugs, alcohol, arguing, and progressive politics at his mother's versus quiet, disciplined adherence to traditional morals at his father's—that he had recurring dreams of being a piece of putty stretched between their warring voices. Both his parents remarried and had children with their new spouses. "Neither of my stepparents treated me the same as they did their own children," Nate recalled, especially highlighting the physical abuse suffered at the hands of his stepfather. "It felt like I was the third wheel, like I was being pushed out of a relationship that was established before either of the stepparents and their children came along."

Over the course of Brandi's childhood, her mother was in three different same-sex relationships. To the watching world, it looked like this modern family was doing her right; Brandi was well behaved, and a good student. What the watching world didn't see was that every time a plane flew over Brandi's house, she would run to the back-yard to look up and wave, hoping her father was on the plane looking down at her. She had love, lots of love from her mother, grandfather, and uncles. Her mother's partners never abused her or harmed her.

But love wasn't enough. Brandi wanted her father. "I yearned for the affection that my friends received from their dads. I wanted to know what it was like to be held and cherished by a man, what it was like to live with one from day to day."

Olivia was raised by a wealthy mother and father who split time between their well-staffed houses in the South of France and in Palm Beach, Florida. She had nannies and was afforded the best education money could buy. But Olivia never felt connected to her mother. "There was no bond." She struggled with feelings of abandonment, and "would scream the place down if her parents left the house." No one in her family looked like her, and even as a young child she "had a sense that something was off" in her family. As an adult, she discovered that her mother was not her biological mother. Olivia had been born via traditional surrogate in Kentucky—a woman who was both her genetic and birth mother. Although she had maternal and paternal love in her life, opulence, and stably married parents, Olivia ascribes the self-destructive behavior she fell into as a teen to the "primal wound" that disrupts the innate connection between birth mother and child.

■ BIG LIES ABOUT FAMILY

Nate, Brandi, and Olivia grew up in different household structures. But they were all victims of the lies we tell about family.

Lie #1: Kids Are Resilient.

The phrase was popularized during the no-fault divorce spike of the '70s and '80s. The idea that children needed things like stability and daily connection with both mother and father was problematic for early divorce advocates. Their answer? "Children are resilient!" Divorce is like a bad cold—it's uncomfortable but kids will get over it.

Then and now, advice columns claim, "Children are resilient. Loving parents can divorce successfully." They'll get over the volleying between homes, the new partners joining and leaving the household, and the often inevitable father absence.

But the "kids are resilient" line didn't quite assuage adults' guilt, because the bed-wetting that reemerged in their ten-year-olds or the declines in school performance seemed to indicate that maybe the kids weren't as resilient as they'd been told. So some experts doubled down—divorce wasn't just neutral; it could be "liberating" for kids as they could "break away from excessive dependency on their biological parents."[1] Divorce actually *strengthens* children, you see.

Take it from one of the greatest beneficiaries of family disintegration—a divorce lawyer: "Divorce, while disruptive in the short term, may offer a healthier and happier environment for the whole family in the long run. It can reduce conflict and provide the opportunity for personal growth and freedom for the parents, which is good for parents and kids alike. Remember, increasing your happiness increases your kids' happiness as well."[2]

The first big family lie was that *marriage doesn't matter*. All that mattered was adult happiness.

Lie #2: Kids Don't Need a Mom and Dad; They Just Need to Be Safe and Loved.

There's nothing special about dads. Or moms, for that matter. Kids just need devoted caregivers. Gender is irrelevant.

This second lie originated with the feminist movement. Unlike the first wave of feminism, which was rooted in the idea that women were *different* from men but *equal* in rights, the second wave of feminism claimed that men and women can't really be *equal* unless they are *interchangeable*. Feminist icons of the '70s like Germaine Greer and Shulamith Firestone raged against the nuclear family as a tool of the patriarchy. Dependence on a man in the context of family was a form of oppression.

Sexual revolution–era feminism insisted that there be no distinction between men and women in terms of career aspirations, attitudes toward (and immunity from the results of) sex, and household roles. Firestone called on women to "seize control of human fertility" so they could create families without fathers. Female equality depended on men becoming unnecessary in the home.

It's not only feminists who have sought to make fathers optional. At the height of its cultural power, the Black Lives Matter website called followers to "disrupt the Western prescribed nuclear family" in the name of antiracism. Their website mentioned Black mothers, Black families, Black parents, and even Black trans women but its creators couldn't bring themselves to include Black *fathers*. Instead, BLM advocated for "extended families and 'villages' that collectively care for one another, especially our children, to the degree that mothers, parents, and children are comfortable."[3]

So the involvement of both a mother and a father in the life of a child was exchanged for the narrative that kids just needed safety and love from a community or "village," not distinctly maternal and paternal love.

The second big family lie was that *gender doesn't matter*. Just love and safety.

Lie #3: Biology Doesn't Matter. Love Makes a Family.

If you have any doubt about this, a quick glance at the dad-dad-kid family pride month mannequin display at Target will set you straight. Their T-shirts declare it, so it must be true. The truth is, the push for gay marriage *required* it to be true.

In most religions and societies in human history, the biological reality that only a heterosexual union can create new life has formed the basis of the family. But when we redefine marriage to remove the "hetero" component, biology can no longer be what makes a family. Our modern family lexicon swiftly replaced kinship bonds with an amorphous idea of "love." The problem is, this brand of modern family *love* requires child *loss*.

In the lead-up to *Obergefell*, the 2015 Supreme Court decision that redefined marriage across the country, armies of sociologists pivoted away from the previously near-universal acknowledgment of the '90s and '00s that married, biological mothers and fathers advantaged kids. Miraculously, they found even though children of same-sex couples were *always* missing one biological parent, *always* missing maternal or paternal influence, and had *always* suffered the traumatic loss of a biological parent, these children were faring "no different" or "even better" than kids with moms and dads. Because "love makes a family."

The big lie was that *biology doesn't matter*. The only thing that mattered was "love."

All three lies serve the same party—adults seeking to justify a decision that will result in the full or partial separation of a child from the mother or father. All three lies elevate ideology over reality. All three lies cause diminished physical, mental, emotional, and relational health for children. All three lies exchange the well-being of children for validation of adult feelings, identity, or desires.

All three lies violate children's right to be known and loved by their mother and father.

HOW THESE LIES HARM CHILDREN

These lies are deployed at different times, in different ways, by different people, with different agendas. They all strip children of things they need to thrive. They deny that marital stability, biological connection, and maternal and paternal influence are relevant in a child's life. Kids fare just as well with one parent as with five; going to bed in the same room every night or shuffling between two homes; raised by their own mother and father; or by adults who purchased their gametes from a sperm or egg "donor"[4] catalog.

These lies destroy the expectation that mother and father will raise their children together for life. What becomes of children who suffer the family breakdown and the father-deprivation that often follows? The outcomes for children (and society) are grim:

- Eighty-five percent of children who exhibit behavioral disorders come from fatherless homes.[5]
- Seventy-one percent of high-school dropouts come from fatherless homes.[6]
- Fatherless females are four times more likely to become pregnant as teenagers.[7]
- Ninety percent of homeless and runaway children are from fatherless homes.[8]
- Seventy-five percent of adolescent patients in chemical-abuse centers come from fatherless homes.[9]
- Sixty-three percent of youth suicides are from fatherless homes.[10]
- Seventy percent of juveniles in state-operated institutions have no father.[11]
- Eighty-five percent of rapists motivated by displaced anger come from fatherless homes.[12]
- Ninety percent of adolescent repeat arsonists live with only their mother.[13]

When we get family wrong, children's physical safety, behavioral health, academic health, relational health, and emotional health are imperiled.

Father deprivation doesn't just increase the likelihood that a child will take his or her own life, drop out of school, or end up in the slammer. It harms children's physical bodies. One 2017 study found that children who lost a parent to death, divorce, or incarceration had shorter telomeres—the endcaps of their chromosomes—responsible for health and longevity. The cells of boys were hit especially hard.[14] Father loss literally shortens their lifespan. Even if they are raised by a stepfather, girls who grow up apart from their biological dads, on average, start their periods one year earlier than their counterparts raised in married, intact homes.[15]

Believing and acting on these family lies, both personally and politically, endangers kids in every way a child can be endangered, from identity formation to child development, from relationship building to physical health and safety.

■ THE TRUTH ABOUT FAMILY

So what is the truth about family? The truth is marriage matters, gender matters, and biology matters.

Truth #1: Marriage Matters.

Whether conceived on a wedding night, during a one-night stand, or in a Petri dish at a fertility clinic, all children come from a man and woman. They have a natural right to be known and loved by that man and woman. When they grow up apart from that man and woman, they are at drastically increased risk for the social ills listed above. The method by which nearly every culture and religion has protected a child's right to that man and that woman is lifelong heterosexual marriage.

When parents are not married, whether cohabiting[16] or divorced, children often experience instability. This means shuffling between homes, or exposure to revolving doors of unrelated adults coming in and out of their homes, sometimes with other children in tow. Rates of abuse and neglect increase, as does poverty. That's why marriage—both its definition and our personal execution of it—is a matter of justice for children.

Truth #2: Gender Matters.

Gender is not a social construct. Men and women are different, and those differences manifest themselves most powerfully within the home. As psychiatrist Scott Haltzman has pointed out, "Parenting styles correlate to biological differences between men and women."

LANGUAGE

Dads speak to their babies like they speak to everyone else; they communicate complex ideas and use adult words.[17] "Dad absolutely crushed his presentation. Definitely going to make partner this year!" Moms simplify their language to the child's level, "Mommy was so busy today, she's pooped!" Gender diversity provides children with one parent who communicates right at their level and another who constantly expands their verbal and cognitive abilities.

PLAY

Mothers tend to *care for* while fathers tend to *play with* children. When mothers do play, they often encourage sharing and fairness. Moms help develop fine motor skills—cutting, chopping, tying shoes. Dad's play is competitive, exciting, and challenging. Dads help develop gross motor skills—running, jumping, climbing.

DISCIPLINE

Mothers tend to discipline more frequently, redirecting children's behaviors to align with social standards, while fathers, although they discipline less frequently, are typically firmer about holding children to family rules.[18]

A dad at home makes for less aggressive boys, fewer police run-ins, and more gentle treatment of women. Daughters who grow up with a father have healthier relationships and fewer trust issues.[19]

Men do not mother and women do not father. Kids need, crave, developmentally benefit from, and have a right to both.

Truth #3: Biology Matters.

A biological connection with parents matters to kids for two reasons: It's a child's best shot at being "safe and loved," and it provides them with access to their biological identity.

SAFE AND LOVED

Children *do* deserve to be safe and loved. And the very people who statistically deliver those household conditions are a child's biological parents who are married to each other. Decades of research shows that a child's own mom and dad are the most connected to,[20] invested in,[21] and protective of kids.

Some heroic stepparents do fill the gap of a negligent biological parent. But in general, the presence of an unrelated cohabiting adult increases a child's risk of abuse and neglect. This phenomenon is so prevalent that researchers have coined the term "Cinderella Effect" to describe the disadvantage suffered by stepchildren.

This is especially true of stepfathers.[22] According to one study, children were 120 times more likely to be beaten to death by their stepfather (or their mother's live-in boyfriend) than their biological father.[23] If you are skeptical, a quick Google search of "mother's boyfriend" should disabuse you of the notion that someone in a romantic relationship with a child's parent provides the same protection as does a biological father.

As data from the National Health Interview Survey testifies, children's risk of experiencing all forms of abuse is highest in homes with a single parent and their partner.[24]

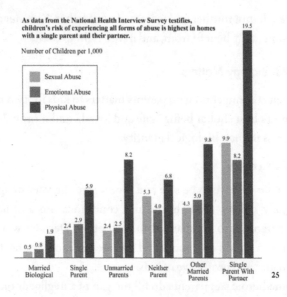

As data from the National Health Interview Survey testifies, children's risk of experiencing all forms of abuse is highest in homes with a single parent and their partner.

Number of Children per 1,000

Sexual Abuse
Emotional Abuse
Physical Abuse

	Married Biological	Single Parent	Unmarried Parents	Neither Parent	Other Married Parents	Single Parent With Partner
Sexual Abuse	0.5	2.4	2.4	5.3	4.3	9.9
Emotional Abuse	0.8	2.9	2.5	4.0	5.0	8.2
Physical Abuse	1.9	5.9	8.2	6.8	9.8	19.5

25

All this is why adoptive parents like me, and like many of you, were rightly required to undergo extensive screening and vetting. From the perspective of child protection, biology and adoption are the only two legitimate pathways to parenthood.

BIOLOGICAL IDENTITY

A child's own biological parents provide something that they crave, something only the man and woman who created them are able to provide—biological identity. If you grew up knowing both your mother and father, you may never have considered how much the answer to the question, "Whose am I?" informs the question, "Who am I?" These kids have. Adoptees[26] are curious about their first parents:

- Seventy-two percent want to know why they were given up for adoption.
- Sixty-five percent expressed a desire to meet their birth parents.

- Ninety-four percent expressed the desire to know which birth parent they resemble most.

Children created through sperm and egg "donors" report similar genealogical bewilderment, sometimes describing a deep-seated feeling that they do not fit in, or a feeling of "otherness." According to the largest study[27] conducted on children created via "donor" sperm:

- Sixty-four percent of donor-conceived adults agreed with the statement: "My donor is half of who I am."
- Seventy-eight percent agreed being donor-conceived was a significant part of their identity.
- Eighty-one percent of children often wondered what personality traits, skills, and/or physical similarities they shared with their donor.

Even the institution of adoption recognizes the importance of biology to children. The past fifty years has seen a dramatic shift away from closed adoption (no knowledge of, contact with, or information about the first family) to nearly 95 percent open adoptions. Social workers recognize that children benefit from as many connections with their biological family as possible, even if they cannot be raised by them.

The same cannot be said for #BigFertility, which routinely, commercially, and intentionally severs children from a biological parent and their dozens, or hundreds, of half siblings.

◾ HOW THESE TRUTHS PROTECT CHILDREN

The truth about family means that adults must do hard things for the sake of children, because the only alternative is to demand that children do hard things for adults.

When adults recognize the truth that biology matters, the event of an unplanned pregnancy results in both mother and father reorienting their lives so the baby is connected to both mother and father. Infertile adults reject surrogacy and gamete selling and purchase, which always separate children from genetic and/or birth parents.

When adults recognize the truth that gender matters, they work to ensure that children are raised by their mom and dad. They will respect and encourage male-female parenting differences within their own marriages, and lavish maternal or paternal love on children in their orbit whose mom or dad is absent. Adults who identify as LGBT who choose to have children will prioritize children's need for both mother and father by marrying their child's other biological parent, rather than constructing a family around their sexual attractions.

When adults recognize that marriage matters to children, they will eschew cohabitation in favor of a public marital commitment to love the child's other parent for life. They will work through struggles in their marriages and reject divorce for grounds other than abuse, adultery, and addiction.

When it comes to family, no one gets a pass. Every adult—single, married, gay, straight, fertile, and infertile—must sacrifice for the rights of children. The only alternative is for kids to sacrifice their rights, well-being, identity, longings, safety, and health for the sake of adult desires. *That* is unjust.

▰ CHILD PROTECTION IN ACTION

We have been arguing about marriage for five decades—from the passage of the first no-fault divorce law in 1969 to the new millennial gay marriage push to current "legalize polygamy" efforts. Opponents of family overhaul efforts often cry, "What about my religious liberty?" But neither gay adults nor religious adults are the primary victims when rulings or legislation doesn't go their way. Children are the victims.

Albania took a better road. Family redefinition activists proposed a bill to replace the words "mother" and "father" in the family code with "Parent 1" and "Parent 2" and demanded that same-sex and unmarried couples have a right to adopt.

One prominent pastor, Akil Pano, and his wife Linda, pushed back. They made it clear that children, not adults seeking relationship validation, would fall victim if mothers, fathers, or marriage became optional in family law. Akil and Linda organized a national conference that included both major political parties as well as Muslim, Orthodox, and Protestant leaders. It was the first time such an Albanian gathering had taken place since the country decided on a national alphabet.

The conference was carried on three national TV channels. Imams, priests, researchers, activists, media personalities and even the Albanian president spoke. In addition to appeals to Albania's distinct authorities—the Bible, church teaching, academic scholarship, Albanian tradition, and their constitution—all addressed the importance of mothers, fathers, and marriage to children.

Within a week, the activists dropped their efforts to gender neutralize the family.

There's power in addressing family as a matter of justice for children. There will be no social justice until we can secure individual justice for children within the family.

Katy Faust is Founder and President of Them Before Us, a global children's rights nonprofit.

RACE

DELANO SQUIRES

Jazmine Barnes was a seven-year-old Black girl who was fatally shot on December 30, 2018, in Houston. Police initially believed the suspect was a White man in his forties. Those reports led Rep. Sheila Jackson Lee, attorney Lee Merritt, and a number of celebrities and civil rights activists to declare the tragedy a hate crime.[1] Bernice King, the daughter of Dr. Martin Luther King Jr., posted the following to Twitter (now X) a few days after her death:

> Just a baby. It is truly unconscionable what's happening to children in America and how the murder of this precious little Black girl isn't permeating our media as much as a wall. Does America care about Black and Brown babies inside or outside of its borders? #JazmineBarnes[2]

The post was accompanied by a portrait of Barnes—smiling, eyes closed, hair braided with the baubles and bows that are common for little Black girls. Vox published an article titled, "Why the Death of a 7-Year-Old Black Girl Became a National Story About Race and Violence."[3] Both local and national coverage of Jazmine's murder focused on the assumption that it was racially motivated.

But when the police apprehended two people within ten days of the senseless crime, both were Black men.

The celebrities who spoke out about the value of Jazmine Barnes' life were conspicuously silent after the arrests. What was even more telling is that none corrected their initial statements framing Jazmine Barnes' tragic death as a racially motivated crime. Black Lives Matter activist Shaun King went so far as to share with his more than one million followers the name and mugshot of Robert Paul Cantrell, a man who fit the initial suspect description. Cantrell took his own life several months later.[4]

The sad reality is that hundreds of Black children like Jazmine Barnes are killed in senseless acts of violence in cities across this country. Rarely do any of them have entertainers, elected officials, and activists bringing national attention to their cases. The response to the death of Jazmine Barnes was different because certain politicians, pundits, entertainers, journalists, and corporations are only interested in crime stories that involve white perpetrators and Black victims. They chant "Black lives matter" with their mouths, but their actions reveal a worldview more accurately described as "White suspects matter."

This "outrage inequity" is the consequence of our nation's long and complicated relationship with race. There is no shortage of public commentary on how this issue has shaped American history. What is needed now more than ever is a greater focus on how it threatens the futures of our children.

▬ BIG LIES ABOUT RACE

Lie #1: Race Exists.

The single biggest lie about race is that it exists, and the first step to understanding this lie is to define the term.

The Merriam-Webster dictionary defines race as "any one of the groups that humans are often divided into based on physical traits regarded as common among people of shared ancestry." In the United States, hair texture and facial features have colored our perceptions of group identity, but the single most important physical trait that has historically been used to classify people by race is skin color. In America, race has most commonly been used—as both a term and tool—for the purpose of creating a social hierarchy based on a set of observable physical traits.

An example of this phenomenon in action is the "one-drop rule" that classified a person with one ancestor of African origin as "Black" for legal purposes.[5] Assigning children of mixed backgrounds to the "subordinate" group is a practice called hypodescent, a common practice in cultures where one's racial group plays a large part in determining social status, political power, and economic opportunity.

This means that a person born in 1920 who had very light skin and straight hair could "pass" as White even if he had a distant ancestor of African ancestry. It also means he would be listed as "Negro" or "colored" on legal documents if his secret was ever discovered.

Lie #2: Race Is Essential.

The second lie of race is that it provides essential information about a person's character and determines the value of their life. The lie of race essentialism ascribes certain beliefs, attitudes, and behaviors—whether vicious or virtuous—to biology and skin color. This lie has endured for centuries and has proven difficult to break.

In 1851, a physician named Samuel Cartwright claimed that enslaved Africans who ran away seeking freedom suffered from a mental condition he called "drapetomania." Cartwright assumed that something was wrong with men and women of a particular hue if they would risk severe punishment and death to escape bondage. He saw enslaved Africans as naturally submissive, a view that paired well with his belief that bondage was the God-given position Blacks were meant to occupy.[6] His distorted worldview made him pathologize an essential aspect of human nature: the innate desire to be free.

Cartwright was a physician for the Confederate Army during the Civil War, but his attempts to blend sin and skin are not confined to his era. Robin DiAngelo became a household name in 2020 when her book *White Fragility*—published in 2018—became the go-to text for liberals who wanted to talk about race after the death of George Floyd.

DiAngelo's flavor of race essentialism is not far from Samuel Cartwright's. She accuses White people of being morally deficient when they refuse to take responsibility for the actions of people who happen to look like them. Only a racial pseudoscientist would find it strange that a person responds defensively when they are accused of racist acts they did not commit or told they should atone for the sins of others.

Lie #3: Different Outcomes Are Always Caused by Racism.

The rise of Ibram X. Kendi shows that racial essentialism is not confined to one particular ethnic group. Kendi is an author who founded an "antiracism" center at Boston University that received millions of dollars and produced little scholarly work.[7] He is also the chief advocate for the third big lie about race—that all differences in outcomes between different groups are caused by racism. The constitutional amendment Kendi has proposed to deal with racial disparities states this lie explicitly: "Racial inequity is evidence of racist policy, and the different racial groups are equals."[8]

Here Kendi uses the term "equal" to suggest that various racial groups—composed of vastly different individuals from different regions and cultures, grouped under color-coded categories—have the same capacities, abilities, beliefs, values and behaviors. He also appears to believe that all groups would have proportionately similar outcomes absent any exogenous interference. His proposed amendment accords with his belief that every policy is either widening or shrinking the gaps in social outcomes between different groups.[9]

Lie #4: We Need "Good Discrimination."

One of Kendi's solutions to racial disparities—specifically between Black and white Americans—is the source of a fourth lie:

> The only remedy to racist discrimination is antiracist discrimination. The only remedy to past discrimination is present discrimination. The only remedy to present discrimination is future discrimination.[10]

The "good discrimination" lie attempts to cure the body politic by bombarding it with more of what has made it ill. There is no reason to return to a race-based system of privileges and punishments based on skin color. It threatened to tear our country apart when Whites were on top and Blacks were on the bottom, and we should expect similar problems if the roles are reversed.

HOW THESE LIES HARM CHILDREN

There is really little difference between the worldviews of Cartwright, DiAngelo, and Kendi. Racist slave traders considered Black people property. Antiracism advocates today consider Blacks pawns. Both groups see Black people as incapable of moral reasoning and, therefore, lacking responsibility for their own actions. The former argues the issue is blood and bone. The latter claims it's a matter of environment and access to resources. The racist was driven by contempt, the antiracist by condescension.

No one suffers more from these warped ideas about race than children, because the lies we tell—and believe—about race lead to bad public policy and even worse moral formation.

Ibram Kendi's claim that racist policies are the cause of racial inequity is accepted as fact by the largest urban school districts in the country. Schools' push for racial "equity" has impelled them to eliminate gifted programs, homework, and even graduation requirements. When disparities in grades and test scores are seen as a reflection of racist teaching methods and assessment tools, no one should be surprised when they fall out of favor.

This way of thinking ignores the real problem of students failing to master subject matter. Changing the admissions test for New York City's most selective high schools will not change the fact that only 40 percent of Black students in the city in grades three through eight are proficient in English language arts and 34 percent are proficient in math.[11]

Promoting excellence and challenging students to exceed the expectations they have for themselves should be the standard for every child, regardless of race. Unfortunately, agency is too often pushed aside for the sake of "equity."

The people making these decisions always claim to do so on behalf of Black students. Their belief that Black students need standards lowered—or even eliminated—to achieve on the same level as their White peers is the progressive "separate but equal" status quo from kindergarten to college.

One high school in a low-income, majority-Black Washington, D.C. neighborhood was celebrated when NPR reported that every graduate was accepted into college. The story in the nation's capital quickly changed when reporters found that half of the graduates missed more than three months of school and 20 percent missed more than ninety days.[12] The soft bigotry of low expectations leads to a hard life of limited employment opportunities when some teens are handed diplomas they can't read.

Schools are not just failing to educate our children. They are infusing the classroom with political ideology in ways that harm both mind and soul. Teachers in Buffalo were being trained to view their job as training activists for antiracism through the use of "culturally responsive" curricula.[13]

The students, some as young as five, are taught that America has created a "school-to-grave pipeline" for Black children and "all White people play a part in perpetuating systemic racism." This is all occurring in a school district where only 27 percent of all students, and 17 percent of Black students, were proficient in English by the time they entered high school.[14]

Racial pseudoscience has no place in American law and culture. This means it has no place in our classrooms. The people who think that the nuclear family, objectivity, and hard work are expressions of "whiteness" are the last ones we need to shape the minds and morals of our children.[15] Teaching White students they need to become "White abolitionists" and attacking Asian students for benefiting from "White privilege" will do nothing to help students flourish.[16] Instead, it will poison how they see themselves and their peers.

Drs. Kenneth and Mamie Clark conducted their "doll test" experiments in the 1940s and found that Black children preferred White dolls to Black dolls. They concluded that even at a young age, children saw being Black in America as a mark of inferior status. Their research was cited in the *Brown v. Board of Education of Topeka* case that banned school segregation.[17] Similar experiments more than half a century later yielded similar results, a good reminder that we should reject any ideas that explicitly or implicitly teach children to assign value to skin color.[18]

▰ THE TRUTH ABOUT RACE

Truth #1: There Is Only One Race—The Human Race.

There is nothing wrong with noticing that skin color, hair texture, and other features vary among different groups of people. A biblical approach to the differences we observe begins by acknowledging there is only *one* race: the human race. This statement does not mean all people are exactly the same or that we must ignore the diversity of the human species across the globe and throughout history. What it does mean is that people from every nation, tribe, and ethnicity all have a common humanity because we have the same Creator.

Truth #2: Every Human Being Is Created in the Image of God and Our Lives Have Inherent—Not Conditional—Value.

The life of Jazmine Barnes was valuable to the progressive outlets and activists who brought attention to her murder because they believed it was politically useful. Once the truth emerged, they all reverted to their default setting that told them a Black child killed by another Black person has very little value in the cultural marketplace.

But murder is not only evil when the perpetrator is White and the victim is Black. An assault should not be deemed newsworthy only when the attacker is Black and the victim is White. Acts of violence against the innocent are always evil.

Truth #3: You Can Combat Racism Without Being "Antiracist."

Frederick Douglass offers a powerful contrast to modern antiracists. He was a patriot who believed in America's founding principles even though he was denied the rights and freedoms his country promised him. He never shied from criticizing the glaring hypocrisies of a nation rooted in the rhetoric of liberty that needed a civil war to end slavery. But he also rejected condescension, however benevolently it was packaged. In contrast with contemporary "antiracist" attempts

to lower standards in pursuit of equal outcomes, Douglass understood that an essential part of being human is the capacity for both
success and failure.

◼ HOW THESE TRUTHS PROTECT CHILDREN

Children who understand that their skin is not a sin are well posi-
tioned to resist the lies about race that pervade our culture. Knowing
that there is only one human race is more important than ever in our
race-obsessed culture.

White children need to know that they do not need to atone for
sins they never committed. Black children need to know that they
are not victims of injustices that occurred to other people in the distant past. Both burdens are too heavy for children to bear.

Knowing that human life has inherent—not conditional—value
protects children in many ways. Affirming this truth has obvious
applications in laws and values that promote life in and outside of
the womb (see this book's chapter on life). With the matter of race, it
should also encourage adults to pursue policies that treat children as
individuals, not members of either favored or disfavored groups. For
example, creating opportunities for gifted K-12 students to receive
more challenging work is one way to improve education outcomes
for students of every background. Promoting agency and excellence
far more effectively improves life outcomes for minority students
than pushing "antiracism" and "equity."

◼ CHILD PROTECTION IN ACTION

Refusing to allow self-serving political interests to weaponize race
also creates opportunities to focus on issues that directly affect social
outcomes. At the top of that list is family structure. Studies indicate
that remaining together as a family unit lowers or prevents school

truancy, criminality, incarceration, and poverty.[19] Having a mom and a dad at home tends to prevent all these pathologies.

This is why efforts to promote marriage and strengthen families should be the top priority for people who claim to care about race and equality. In fact, a "Black Wives Matter" movement that reestablishes marriage as the foundation of Black family life would do far more good for the country than a Black Lives Matter movement that wants to destroy the nuclear family.[20]

Given the fact that 40 percent of all American children are born to unmarried parents, a "marriage before carriage" movement would benefit children of every background.[21]

This is why some schools are looking for ways to incorporate the "success sequence" into character-development instruction. Students need to know that people who finish high school, secure stable employment, and marry before having children have a single-digit poverty rate by their mid-thirties.[22] This is particularly useful knowledge for students who have not grown up in two-parent, middle-class homes. One educator named Ian Rowe is incorporating the success sequence into the curriculum at Vertex Partnership Academies, a charter school network he cofounded that is based in the Bronx.[23]

One of the best ways for students to attend schools that teach the success sequence is to promote and advance education choice at the K-12 level. All students should have access to learning environments that are the right fit for them, reflect their families' values, are safe, and provide rigorous academic preparation. For too long, low-income and minority children, in particular, have been consigned to poor-performing and often unsafe public schools because that's where their family can afford to buy or rent a home.

But school choice does more than offer value-based education to minority students; it offers effective education as well. One of the best examples of the power of choice is the Success Academy charter school network in New York City. Success Academy students largely come from working-class and low-income Black and Hispanic families, but neither their skin color nor zip code keeps them from achieving. Nearly 100 percent of Success Academy students passed the state exams in math, English, and biology.[24] Success schools also outperform district schools in their neighborhoods, often by a significant margin.[25] The progressives who claim to care about race and equality should be doing more to replicate these outcomes, not fanning the flames of racial grievance.

If Jazmine Barnes were alive today, she would probably be thinking about what high school she would want to attend. Unfortunately, her life was cut short by people who did not care about her dreams and aspirations. Their actions reflect who they are, but the reaction to her tragic death reflects many of the lies that cloud our cultural thinking around race.

To some people, she was valuable to the extent that her death perpetuated their narrative about this country's racist past—and present. But the truth is that her life mattered because she was created in God's image, not because of her skin color. The same can be said for us all.

Delano Squires, research fellow at the Heritage Foundation

Delano Squires is a Research Fellow in the Center for Life, Religion, and Family at The Heritage Foundation. Delano's articles and essays on his marriage, family, fatherhood, race, and culture have been published by *Black and Married with Kids*, *The Root*, *The Grio*, *Newsweek*, *The American Conservative*, *The Federalist*, Blaze Media, and the Institute for Family Studies.

Delano earned his bachelor of science degree in computer engineering from the University of Pittsburgh and a graduate degree in public policy from The George Washington University. He resides in Maryland with his wife and their four young children.

GENDER IDEOLOGY

CHRIS ELSTON

I can't believe this happened. I ruined my life. When you break it down, I decided that I didn't want to be a woman before I had ever even experienced being a woman. I had no idea what being a woman was like because I was a child, and now I feel like I will never entirely know.

I want to say that I really feel like some people in the trans community—and the trans medicalists, and the doctors—really target the most vulnerable of us. I have borderline personality disorder and I know for a fact that this is the reason for my transition. It's a very difficult mental illness and one of the core features is not having any sense of self or identity, and my doctors knew this. I told them, even though they didn't ask, that I had been diagnosed with BPD and it was all fine to them.

I wasn't happy as a girl so that meant I was a boy, and I was trans. And so I...I just took the cure that was handed to me.

I was told that I was being given a cure, and I wouldn't want to kill myself anymore, and it wasn't true! I lost a lot of things to this, and I just hope that anyone else who's going through what I went through as a young girl will not be prescribed hormones and surgery because of other things. There are many mental health disorders that make you hate your body, and the solution isn't to change your body; it's to fix your brain.

I just don't want anyone else to ever feel this way. I lost my voice. I lost my chest. I don't know if I'm going to be able to have kids. I feel like no one wants to date me or love me, because I'm ruined.

—*Prisha Mosley, detransitioner*

You just read the transcription of a video by Prisha Mosley in 2022.[1] Like so many other young women and girls dealing with a variety of mental health issues, Prisha was lured into a modern-day cult which has swept across the Western world: the cult of trans, also known as gender ideology. It is a radical movement teaching the quasi-religious, psychologically abusive madness that children are sometimes "born in the wrong body."

At the age of fourteen, Prisha had suffered a sexual assault. At fifteen, she was hospitalized for depression. At sixteen, she was diagnosed with major depressive disorder, obsessive-compulsive disorder, borderline personality disorder, and an eating disorder. She was also cutting herself, resulting in a visit to the emergency room.[2]

None of that mattered to the gender doctors. It almost never does. They didn't even ask about her history. Prisha was given the standard "cure" they are giving to tens of thousands of distressed children. She was prescribed irreversible harm: testosterone and a double mastectomy.

BIG LIES ABOUT GENDER

Lie #1: We All Have a Gender Identity.

The principle lie forming the foundation of this entire movement is that we all have a gender identity. We do not. We have personalities.

The term "gender identity" was first coined in 1964 by psychiatry professor Robert Stoller,[3] and popularized by John Money, a psychologist, sexologist, and professor at Johns Hopkins University.[4] It is an utterly meaningless term that should never have been invented. Indeed, if you ask one thousand people on the street what it means, as I have done, you'll have great difficulty finding a single coherent answer. The dictionary defines it as "each person's internal and individual experience of gender." This, of course, is a circular definition which begs the question: what is gender?

Until a few years ago, we all knew what gender was. It was a more polite word for sex. But the political Left, led by academics and feminist scholars such as Judith Butler, have redefined gender to mean something entirely different than sex. Gender, to them, is a feeling of what it means to be a man or woman, and it is entirely based on regressive, sexist stereotypes.[5]

The go-to remedy for a "gender identity" that does not align with a child's "sex assigned at birth" is to simply affirm a child's delusion that they were "born wrong," or to plant that idea in their vulnerable minds in the first place. Children are celebrated for finding their "true selves" and encouraged to "socially transition" with a new name and pronouns.

Social transition is not a benign intervention. It is causing grave psychological harm. People may say, "What's the problem? Just go along with the pronouns." But when you call a girl a boy, or when you call her "he/him," the message is clear. You are affirming that she was supposed to be something she's not. You're encouraging self-hatred. It's psychological abuse, and we should never play along with it.

Lie #2: Children Can Consent to Puberty Blockers, Cross-Sex Hormones, and the Removal of Their Sexual Organs.

In what is undoubtedly the greatest child abuse scandal in modern medical history, children who have suffered trauma, abuse, or who are struggling with various mental health comorbidities are being taught that "gender" is the source of their distress, and the solution is to modify their bodies with experimental puberty blockers, cross-sex hormones, and surgeries. They are told that puberty blockers are reversible, and they just buy the child time to explore their gender identity. Puberty blockers are not reversible any more than time is reversible. Once years of development are lost, there is no going back.

What are puberty blockers? Technically, they are gonadotropin releasing hormone (GnRH) analogues. They work by suppressing the production of estrogen in girls and testosterone in boys. Without these hormones, a child's secondary sex characteristics won't develop.[6] Girls' breasts won't grow, their hips won't get wider,[7] boys' penises won't grow, they suffer testicular atrophy,[8,9] and one widely known side effect is bone demineralization.[10] Some studies even point to IQ loss.[11] Because there have never been any long-term studies or clinical trials into the use of these drugs for the purpose of child transition, there remain many unanswered questions about the harms they are causing.

Cross-sex hormones are very simply the hormones associated with the opposite sex. Girls are prescribed testosterone, and boys are prescribed estrogen. Our bodies are not equipped to function with high doses of the opposite-sex hormones. While on testosterone, girls will develop facial and body hair, their voice will deepen almost immediately and irreversibly, body fat gets redistributed and they will gain muscle mass.[12] They may develop male-pattern baldness,[13] and will suffer from vaginal[14] and uterine atrophy.[15] After a number of years, it is common for females to require a hysterectomy due to the damage caused.[16] They may also get an oophorectomy, the removal of their ovaries.[17] Teenage girls are being sent into menopause.

For boys, excess estrogen may cause gynecomastia, erectile dysfunction, infertility,[18] thinning hair, and fat redistribution to the hips.[19]

In addition to the above side effects, there are also indications that puberty blockers and cross-sex hormones are leading to cancer.[20, 21]

The final step in this medical pathway of child transition is what trans activists call "gender-affirming surgery." As with almost all of the terminology they use, this is a misnomer. There is nothing affirming about cutting body parts off of children. It is mutilation. Girls as young as twelve years old in the United States have received double mastectomies, cutting off their healthy breast tissue.[22] Boys as young as sixteen are receiving penile inversion vaginoplasties. This is where surgeons castrate the boy, and then invert the penis to form what is called a neovagina.[23] Oftentimes, because puberty blockers stunted the growth of the penis, there is not enough tissue to do this surgery. In what is an unregulated experiment on children, doctors will then cut out some of the boy's colon, or some of his peritoneum, and use that tissue to form the lining of his false vaginal cavity.[24] It is really just a wound. A wound that has to be dilated for the rest of his life to prevent it from closing up.

HOW THESE LIES HARM CHILDREN

Gender ideologues have tried to convince all of society, loudly and angrily, that to not go along with a child's new name and pronouns is misgendering, and a form of discrimination based on their gender identity. And to a large extent, they have been successful. There's been a meteoric rise[25] in both trans-identifying children, and gender clinics to meet their medical demands. The average age of a little girl seeking to transition is eleven, for boys it's age thirteen.[26] Many of those kids are put on a highway littered with pharmaceuticals and surgery.

The number-one activist justification for this abuse is that if we don't affirm children as the opposite sex and modify their bodies with chemical castration drugs, hormones, and surgeries, they will kill themselves. This is a despicable lie with not an ounce of evidence to back it up,[27] but this lie is repeated in virtually every conversation they have. Gender doctors even coerce parents to go along with transition by saying they can have "a dead daughter or a live son."

Some of those activists have coopted groups[28] that swear to "do no harm," like the American Academy of Pediatrics, into endorsing the unnecessary medicalization of children.[29] Several countries have codified child transition in law, or through human rights statutes. In some places, it is now a crime, punishable by hefty fines and/or prison sentences, for a parent to object to the transition of their own child.[30] It is a criminal offense to reject your child's trans identification, and to help them feel comfortable with their bodies.

Gender identity indoctrination is officially part of school curriculums starting as early as kindergarten. The most popular resource in the world used to teach children about gender identity—it's even used in children's hospitals to teach staff—is a cartoonish image called the Genderbread Person.

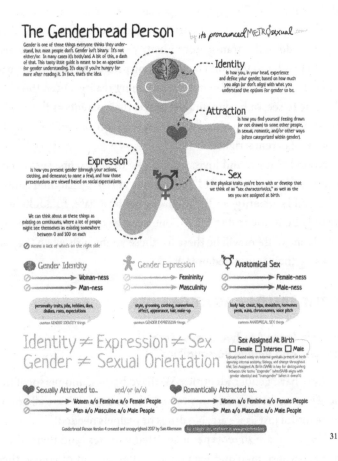

The Genderbread Person

Gender is one of those things everyone thinks they understand, but most people don't. Gender isn't binary. It's not either/or. In many cases it's both/and. A bit of this, a dash of that. This tasty little guide is meant to be an appetizer for gender understanding. It's okay if you're hungry for more after reading it. In fact, that's the idea.

b/g it's pronounced METROsexual

Identity is how you, in your head, experience and define your gender; based on how much you align (or don't align) with what you understand the options for gender to be.

Attraction is how you find yourself feeling drawn (or not drawn) to some other people, in sexual, romantic, and/or other ways (often categorized within gender).

Expression is how you present gender (through your actions, clothing, and demeanor, to name a few), and how those presentations are viewed based on social expectations.

Sex is the physical traits you're born with or develop that we think of as "sex characteristics," as well as the sex you are assigned at birth.

We can think about all these things as existing on continuums, where a lot of people might see themselves as existing somewhere between 0 and 100 on each

⊘ means a lack of what's on the right side

Gender Identity	Gender Expression	Anatomical Sex
⊘———→ Woman-ness	⊘———→ Femininity	⊘———→ Female-ness
⊘———→ Man-ness	⊘———→ Masculinity	⊘———→ Male-ness
personality traits, jobs, hobbies, likes, dislikes, roles, expectations	style, grooming, clothing, mannerisms, affect, appearance, hair, make-up	body hair, chest, hips, shoulders, hormones, penis, vulva, chromosomes, voice pitch
common GENDER IDENTITY things	*common GENDER EXPRESSION things*	*common ANATOMICAL SEX things*

Identity ≠ Expression ≠ Sex
Gender ≠ Sexual Orientation

Sex Assigned At Birth
☐ Female ☐ Intersex ☐ Male

Typically based solely on external genitalia present at birth, ignoring internal anatomy, biology, and change throughout life. Sex Assigned At Birth (SAAB) is key for distinguishing between the terms "cisgender" (when SAAB aligns with gender identity) and "transgender" (when it doesn't)

♥ **Sexually Attracted to...**   and/or (a/o)   ♥ **Romantically Attracted to...**

⊘———→ Women a/o Feminine a/o Female People		⊘———→ Women a/o Feminine a/o Female People
⊘———→ Men a/o Masculine a/o Male People		⊘———→ Men a/o Masculine a/o Male People

Genderbread Person Version 4 created and uncopyrighted 2017 by Sam Killermann   *For a bigger size, read more at: www.genderbread.org*

It defines gender identity as being based on your personality, jobs, hobbies, likes, dislikes, roles, and expectations. The entirety of gender ideology hinges on stereotypes of what it means to be a man or a woman, a boy or a girl. Gender ideologues believe that our gender is on a spectrum, which is entirely based on regressive stereotypes.

Those who push the idea that children can be born in the wrong body are also harming children by driving a wedge between them and their parents. This applies especially to public school teachers. It is official policy in many districts to hide from parents that their child has adopted a transgender identity.[32] Other students are also directed to refer to the child by the wrong pronouns, leaving the parents as the only voice who may be affirming reality. Often the child will come to see, or be encouraged to see, their parents as the enemy. This is a dangerous psychological intervention on children, and a violation of parental rights.

Nobody knows and loves a child like their parents, yet schools are undermining parents and putting kids at risk by handing control of the child's identity, and sometimes medical care, to adults who may only be in the child's life for one year, or one doctor's appointment. None of them will be there for these young girls when they are mourning their amputated breasts.

▨ THE TRUTH ABOUT GENDER

Truth #1: There Are Two Sexes, Zero Genders, and Infinite Personalities.

We don't have gender identities. We have bodies, and personalities. There is no right or wrong way to be a boy or a girl. We are all unique and beautiful just as we are. No drugs or scalpels needed!

Yes, there are stereotypes associated with sex, and there always will be, because men and women are different, but of course there is deviation from the "norm." There are girls who like to play football, work on cars, and play with the boys. There's a term for them. They're called beautiful girls! They're also sometimes called tomboys, and there's a good chance if you're a woman reading this, you were a tomboy. It didn't mean you were an actual boy!

There are boys who prefer to cook, draw, read and dance. There's a term for them. They're called amazing boys. They might not like football, but are destined to become a top chef, great artist, and connected dad.

Truth #2: There Is No Such Thing as a Transgender Child.

No child is born in the wrong body. No child has a "gender" that is different from their biological sex. And the lie that you can have a "living daughter or dead son" is crumbling under the weight of new evidence.

With the adult population, evidence clearly shows that suicides go up, not down, after transition.[33] When it comes to kids, a recent study out of Finland revealed that over twenty-three years, there were only seven suicides out of more than two thousand children who attended the gender clinic. This includes those children in distress who were not medicalized. Annualized, the suicide rate was .051 percent.[34] Every suicide is a tragedy, but this showed that there was no epidemic of pediatric suicides for children experiencing distress about their sex.

Historically, 80–95 percent of gender-confused children who had no medical intervention embraced their natal sex after undergoing natural puberty.[35] Those who are denied that critical developmental phase suffer irreversible harm.

"...the process of transition didn't make me feel better. It magnified what I found was wrong with myself...I expected it to change everything, but I was just me, with a slightly deeper voice."[36]

"It's like a virus...infected me and it happened so quickly and I was right there agreeing to every single thing, but I don't know how it happened...I can't have kids...I feel like I just have to accept the scraps of the life I should've had...."[37]

These children were told they were transgender. They were lied to. They didn't need surgery or drugs. They needed to be loved for the boy or girl that they actually were.

It is impossible for anyone to "transition." Take it from Dr. Paul McHugh, distinguished professor of psychiatry at the Johns Hopkins University School of Medicine, who finally shut down the hospital's sex-reassignment surgeries because he saw no improvement in the mental well-being of his patients:

> Transgendered men do not become women, nor do transgendered women become men. All (including Bruce Jenner) become feminized men or masculinized women, counterfeits or impersonators of the sex with which they "identify." In that lies their problematic future.[38]

Truth #3: Children Cannot Consent to Puberty Blockers (or Cross-Sex Hormones, or the Removal of Their Sexual Organs)

We have no idea what the lack of their natural hormones are doing to children's developing brains because this has never been done before in the history of the human race, and there has never been a single clinical trial. Puberty blockers are not approved by the FDA to treat gender dysphoria. They are used off-label all across the world[39] The approved use for these drugs, typically Lupron, is to treat prostate cancer, endometriosis, uterine fibroids,[40] and they are still used to this day to chemically castrate pedophiles.[41]

Puberty blockers are given as early as Tanner stage 2, which for girls is around ten or eleven years of age. Boys are typically six months to a year later.[42] One result of puberty blockers—which Marci Bowers, president of the World Professional Association for Transgender Health (WPATH) admitted to on a leaked Zoom call—is that none of the boys who started on puberty blockers at Tanner stage 2 have ever been able to have an orgasm as an adult.[43] Children are being turned into anorgasmic, mutilated, sterilized, lifelong pharmaceutical patients, forever reliant on cross-sex hormones.

...I really didn't understand all the ramifications of any of the medical decisions I was making...I wasn't capable of understanding...I don't know if I'll be able to fully carry a child, and I might be at increased risk for certain cancers, mainly cervical cancer...no child should have to experience what I have.[44]

It is impossible for a child aged ten, or twelve, or sixteen, or arguably even eighteen years of age to comprehend, and thereby consent, to such dangerous, untested, and permanent interventions.

When the AAP, AMA, Endocrine Society, and WPATH are forced to finally show their evidence to justify child transition, they will fail. This entire movement has been led by activists, not science.

This is child abuse, pure and simple, and we must not tolerate it a moment longer.

▆ HOW THESE TRUTHS PROTECT CHILDREN

When people know the truth about gender—that there's no such thing as a "gender identity," just a beautiful array of personalities; that there's no such thing as a transgender child; and that children cannot consent to experimental transgender treatments—they take action.

Just two or three years ago, almost no politicians would touch this issue. Now, half of the states in the U.S. have passed legislation to stop this child abuse.[45]

Several countries in Europe are also applying the brakes. In England, the so-called "gender-affirming care" model is all but dead. Puberty blockers have been banned, not by politicians, but by the pediatricians after conducting a systematic review of all of the evidence.[46] Scotland went even further, also banning cross-sex hormones for children. Similar progress has been made in Sweden and

Finland.[47] Denmark[48] and Norway[49] look to be following suit, along with progress in Germany and France.

Another recent development in the fight to protect our kids, and perhaps the most encouraging one, is that lawfare is finally underway. Several detransitioners are suing, and a new law firm even formed in Texas just to represent them. Four dads with seventeen kids between them all left their previous law firms and formed a new one, feeling called to fight for these kids who were harmed by the cult of gender.[50]

Javier Milei, president of Argentina, gave a speech where he said he "did not come here to guide lambs" but to "awaken lions."[51] With every bit of awareness that is spread about the truth of child transition, we're also awakening lions—moms and dads who have had enough of this assault on our kids.

▉ CHILD PROTECTION IN ACTION

What can we do to stop this? It's a monumental undertaking, but we can't let the scope of the problem deter us. For myself, I have one conversation at a time, and I've been doing so out on the streets and at university campuses in about eighty cities around the world, wearing my trademark sign that reads "Children Cannot Consent to Puberty Blockers."

It may be unconventional, but it works. I have always had 100 percent confidence that when enough parents learn what is going on, we will put a stop to this, and it is happening.

Gender ideology is one of the greatest lies ever told, and we must keep exposing the absurdity of it. Even activists who support the trans agenda who approach me on the street can't help but agree with me that we shouldn't push stereotypes on kids, but they have a blind spot. They can't see that not only are they promoting these stereotypes, they're suggesting children should change their bodies to more closely match them.

For those with people in their life who support this negative, child-destroying cult of the gendered soul, I have two recommendations:

1. Say things they agree with. A statement like "There's no right way to be a boy or a girl" is something that almost everyone will instinctively support. Even the angriest Far Left social-justice warrior will have to pause and agree with you, and that's powerful. In that moment, you will have caused something called cognitive dissonance—the discomfort that arises in someone when they simultaneously hold two contradictory beliefs. They might have started off the conversation thinking you are some terrible bigot for not believing in the existence of transgender children, but when you say something they can't help but agree with, they get confused. That's a wonderful outcome with a trans activist. Confusion leads to questioning, which brings us to my second tactic.

2. Ask them questions. People who push gender ideology don't allow themselves to question it. They police their own thoughts, and shut out any external sources of information which will challenge their beliefs. It's too much for them to confront that this ideology they've been promoting is literal child abuse, but by asking them questions, you're not arguing with them; you're getting them to think.

This fight has been led by parents doing what they can, with no money, but with an abundance of heart. Against what seem to be insurmountable odds, we are winning. We have the truth on our side, and the truth spreads for free.

Keep having conversations.

Chris Elston, aka Billboard Chris

Chris Elston, aka Billboard Chris, is a father of two girls from Vancouver, Canada, who has been traveling the world since 2020, having street conversations, generating media, and reaching millions of people about the dangers of gender ideology—specifically, the practice of giving children harmful puberty-blocking drugs, cross-sex hormones, and surgeries.

PORNOGRAPHY

JON SCHWEPPE

"I first found porn when I was eleven years old," a young Christian named Connor confessed to me recently. "That was almost twenty years ago."

Like so many, Connor's first exposure to pornography was accidental.

"I was on my parents' old computer playing an online game. I think it was *RuneScape*. And while scrolling the internet, I stumbled upon a pop-up window full of naked women. They were performing sexual acts with one another."

He paused.

"At the time, I didn't know exactly what I was seeing," Connor explained. "But my body became weak and numb as I just kept staring. I don't know if I sat there for thirty seconds or thirty minutes. No idea. I just remember being stunned."

That initial shock quickly gave way to curiosity. And then obsession.

"It actually started with Hollywood. Nothing rated R. We're talking like PG-13 films. I started searching for some of those scenes on YouTube to watch and rewatch," Connor told me. He would notice his imagination running wild every time he came across even the most inoffensive romantic scene from a movie.

After a year or two of this, the initial excitement wore off, and Connor began looking for something more provocative to satisfy his appetite. He ultimately found his way toward online pornography websites like Pornhub.

"Each time I would get a rush. And I wanted more of it," he said.

Connor was trapped.

"I was a Christian teen with a deep desire to be pure in my love life," Connor explained. "But I was in a vicious cycle where multiple times a week, I'd watch porn, masturbate, immediately experience deep regret, and then start all over again."

This story, which is all too common for American children today, continues in a predictable way: Connor lost his virginity as a teenager. He went on to struggle with relationships and physical boundaries. He was exposed to "nearly all forms of sexual acts" despite his faith and conscience convicting him otherwise.

"I was a sex addict lacking the willpower to fight," Connor lamented. This went on for ten years.

Connor did manage to turn it around. "I finally said I had had enough," he told me. "I called on God for help, and through immense effort where I literally slept in the same room with other guys struggling with this addiction, I managed to kick the habit for good." He is now married with children.[1]

Connor's happy ending is an outlier. What happened to him has unfortunately become all too common. Online pornography is everywhere—according to a survey from Common Sense Media, 73 percent of teenagers report having watched online pornography at some point. The survey also found that the average age a child first consumes online pornography is now just twelve years old. Fifteen percent of respondents said they first saw online pornography at *age ten* or younger.[2]

Ubiquitous, normalized porn is destroying our kids' innocence and wreaking grievous mental, physical, and emotional harms on them. It doesn't have to be this way.

▪ BIG LIES ABOUT PORN

Most people concede that pornography is bad. Outside of a few paid shills for the adult industry, there isn't much of a propornography movement. But despite the lack of defenders, the adult industry benefits from several big lies.

Lie #1: Parents Should Be Able to Handle This Problem All by Themselves.

Don't they purchase porn filters for their devices? Don't they pay attention to their kids' screen time? Aren't they adequately supervising sleepovers and playdates? Why does the government need to get involved in something that is fundamentally a responsibility of parents?

These arguments fail to account for reality. Filter technology is always playing catch-up to the fast-paced world of porn distribution, and device manufacturers do parents no favors on this front. The true efficacy of these filters, especially against kids trying to evade them, is dubious.

Even if technologically savvy parents somehow managed to install functional porn filters on every device in their own home, that doesn't account for the fact that kids will have plenty of access to unfiltered internet outside the home among their peers. It is ludicrous to suggest that filters are enough. They've been around for decades, and online pornography has become more pervasive and more easily available to children than ever before.

But there's an even bigger reason that online pornography has flourished and been allowed to maintain its unfettered access to our kids—and it's the biggest lie of them all.

Lie #2 Pornography Is Free Speech.

This modern understanding views pornography as protected speech under the First Amendment. Therefore, it is unconstitutional to pass legislation that would punish adults for distributing harmful material to kids.

This is a lie. But it's understandable why so many people have fallen for it. Blame the Supreme Court.

During the early days of the internet, a number of forward thinkers saw the threat that online pornography would pose to children, especially as technology advanced. These leaders pushed Congress for action, and eventually succeeded.

In 1996, Congress passed a federal antipornography bill called the Communications Decency Act (CDA). The law sought to limit the online distribution of obscene and indecent material to minors—a huge win for families.

But left-wing groups asked the Supreme Court to intervene, and it did.

In *Reno v. ACLU* (1997), the Supreme Court struck down the CDA, finding numerous inventive ways to distinguish it from other laws bound by the Court's numerous precedents covering brick-and-mortar institutions. This allowed the Court to uphold ID-check laws in the states, while still prohibiting their equivalent online.

After granting this special right to online pornographers, the Supreme Court conceded the government's interest in protecting kids from online pornography, but insisted that Congress could pass a law so long as it used the least restrictive means possible to prevent a broad suppression of nonobscene adult "speech." In other words, protecting kids from the most horrific pornographic content imaginable must come second to the satiety of adult desires.[3]

For many bills, a Supreme Court ruling like this would have been the end. Once the Supreme Court speaks, Congress often lacks the willpower to revisit an issue. Not so in this case. In a rare case of bipartisan statesmanship, our leaders were insistent.

Enter the Child Online Protection Act (COPA), an age-verification bill that specifically addressed the Court's main concerns. COPA explicitly targeted the internet transmission of "material harmful to minors."

Congress's findings in COPA were crystal clear—the problem was very grave. And the least restrictive means it could find to effectively combat the problem was the same that legislators have always found in the context of the real world: requiring the purveyors of commercial pornography to limit access to their content to adults, through whatever age-verification measures were reasonably technologically available.[4]

In October 1998, a little more than a year after the Supreme Court struck down the CDA, Bill Clinton signed COPA into law. But it never went into effect.

Left-wing groups once again sued, and ultimately, in *ACLU v. Ashcroft* (2004), the Supreme Court ruled five to four that COPA was also unconstitutional. In his majority opinion, Justice Anthony Kennedy argued that parents who wanted to protect their kids from pornography should just suck it up and pay for filters:

> Filters are less restrictive than COPA. They impose selective restrictions on speech at the receiving end, not universal restrictions at the source. ... [T]he Government failed to introduce specific evidence proving that existing filtering technologies are less effective than the restrictions in COPA.[5]

Justice Stephen Breyer's dissenting opinion, joined by Justices William Rehnquist and Sandra Day O'Connor, belittled this argument: "The presence of filtering software is not an alternative legislative approach to the problem of protecting children from exposure to commercial pornography. Rather, it is part of the status quo, i.e., the backdrop against which Congress enacted the present statute." [6]

This was true—in fact, the congressional findings explicitly contemplated and then *rejected* a filter-based approach as ineffective. Another dissenting opinion, by Justice Antonin Scalia, suggested that the Court's requirements were far too strict—the type of sexually provocative pandering covered by the bill enjoyed no First Amendment protections whatsoever. Scalia argued Congress shouldn't even have to show that its solution was the least restrictive means of fixing the problem.

But the damage was done. There would be no third attempt at federal legislation. Even though the people demanded it. Even though the legislatures had gotten it done. The Court ruled, and it said "game over."

As a result, online pornography proliferated, and a generation of America's children dealt with the consequences.

HOW THESE LIES HARM CHILDREN

As mentioned, some three-quarters of teens (73 percent) have viewed porn, either intentionally or accidentally. Nearly half (44 percent) indicated they had done so intentionally, including 52 percent of boys.[7] But girls are being ensnared by online pornography, too, with 36 percent of girls indicating they had viewed porn intentionally.

Grammy Award–winning singer Billie Eilish has spoken out about her early encounters with pornography, which she calls a "disgrace."

"I started watching porn when I was, like, eleven," Eilish told Howard Stern on his Sirius XM radio show in 2021. This led to serious problems for her. The pop star suggested that viewing violent forms of pornography at an early age led to unhealthy sexual encounters early on in her dating life.

"The first few times I, you know, had sex, I was not saying no to things that were not good. It was because I thought that's what I was supposed to be attracted to," she said.[8] The data backs up Eilish's experience. When it comes to porn, what happens online doesn't stay online. According to a survey conducted in the mid-2000s, kids between the ages of ten and fifteen who had been exposed to pornography were six and a half times more likely to report sexually aggressive behavior—and twenty-four times more likely if they had been exposed to violent material.[9]

According to another more recent study from Middlesex University in London, some 44 percent of males and 29 percent of females reported that online pornography had given them ideas about the types of sex they wanted to try out.[10] The desire to practice what they had learned increased as kids got older: 21 percent for eleven- and twelve-year-olds, 39 percent for thirteen- and fourteen-year-olds, and 42 percent for fifteen- and sixteen-year-olds.

Evan Myers documented particularly horrifying examples of this "try it out" phenomenon in *National Review*:

> Heidi Olson, a pediatric sexual-assault nurse examiner in Kansas City, has similarly disturbing stories. "I always assumed that whoever would be acting out on a child would be a creepy old man in a basement," Olson tells me. "No one prepared me for the huge number of violent sexual acts in which children and teenagers are often the perpetrators themselves."

According to studies, at least 33 percent of sexual assaults against children are perpetrated by other children or teens, and though Olson did not initially conclude porn was to blame for these horrible incidents, the evidence kept mounting: "One time," she explains, "we were taking care of a thirteen-year-old girl who had been raped by her sixteen-year-old brother and she spontaneously disclosed that he said, 'I was looking at pornography and I can't stop thinking about it' just before he raped her."[11]

Exposure to online pornography, especially its more extreme variations, such as BDSM, choking, rape, incest, bestiality, multiple partners, humiliation, adult/teenager, and scatological porn, dramatically warps kids' views about sex and relationships.

These more extreme variations—often called "fetishes" or "kinks"—are quite prevalent. Many of the categories listed above feature prominently on the most highly trafficked online porn websites.

Elementary school kids are just one or two clicks away from the most violent sadomasochistic pornography imaginable. And these porn websites have been freely distributing this content to young children unperturbed by the U.S. government for more than twenty years.

When the CDA was passed in 1996, most people still used dial-up modems. Online porn at that point consisted almost entirely of still images, and the few videos that existed took hours to download and often included viruses and malware. The logic of *Reno* in 1997—which relied in part on the idea that "the Internet is not as 'invasive' as radio or television"—made some amount of sense for that moment in time.

But the introduction of broadband and modern internet speeds have changed the game entirely. Download speeds quickly increased fiftyfold and even hundredfold.[12] This led to a transformation in how Americans consumed pornography, moving it ever more into the digital realm. While adult movie theaters, sex stores, and nudie magazines were covered by age-verification requirements in the real world, their online equivalents were entirely outside the law's reach. Pornography could now be peddled to children without any threat of legal consequence.

Today, the problem has only been exacerbated by the ubiquity of video and live streaming. A child doesn't even need to enter a website's domain name to find pornography. They can find exactly what they're looking for on Google. They can browse for it on a social-media platform like TikTok. In some cases, like on X (formerly Twitter), the porn might even come looking for them!

Because of this, children are seeing more obscenity—and *more graphic* obscenity—than at any point in our nation's history. Yet we continue to operate under the logic of the 1990s. Adults, we are told, have a First Amendment right to seek out pornographic content and enjoy it how they see fit. Protecting children is an afterthought.

That's no longer acceptable. It's time to leave the 1990s behind.

■ THE TRUTH ABOUT REGULATING PORN

Truth #1: We Should Regulate Porn.

Addictive behaviors of all sorts are regulated to minimize the dangers to minors. Online sports gambling has been legalized in dozens of states, and all the gambling firms require age verification. Customers must also undergo age verification to buy tobacco or alcohol online. Obscenity has never been classified as free speech protected under the First Amendment, and the effects of pornography on young minds are arguably more devastating than those substances we already regulate.[13]

Are we really going to require age verification for all these other industries and then say it's a bridge too far for online pornography? Come on.

Truth #2: We Can Regulate Porn.

The best way to do that is by requiring online porn websites to verify the ages of their users and allow only adults to access their content. It's obvious that the compelling state interest in protecting kids from online pornography identified in both *Reno* and *Ashcroft* has become more compelling over time. And it's clearer than ever that age verification is the least restrictive means of achieving that interest.

I've spoken with several experts within the age-verification industry, including some that work directly with the adult industry. The technology has improved dramatically. All of these processes take great care to anonymize customer data and discard it after use. We have the means to effectively regulate—let's use them.

The Supreme Court obviously got it wrong on the CDA and COPA, but even if we accept those decisions' arguments, the set of facts has changed dramatically in twenty years. That alone should encourage the Supreme Court to revisit the question. Justice Kennedy's best argument in his majority opinion was that parents could protect their kids by buying internet filters from private companies. Today, that argument is laughable on its face. Who should be held responsible for paying for technology to protect kids? Parents, or the porn websites knowingly distributing obscene material to any fifth grader with access to a search engine?

It's time to relitigate all of this, and that's exactly what the new batch of age-verification bills passing all over the country set the stage to do.

■ HOW THESE TRUTHS PROTECT CHILDREN

Combining the willpower to protect kids with the tools of age-verification technology prevents a lot of avoidable damage to children. Since 2022, sixteen states have passed age-verification bills requiring pornography websites to verify the adult age of their users prior to distributing sexually explicit content. These states are: Louisiana, Utah, Virginia, Mississippi, Arkansas, Montana, Texas, North Carolina, Florida, Idaho, Indiana, Kansas, Kentucky, Alabama, Nebraska, and Georgia.[14]

The constitutional argument is simple: states have an interest in defending children within their boundaries from harmful material on the internet, and requiring age verification from online porn distributors is the least restrictive means to do so.

These bills are tremendously popular and have consistently passed with bipartisan majorities. They've also weathered legal scrutiny quite well. U.S. district courts have thrown out legal challenges to both Utah's and Louisiana's age-verification laws. And although a federal judge issued an injunction on the Texas bill, the 5th Circuit Court of Appeals not only stayed the injunction, but expedited the appeals process, allowing the bill to temporarily go into effect.

These age-verification laws are also starting to change the behavior of pornography websites—at least in part. Pornhub, one of the most-trafficked pornography websites in the United States, has implemented Louisiana's state-ID requirement, but has pulled out of several states, including Virginia and Texas, rather than comply with their age-verification laws.[15]

But state laws on their own will not solve the problem. Jurisdiction matters, and it will be difficult for a state attorney general to rein in a pornography website based out of Romania. Ultimately, this makes the case for federal legislation.

▮ CHILD PROTECTION IN ACTION

A recent RMG Research poll commissioned by my employer, the American Principles Project, found that 83 percent of Americans supported a federal age-verification law to protect kids from online pornography.[16] This has never been a problem of public opinion or even political leadership. The problem has always been bad court rulings.

The overwhelmingly bipartisan support in the states indicates that we could move an age-verification bill at the federal level. There are a number of options, such as Senator Mike Lee's SCREEN Act, or even a section 230 reform bill like Representative Greg Steube's CASE-IT Act that strips immunity from civil liability away from online pornography websites.

We could also simply enforce existing obscenity laws, especially as they relate to minors. The Supreme Court left federal obscenity statutes alone in both *Reno* and *Ashcroft*. The laws are already on the books, waiting for an administration with the political will to enforce them.

Maybe there's something we haven't thought of yet. Perhaps a creative age verification law could direct the Department of Justice to seize domain names, block traffic, and/or explore other ways to prevent foreign pornography websites from ensnaring American kids.

Much more discussion about strategies lies ahead. The bottom line is that we're going to get this done. There's a national consensus that we should protect kids from online pornography—there always has been—now we just need the Supreme Court to get out of the way and let us keep our children safe.

Jon Schweppe, policy director, American Principles Project

Jon Schweppe is the policy director for American Principles Project. In this role, he has served as an important advocate in the fight to protect kids from online pornography. He coauthored the groundbreaking 2020 report, *Protecting Free Speech and Defending Kids: A Proposal to Amend Section 230*, which advocated for imposing civil liability on websites that distribute pornographic content to minors. Schweppe has developed model legislation, lobbied legislators, and testified on behalf of age verification in half a dozen states. He is now working on a federal antipornography initiative that he hopes will be implemented by the next Republican administration.

ECONOMIC

THE ECONOMY

CHRISTOPHER BEDFORD

In 2011, the Sierra Club launched an advertising blitz in Washington, D.C.'s subways.[1] The posters showed a darkened picture of a coal plant emitting fumes next to a toddler holding an inhaler to his lips. "Your local coal burning power plant has a new filter," the ads read. "His name is Danny."[2]

Coal, an industry already in decline, was an easy target. An economic driver for two centuries, it was less sexy than liquid natural gas, or the "green" newcomers. Songs about the hard life of mining coal were a part of the American canon. "Who," the Sierra Cub might have wondered, "doesn't want to move past all of that?"

Coal's competitors in the energy industry certainly did. They were eager to grow their own market shares, even if that meant donating millions to groups claiming that American energy is bad for American children. President Obama agreed: he was happy to rack up a win with the green wing of his party.

How to handle the massive economic shifts this sort of change would bring to the country was a question for "the markets" to figure out. Then presidential candidate Joe Biden would help laid-off miners and their families navigate the transformation by championing an initiative to teach them how to write code.[3]

One by one, the plants and the mines shut down. The "good guys" won. "In 2010," the Sierra Club brags in one brochure, "burning coal generated 45 percent of US electricity. Today, it generates only 27 percent."[4]

But what of the people left behind in a supposedly dynamic and modernizing economy? The vice president's coding plan turned out to be little more than a fraudulent public-relations campaign. Even if the market for middle-aged, American, novice computer coders had been booming (which it was not), the training and job placement necessary for success would have made for a heavy lift. But the promise had served its purpose: answering any uncomfortable questions that might arise about the human consequences. People worried least of all about the children of West Virginia and eastern Kentucky and the other regions affected.

Depression descended on towns that had once seen gainful employment. Drug and alcohol abuse climbed steadily, and with them, the "deaths of despair" D.C. finally began to notice after *Hillbilly Elegy* became a bestseller. Families came apart. The tax base collapsed. In 2021, a decade after the subway ads pleading to protect the children of Appalachia from the coal industry, three[5] elementary[6] schools[7] closed[8] down in Boone County, West Virginia alone. These closures are part of a broader trend across coal country, where families have collapsed or left town. No glossy advertising campaign foregrounded the plight of kids left behind with no school and few future prospects: just welfare and pills.

No family in Boone County would have made these decisions about their future. But they weren't the ones who made the calls. That fell to men and women in Washington, D.C., New York City, Seattle, San Francisco and other distant power centers—men and women who had the gall to claim it was all about the kids.

■ BIG LIES ABOUT THE ECONOMY

Lie #1: Depressing the Economy "for the Children."

Grover Norquist, who is also featured in these pages, likes to joke that when politicians say they need to raise taxes for X "because X is a crucial priority!" what they really mean is X is so low on their list of priorities they aren't going to pay for it with any of the dollars they already raised with existing taxes. If it was a priority, it would be taken care of. Since it's not, up go the taxes.

More often than not, the same is true when they tell you, "It's for the children."

Politicians and activists love to use kids as political props. Those millions of military-age young men streaming illegally across the border? They're just families with kids! Laws phasing out your truck or family minivan? It's for the children, who will die of global warming otherwise. Shutting down coal plants and mines? For the children, whose father is now laid off and whose neighborhood school is now closed.

Lie #2: The Government Will Fill the Gap.

Those same politicians had a plan to prop up all those broken households and left-behind children in Boone County and across the country. In 2012, as president Obama and vice president Biden campaigned for another four years on the job, the White House released a storyboard called "The Life of Julia."[9] The campaign walked through the life of a character named Julia who from birth until death would be taken care of by different government services.

Julia is the main character. She's also the only character. While she is indeed born, and "[u]nder President Obama...decides to have a child," there are no parents in the ad, nor a husband, nor any town or community; just Julia, eventually a baby, and the benevolent hand of the state. No need for a mother and a father. Even gainful employment could take a back seat.

This isn't the sort of life parents would ever want their little girl to have, nor is it the kind of life responsible parents would want for themselves. It's paternalism without parental instincts. And when it's all done, and you're trying to charge your car during regulated rolling blackouts in a neighborhood that industry left behind, our leaders will pretend your sad story and others like it across the country are just "the way things go." But this isn't the case, which brings us to the next big lie.

Lie #3: The Economy Is Out of Our Hands.

It's true, "the economy" is massive and unwieldy. It's true that market forces are difficult things to defy. But that doesn't mean that the economy, as we experience it in our daily lives, hasn't been seriously tinkered with. So many of the realities of our boom-and-bust economic life derive not from naked market forces, but from conscious decisions made by men and women in power. These decisions affect inflation, soaring and falling stocks, housing crises, how labor is incentivized and how capital moves freely, who can sell what to whom, and who can label their beef "Made in the USA." Many of these realities do not arise from nature but from the American legislature, or the Federal Reserve Bank, or a bureaucrat at the World Trade Organization (WTO).

This is not simply a Left-Right issue. Both free-market dogmatists and zealous regulators benefit from citizens' broadly held assumption that child care costs so much because it just *does*; or that taxes on our labor inevitably exceed taxes on other people's investments; or that an American company's decision to move production abroad isn't the sort of thing politicians enabled—or can stop. The 2012 Republican nominee for president, Mitt Romney, perfectly encapsulated the modern GOP's blind spot for Main Street American entrepreneurism with his now infamous claim that "corporations are people."[10] His opponent perfectly encapsulated his own party's blind spot for the same small businesses with his retort: "You didn't build that."[11]

HOW THESE LIES HARM CHILDREN

The statist "Life of Julia" dream traps children in poverty and broken homes. It's well documented how the welfare state constructed over the course of the late twentieth century has disincentivized marriage,[12] leaving hundreds of thousands of children poor, fatherless, and lacking opportunity.

The government's attempt to usurp the role of parent—to children's detriment—appears also in the inheritance tax, or "death tax." This is one battle for the soul of the economy that is still divided by partisanship, with liberals lining up behind the antichild stance here. The death tax weighs most heavily[13] on small family businesses, and hinders Americans from handing down their businesses to their children in one piece. Big corporations, meanwhile, easily dodge these difficulties. Repealing such taxes would help refocus America's economy on securing a future for the next generation.

On the other side of the aisle, Republicans' rejection of organized labor (entrenched, in part, by union leadership's slavish allegiance to Democrat politicians) has hurt American children, destroying well-paying jobs able to provide for whole families. A workforce that can negotiate with management and ownership makes the economy healthier and more truly free. Isolated workers are easier to take advantage of in matters of pay and scheduling.

The mundane but important matter of scheduling deserves more notice. In his book *Tyranny, Inc.: How Private Power Crushed American Liberty*, Sohrab Ahmari tells the story of a thirty-two-year-old waitress and mother of a young baby, who struggles to find child care and make ends meet when her shifts are scheduled only the week before. While restaurant management must often juggle competing interests to find shift time for a loyal and hardworking few—and cover for an often flaky and unreliable many—the situation is untenable for young children.[14]

"Parents with irregular schedules," the *New York Times* reported, citing a University of California study, "had less money and time for family meals, playing with children or helping them with their homework. The biggest way parents' work schedules affected their children? Those with unpredictable schedules were more likely to feel stressed, irritable or depressed."[15, 16]

The lie that nothing can be done about such realities amounts to shrugging at children's suffering. Many are the regulations, incentives, and initiatives that policymakers pursue in the service of private equity, but when it comes to making shift work a more reliable means of putting food on the table, or bringing back manufacturing jobs to empower American fathers to provide for their kids, they throw up their hands.

▨ THE TRUTH ABOUT THE ECONOMY

Truth #1: We Should Put Children's Futures Before Foreign Companies.

On a cross-country reporting trip in the spring of 2020, I pulled over at Allen Etzkorn's cattle ranch, twenty miles east along the Missouri River in Pierre, South Dakota. His wife Mary owns a steakhouse in town, where her mother's French onion soup will warm you up while you wait for dinner.

The day I visited was branding day, and Allen and a group of cowboys were hard at work. The industry had been hard hit by COVID and tough markets in general, but even more insulting was a rule handed down six years earlier by the WTO forbidding them from labeling their products "Made in America." "Some bureaucrat made a deal," surmised one of the younger men.

He was right. Mexican and Canadian cattle companies in particular, knowing American consumers would pay a premium for beef made at home, sued repeatedly at the WTO and won. The Trump administration was working to repeal, but these things take time. It was just this March (2024) when the United States finalized a rule enshrining the "Made in America" label for meat and eggs "born, raised, slaughtered and processed in the United States."[17]

It's the kind of decision that puts generational family ranches and small businesses ahead of multinational corporations. It's the kind of decision that prioritizes our kids and their future over international relations and bureaucratic ease. Victories like these are not impossible if we approach economic policy valuing children more highly than we value foreign corporations and the WTO.

Truth #2: A Pro-Child Economy Isn't Utopian.

When Donald Trump was running for president in 2016, he pledged to bring American manufacturing back to the United States. It was a straightforward idea: countries have insulated key industries from outsourcing for centuries, and the trade regime that made profitable outsourcing possible was only twenty years old. But to so many patronizing politicians and snickering pundits in the Acela Corridor, the American economy that had nurtured families and provided stable employment for generations was a pipe dream.

How exactly are you going to do that?" President Barack Obama asked at an election town hall. "What exactly are you going to do? There's no answer to it."

Trump said "Well, I'm going to negotiate a better deal."

"Well, what, how exactly are you going to negotiate that? What magic wand do you have?"[18]

The wisecracks on the audacity of resurrecting the American Dream were particularly ironic when delivered by the author of *The Audacity of Hope: Thoughts on Reclaiming the American Dream.*

Of course it was possible. No magic wand was needed. In many cases, strong words, a few promises, and the threat of tearing up bad trade deals was enough for a number of companies to bring manufacturing home. Were future administrations to continue and develop these policies, the United States could experience a resurgence in manufacturing, rekindling the sorts of jobs families rely on.

There are many more reasonable, attainable policy steps that can promote child flourishing. We can abolish the death tax, allowing children to take up the work of their parents' hands. We can follow Ahmari's call to[19] pursue a "fairer distribution of the expenses that come with periods of low demand" to bring balance to the lives of workers and their children, resulting in a happier workforce.[20] We can reform welfare: the Heritage Foundation's Robert Rector points out[21] that "eliminating all anti-marriage incentives in these programs overnight would be very expensive," but suggests that "policymakers can reduce welfare's anti-marriage penalties incrementally. A positive first step in this incremental process would be to reform the [Earned Income Tax Credit] EITC. For the most part, the EITC provides refundable tax credits (i.e., cash benefits) to low-income parents who have no federal income tax liability."[22]

Truth #3: A Strong Economy Depends on Strong Parents.

Of course, the problems that beset families can't be fixed solely from the top down (though claims that government "has no role" in a solution are gravely mistaken). Building a more just economy begins with the family, and depends on what we each do to configure our lives and obligations to better care for our kids. Modern culture and its accompanying economic structure demand that women find "self-worth" in the workplace, while often denigrating those who focus more on raising their children.

Today it's very difficult for parents to realize their personal dreams on one salary, but that shouldn't stop them from weighing the costs and benefits of going to work while paying for child care, and perhaps forgoing this path if it's what is best for their kids in the long run. Too often, we fall into the dual-income trap without even considering alternatives.

More and more young people say they don't want to bring kids into this world.[23] Those who do fret they're not wealthy enough yet to afford it. The reality these folks miss is that children are not the jewel in the crown of a happy family or a successful economy—they are the very foundation of a happy family and a successful economy. Adults have the power to model a different way, and consciously teach its precepts to their children.

Teach them that the family is more important than the individual. That the past matters, and should inform the future. That they are links between the family that came before them and the children that will come after them. That we are all interconnected in this thing called the economy, which is about more than individual profit making.

■ HOW THESE TRUTHS PROTECT CHILDREN

A healthy national economy farms food to feed its citizens, manufactures products for use at home and for selling abroad, and is powered by domestic energy sources. A healthy national economy supports Main Street businesses, not because it makes for a catchy political slogan, but because these are where families live and thrive and enter the middle class. A healthy national economy is powered not by massive multinational corporations (though these are essential to global competitiveness), but by these small- and midsized businesses. A healthy national economy is one in which children flourish.

The United States used to have such an economy. Its centers were wide ranging and disparate. Chambers of commerce in Wichita, Kansas; Columbus, Ohio; and Milwaukee, Wisconsin held important sway over both business and politics. This more even spread of capital and opportunity made the American Dream a real and attainable thing. The business owners who achieved it donated to their local churches, joined the Lions Club, and sponsored school sports teams. Neighbors knew and trusted each other. Kids rode their bikes far and wide, and played on those sports teams. When they grew older, they found jobs and opportunities in town that would keep them there, among people they knew and trusted. The cycle continued.

Today, in all but a few special places, this America is a distant memory. The economic conditions that made these sorts of towns possible have been swept away by global trade winds, ushered in by politicians and bureaucrats in Washington. Welfare in its current form has not filled the gap. Civic organizations have collapsed,[24] as has church attendance.[25] Kids are as isolated and atomized as adults, and trust has broken down.

It's a hard outlook, but the problems are not irreversible. We can help guide our economy back toward health, and once again nourish a world where our children flourish.

CHILD PROTECTION IN ACTION

An economy geared toward protecting and promoting kids isn't an abstract idea for dreamers. As the industrialized world tackles declining birth rates and increasingly broken families, it is a practical necessity.

Countries such as Israel,[26] Hungary[27] and Germany[28] have successfully pursued pro-child economic measures using tax benefits, health care policy, and other programs that support the growth of large, intact families. Hungarian president Viktor Orbán in particular has made it a focus of his government to grow and support Hungarian families.

One policy, introduced five years ago,[29] is making interest-free loans of up to 10 million Hungarian forints available to women in their first marriage, where repayment is suspended after her first child is born, suspended another three years and reduced by 30 percent if she has a second, and totally forgiven if she has a third. Other examples[30] include home-buying grants to families with two or more children, mortgage deductions for each child born after the first, grants for families of three children or more to purchase a vehicle, and a lifetime suspension of income taxes for women who have four or more children of any age.

Hungary's progress has been slow, but positive. While 2010 birthrates languished at 1.21 per couple, by 2022 the birthrate had risen to 1.56 per couple—still below the 2.1 level necessary to maintain and slowly grow population.[31] Nearby countries like Italy have taken notice, pledging to learn from Hungary's model to try to reverse their own population decline.[32]

No two situations are the same: tax codes and cultures necessitate differences between the policies various countries can pursue. American thinking, however, must extend beyond immigration and welfare to deal with low native birth rates, and into more creative, child-focused policies that transcend the accepted Republican-Democrat matrix.

We can put our children before ourselves, but it will be difficult. If we want to survive, we have no choice.

Christopher Bedford, writer based in D.C.

Christopher Bedford is the senior editor for politics and Washington correspondent for The Blaze. His work has also been featured in *The Telegraph*, *The New Criterion*, *Compact*, *The American Mind*, *The Washington Examiner*, *National Review* and the *New York Post*. His first book, *The Art of the Donald*, was published in 2016.

GROVER NORQUIST

Mary is now in high school in northern New York state.

Her dad is between jobs again. His company began layoffs a few years ago because a Chinese company sold products at a lower cost. Dad's company had to pay a 7.25 percent[1] New York state business tax and on top of a federal corporate income tax of 35 percent, the highest in the world. China has a 25 percent[2] corporate tax rate and other countries' rates are even lower.

New York's high property taxes, high income taxes, and high business taxes have kept employers from hiring or expanding in the area. Mary's older brother graduated from college nearby and wanted to stay close to home, but he had to leave the state for work.

When the government imposes higher taxes than America's competitors, American workers have to compete on lower wages or go out of business.

Mary's mom had similar challenges when she was looking for work. It was tough to make ends meet with one family paycheck. Mom would have liked to stay home with the children as they grew up, but it is tough for a family to pay the bills with after-tax dollars from Dad's work alone.

The amount of Dad's salary available to the family is reduced by every tax. New York state has income taxes as high as 10.9 percent.[3] State residents face a combined state and local sales tax rate of 8.53 percent.[4] And the property taxes are also rising. Almost every family needs a second income just to pay the taxes.

Mary's older sister used to work in local restaurants, but with property and other taxes hitting the restaurants and its customers, more are closing down and there are fewer and fewer options. And traveling to other towns for work is harder with the New York state gas tax of 36.7 cents[5] per gallon.

It is tough to see how this will turn around, because high taxes flow from high levels of government spending.

New York state will spend $245.8 billion[6] in fiscal year 2024.

Florida, by contrast, will spend $116 billion.[7] Florida has 3.4 million[8] more people than New York. So New Yorkers pay more than twice as much for the state government as people in Florida. They both have roads and schools and police.

New York's higher taxes pay for more government bureaucrats, higher pensions and more days off (for government workers not ordinary citizens like Mary's dad). This is a case of higher taxes with nothing to show for it.

Florida does not have a state income tax. It doesn't need it. It spends half as much per capita as New York.

As a result, more investment and jobs are moving to lower-taxed states. First the investment leaves, then the jobs, then the young men and women.

Mary's older three siblings have moved to states with lower costs, lower taxes, more jobs. But they are far away, and Mom and Dad are hoping Mary might be able to raise a family in New York. Still the property taxes and high housing costs make that look less likely. It was nice when all the family could be together for weekends.

Travel costs with higher taxes on fuel (cars and planes) are tough and getting worse.

■ BIG LIES ABOUT TAXES

Lie #1: You Are Greedy

Families—Mom and Dad and older children—earn income and build up savings and property by working, earning, and investing. Governments accumulate dollars by taking some of that income and savings and property from you. Year after year. That is difficult to justify to taxpayers who are also voters. That is why politicians often lie.

The first lie politicians unleash is to smear and demonize those they intend to tax.

They like to say you are "greedy" when you oppose having more of your income taken away. Greed and avarice are sins. You know that working on Saturday to provide for your children is not greedy. You are not demanding or envying other people's stuff. Or money. Hard work is a virtue, as is caring for one's family and fulfilling one's responsibilities to others.

But the politician who wishes to seize money from you in property taxes, income taxes, and sales taxes is acting out of greed. He wants what you earned. He wants to take away from you and spend what he did not earn. He wants to deny this to your children. He will use your work, your creation of wealth. He will take it and give it to special interests who reelect him. And too often, he will keep some himself.

Lie #2: Don't Worry. Someone Else Will Pay This New Tax I Am Proposing. Not You. "Them."

This lie comes during a campaign: "I will not raise taxes on you."

Bill Clinton won the presidency in 1992 promising that he would only raise taxes on those earning more than $200,000.[9] Not you. In 2008, Obama promised to tax only those earning more than $250,000.[10] Not you. In 2020, Biden promised that he would only raise taxes on those earning more than $400,000.[11] Not you.

In each case, middle-class Americans were among the first ones to see their taxes raised. In Clinton's first year, he raised the gas tax and also moved to tax your energy use.

And Obama also imposed eight taxes in Obamacare that hit those earning less than $250,000.

The outright promise to not tax low- and middle-income people was used as a lie in three recent presidential campaigns. It worked each time.

Politicians learn. There are two—more subtle—ways to lie to Americans in promising that "you" will not face higher taxes.

Lie #3: The New Tax Will Hit Only "The Rich."

When politicians promise that a new tax will only hit the rich, they have not finished the sentence. This will hit the rich...first. Then eventually everyone else.

This is called trickle-down taxation. Start with a tax on "the rich" and expand it slowly, then faster, to hit more and more Americans.

In 1898 the United States declared war on Spain, which occupied Cuba. To pay for this war, a federal excise tax (FET) was imposed on long-distance phone calls. Back in 1898, only rich people had phones. But by 1960, 79.5 percent[12] of households had a phone, and the tax was hitting Americans rich and poor for decades.

Another example: in 1966, president Lyndon Johnson's administration asserted that there were 155[13] "high income people" who paid almost no federal income taxes—mostly retirees who had their life savings in municipal bonds that were not taxed by the federal government.

To fix this, a "minimum tax" was imposed in 1969, restructured in 1982 as the "alternative minimum tax" or AMT. The AMT gradually hit more and more Americans and threatened to hit thirty million[14] households by 2010.

"Them" (155 people) grew to thirty million of "us." (The 2017 Trump tax reform reduced the number of Americans hit to 0.1 percent of households.)[15]

The most prominent example is the federal income tax created in 1913 to "soak the rich." Back then, you had to earn the equivalent of $11.8 million[16] in 2017 dollars to pay the top rate of 7 percent.[17] Today the *lowest* rate is 10 percent, higher than the original 1913 "top rate" on rich people. Americans now begin to pay income tax at $23,200[18] (married filing jointly.)

And the top individual tax rate on Americans earning more than $609,350[19] is now 37 percent.[20] (When Reagan left office in 1989, it was 28 percent.)[21]

Who are these "rich" people who pay that 37 percent rate?

Many of them are not individuals, but rather small businesses that pay their taxes though the individual rate. They are Subchapter S or pass-through corporations. Partnerships. That "business income" pays salaries, benefits, pensions for workers in many smaller firms.

So, these "rich" are mostly small- and midsized businesses and their employees. These are the key employers on Main Street. The sponsors of youth sports leagues and key donors to local charitable giving. These businesses are deeply embedded into the community.

The politicians who simply want more of your money do not care.

Lie #4: "Big Corporations," Not You, Will Pay "Business" Taxes.

Corporations compose the other group that the big government, big-spending politicians like to promise to tax. Not you, of course. Not your family paychecks and life savings. No. "Big corporations." Like General Motors.

But Mr. General Motors does not simply write a check to pay the tax: it gets passed on to *you*. Your family pays corporate taxes every time you buy something.

When a politician raises taxes "on corporations," the burden of that tax increase is on your shoulders in the form of higher prices and slower wage growth. One problem for tax and spend politicians is that increasing numbers of Americans now understand this.

A HarrisX poll commissioned by Americans for Tax Reform found that Americans recognize (by a margin of 81 percent to nineteen percent[22]) that a corporate tax increase will increase the cost of goods and services.

Still the lie is told.

Lie #5: "We Will Only Bring in This New Tax to Replace or Reduce an Existing Tax. Trust Us."

In 1965, New Jersey had no sales tax or state income tax.

Garden State voters noticed that spending was going up, and property taxes were becoming more painful. The politicians were not willing to curb their abusive spending, but they did offer to "fix" the high property taxes by imposing a brand-new sales tax. Sales tax revenues would allow the property taxes to be reduced. Promise.

Fast-forward to 2024. There is a 6.6 percent *combined state-local sales tax*[23] in New Jersey on top of high property taxes.

The new sales tax allowed more spending and that demanded even higher sales and property taxes. Did New Jersey politicians then offer to spend less? Of course not. Instead, they decided to add an income tax to the sales tax and property tax. Now New Jersey has a top personal income tax rate of 10.75 percent.[24]

In many states, politicians cover for high-spending mayors and city councils and school boards by offering to hike state taxes to "restrain" property taxes. The state ends up with high spending paid for by two taxes rather than spending restraint.

▬ HOW THESE LIES HARM CHILDREN

How do the lies of politicians that lead to higher taxes harm children?

It is often said that you used to be able to support a family on one income. Dad could work full-time and cover all family costs while Mom was able to spend full time with children. What changed? The cost of government.

Local, state and federal taxes have increased to the point that many families find that one spouse working part-time or full-time is actually working all week to pay taxes on the breadwinner's original salary. Mothers are being taxed out of the house. Full-time or part-time.

The saying goes: time is money. One adds now that earning money takes time.

When politicians tax the income of parents, they are taxing away the time parents can spend with their children. Every tax hike forces Mom and/or Dad to stay at work longer and longer each week to earn the same after-tax paycheck. Taxes mean less time with each child. Each week. Every year.

Taxes also break up families as the next generation often moves not across town, but to a different state to find work.

High state taxes on businesses in your state reduce the ability of existing companies and new ones to start. Businesses die in high-tax states and new ones are created in low-tax states.

Mom's job might move. Dad's job might move. But first new businesses will start in low-tax states farther away from home. That is where your children will move, marry, and raise families. Far away from siblings and parents and grandparents.

And higher taxes on gasoline make it more expensive to visit far-flung relatives. Or to find a job family members can commute to while staying together in the same town.

High taxes in your city and state make it hard to keep your family together over time.

▬ THE TRUTH ABOUT TAXES

Truth #1: Lower Tax Rates on Americans Lead to Economic Growth: Higher Taxes Slow Growth, Job Creation.

In the 1920s, Harding and Coolidge cut tax rates down from 73 percent to 24 percent[25] and we had the Roaring Twenties.

Hoover raised taxes up to 75 percent, FDR took them higher, and we had a decade of the Great Depression.

John F. Kennedy pushed for an across-the-board tax cut that passed in 1964 and gave us a strong economy in the 1960s.

Richard Nixon increased taxes, and we had the stagnation of the 1970s.

Carter increased taxes: stagflation. Double-digit inflation.

Reagan cut tax rates across the board and America boomed for the next seven years—until Bush raised taxes.

There is a trend here.

Truth #2: Cutting Taxes on High-Income Americans Does Not Shift the Tax Burden to Lower-Income Americans.

Let's look at what has actually happened as we reduced the top tax rate of the federal income tax that was once 90 percent.

When Reagan took office in 1981, the top rate was 70 percent[26] and the top 1 percent paid 17.6 percent[27] of all personal income taxes. By 1988, Reagan brought the top rate down to 28 percent[28] and the top one percent of taxpayers paid 27.5 percent[29] of personal income tax revenue.

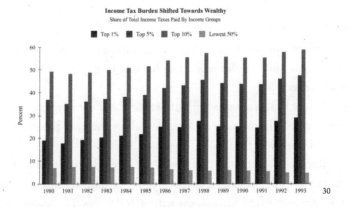

Income Tax Burden Shifted Towards Wealthy
Share of Total Income Taxes Paid By Income Groups

■ Top 1%   ■ Top 5%   ■ Top 10%   ▨ Lowest 50%

30

Truth #3: Lower Taxes on Businesses Create Jobs and Increase Family Pay.

When Trump cut the corporate income tax in 2017 from 35 percent to 21 percent, the Congressional Budget Office (CBO) estimated[31] that corporate income tax revenue would total only $389 billion in 2022. Instead, even with the tax rates falling from 35 percent to 21 percent, the 2022 corporate income tax revenue came in at $424.9 billion,[32] a record high. Growth. And lower corporate rates also drove up employment by 2.1 million jobs[33] in 2019 and median family income by 6.8 percent[34] in 2019 alone.

■ HOW THESE TRUTHS PROTECT CHILDREN

When parents and politicians understand that lower taxes create new businesses, more jobs, increase paychecks, and create new opportunities for family members of all ages, then public policy can focus on reducing the tax burden.

Lower property taxes will make it easier for families to buy a home that can allow for larger families. Larger backyards. And the next generation will be able to buy a home as large and family friendly as Mom and Dad did.

Lower individual income taxes will increase the take-home pay such that many families will again be able to support a family on one paycheck.

Lower business taxes will attract new and growing businesses that offer jobs for teenage children and allow the next generation to live and work near the family.

Knowing the truth: that lower tax rates do *not* enrich those who are already successful at the expense of middle- and lower-income Americans strengthens the nation. It defangs the arguments of envy and greed. Your family's success does not come at the expense of anyone else's. Growing economies empower and help all Americans of all backgrounds and income levels. Greed and envy poison the public square. Knowing the truth about lower taxes, growth and how all benefit from them creates a safer environment for all American families.

When parents, taxpayers, and eventually political leaders understand that taxing businesses is simply a hidden tax on workers, consumers and those saving for retirement—then policies can be enacted at the federal, state and local levels to attract rather than repel new jobs and opportunities. Families will have more choices of where to work, what career to choose, and how best to save for retirement.

Lower taxes on businesses will make American products more competitive in the world. They will make higher pay possible. No more closed factories because politicians shut down the "Rust Belt" with taxes (and regulations) that bankrupt the jobs and future of American families.

■ CHILD PROTECTION IN ACTION

Americans understand the damage done by high taxes when they understand how it harms families and children.

When gas taxes are increased, how many hours will you have to work to cover the cost of driving to your daughter's home for Christmas or Thanksgiving? Do you take that additional time away from the day before Thanksgiving or the day after? Every tax hike shrinks vacation family time at both ends.

A state with no personal income tax makes it easier for Mom or Dad to homeschool while one parent travels to work. Vermont, New York, California, New Jersey—all have high income tax rates. The seven states[35] with a zero-rate income tax and the ten now moving toward zero will make it easier for one parent to work and a second parent to homeschool.

Lower Taxes Can Come in Various Forms

Education savings accounts (ESAs) allow state funding for education to "follow the child" as if in his backpack. Parents who choose homeschooling or parochial schools or private schools of any form no longer have to pay for the government-run schools (which their children do not attend) and their child's education. They have more control over what their children will learn. What values will be upheld? What subjects will be taught?

Tax-free savings accounts such as *individual retirement accounts (IRAs) and 401(k)* accounts allow parents to save for their retirement and have peace of mind that they will not be a burden on their children.

Ending the death tax strengthens the bonds between generations when parents can pass on a small business or farm, ranch, or other property without it being cut in half by the death tax.

Children see the family farm or small business not as Mom's or Dad's job, but the family's joint project. The family's savings. And family retirement plan. Three generations can work on a small business. The death tax tears apart a business at the death of the founding parents because the payment the tax demands can often be paid only by selling off the business.

Some progress has been made here. The death tax has, thanks to recent reductions, been removed from the backs of many families— *but in the past, the death tax has been repealed three times and returned three times.*[36] Sadly, it remains a threat to family farms, ranches, and businesses today.

Think of any tax increase. There is a story to be told on how that tax hike damages every family in America, robbing it of autonomy, time they can spend together, ability to homeschool or supplement other education and limiting parents' ability to save for children's college or parents retirement/health care.

And conversely, every state, local, and federal tax cut increases opportunities for all families to manage their time, their finances, and their plans together. It boosts their ability to have children grow up and live near parents without being pulled or pushed to lower-tax states.

What would you do for your family if you had more time? Every tax hike robs you of that opportunity. Every tax cut makes your plans for family time more attainable.

Grover Norquist, president of Americans for Tax Reform

Grover Norquist is president of Americans for Tax Reform (ATR), a taxpayer advocacy group he organized in 1985 at President Reagan's request. ATR works to limit the size and cost of government and opposes higher taxes at the federal, state, and local levels.

ATR organizes the Taxpayer Protection Pledge, which asks all candidates for federal and state office to commit themselves in writing to the American people to oppose all net tax increases.

Norquist chairs the "Wednesday Meeting," in Washington D.C. a weekly gathering of more than 150 elected officials and conservative movement leaders. There are similar coalition meetings in forty-two states and twenty nations.

He serves on the board of the Parental Rights Organization, the Goldwater Institute, and the Center for the National Interest.

DEBT

PHIL KERPEN

My friend's first grandson, Noah, was recently born. As he took his first breaths, he was already saddled with over $78,000 in federal debt that he had no say in accumulating. A staggering burden, courtesy of a generation—ours—that prioritized short-term gratification over long-term responsibility. This is the grim reality facing every child born in America today. And it is getting worse.

The U.S. national debt currently sits at an obscene $35 trillion, with over $27 trillion of that "debt held by the public," which is the debt excluding what the government owes to itself to cover Social Security and other trust-fund obligations.

These numbers are so large that they become abstractions. Let's translate them into starker terms. Every single American citizen, including baby Noah, owes a share of this debt. As fertility rates decline while federal spending explodes, the burden of that share will grow heavier.[1] On our current trajectory, Noah's share of federal debt will be over $140,000 when he reaches age eighteen and $226,000 at age thirty. These debts must be paid—either through steeply higher taxes, chronic inflation, or perpetual refinancing.

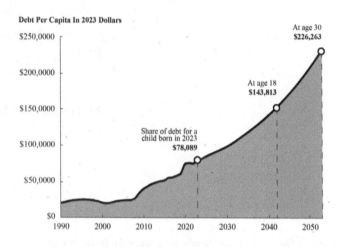

This isn't just about numbers on a spreadsheet. It's about stolen opportunities. It is about children like Noah being born into serious debt. It is perhaps best described as fiscal child abuse.

Every dollar wasted on government spending today is a dollar stolen from future generations' ability to make their own decisions; to spend their dollars on the things they value and enjoy; and to invest in infrastructure, education, and scientific progress.

Think about the dreams baby Noah will have. Maybe he will aspire to be a doctor, an engineer, or an athlete. Maybe he will want to be a scientist, a software developer, or an entrepreneur. But under the weight of this crushing debt, those dreams become an uphill battle. The resources needed for education, housing, and business formation will be increasingly scarce, choked by our insatiable appetite for government handouts.

BIG LIES ABOUT FEDERAL SPENDING AND DEBT

In the grand theater of American politics, few performances are as enduring and deceptive as *The Big Lies About Federal Spending*. These lies are not just falsehoods; they are carefully crafted narratives designed to mislead the public about the nature of government expenditure and its impact on our nation's future.

Lie #1: Federal Spending Stimulates the Economy.

Proponents of this myth argue that government outlays on programs and services inject money into the economy, creating jobs and boosting consumer spending. However, this Keynesian view fails to acknowledge that every dollar the government spends is a dollar taken from taxpayers, now or in the future. It is at best a zero-sum game where the government's gain is the private sector's loss, but in practice, it is much worse than that. Deficit spending misallocates resources, undermines prosperity, and funds government bureaucracies that actively harm the public good. One study found that the average federal bureaucrat destroys up to ninety-eight private sector jobs per year.[3]

Lie #2: Federal Spending Is an Investment in Our Future.

The second lie equates all federal spending with investment. While it's true that some government spending can be beneficial, such as providing for the national defense, the court system, and interstate infrastructure, the blanket statement that all spending is investment is misleading. Much of federal spending goes to consumption rather than investment, with little to no consideration for the return on investment. True investments yield long-term benefits exceeding their costs. Unfortunately, the vast majority of federal programs fail to meet this criterion.

Lie #3: We Can Solve Our Fiscal Problems by Taxing the Rich.

This third lie is attractive because it suggests an easy solution that doesn't require sacrifice from the majority. However, the math doesn't add up. Even if we imposed every possible proposed tax on the rich, it would plausibly amount to only about 1 percent of GDP in revenue, making little difference to the large fiscal gap we already face, let alone paying for progressive wish-list items.[4] The problem is not a lack of revenue, but an addiction to spending. In fact, revenue under the 2017 tax cuts exceeds the historical average. The entirety of forecast debt stems from out-of-control spending.

Total Outlays and Revenues

From 2024 to 2054, federal spending is larger and faster, on average, than revenues are. Spending and revenues each represent a larger percentage of GDP over that period than they did, on average, over the past 50 years.

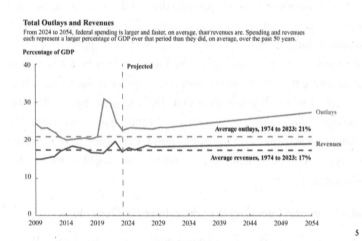

Lie #4: More Spending Means Better Outcomes.

The fourth lie peddled in the halls of Congress is that increased federal spending will translate into better social outcomes. This is a fallacy. Throwing money at problems does not guarantee improvement. More often, it reduces quality and increases costs as the government replaces competitive private markets that would provide downward pressure on prices with an endless stream of taxpayer largesse.

Lie #5: Cutting Spending Will Hurt the Poor and Vulnerable.

This is a scare tactic used to stymie fiscal reform. This narrative fails to recognize that unchecked spending and growing debt can lead to economic instability, which ultimately harms everyone, especially the poor and vulnerable. Responsible spending cuts, coupled with reforms, can lead to a more efficient allocation of resources and a healthier economy that lifts all boats, providing a stable foundation for the prosperity of future generations.

Lie #6: Social Security Is Fair to All Generations.

The sixth lie is the belief that Social Security is a secure and reliable retirement plan for future generations. The truth is, the Social Security Trust Fund is projected to be depleted by 2034, after which the program will be able to pay out only about 78 percent of promised benefits.[6] The program's pay-as-you-go structure is not a savings account but a transfer from current workers to current retirees, with no guarantee for future beneficiaries. Declining birth rates and longer life expectancies mean that such a system badly shortchanges children born today, who will face higher taxes or reduced benefits as they enter the workforce.

These lies about federal spending are not just intellectual errors; they are moral failings. They betray a lack of responsibility and a willingness to sacrifice the well-being of future generations for present comfort. It's time to confront these lies with the truth: that a government that lives beyond its means creates a society that lives beneath its potential.

We owe it to our children to be honest about federal spending and to make tough choices today to secure their prosperity in the future.

▨ HOW THESE LIES HARM CHILDREN

The stimulus myth leads to a ratcheting up in government spending after every war, recession, pandemic, or other crisis. In his classic *Crisis and Leviathan*, Robert Higgs traced the history of American government as a series of crisis responses in which the size and intrusiveness of government ratcheted up, never to fully recede.[7]

Government expands significantly during crises—whether wars, economic downturns, or pandemics. The government's response to these crises often involves increased spending and intervention, which Higgs argues becomes a permanent fixture, rarely retracting to pre-crisis levels. Stimulus spending, particularly in the wake of the COVID-19 pandemic, is a textbook example of Higgs's argument. The government unleashed trillions in spending to mitigate the economic fallout, ostensibly as a temporary measure. Yet, as the graph above shows, the decline from the emergency peak was at a level higher than before the crisis, and the spending continued upwards from there.

The lie that the response to every crisis is to pile trillions of dollars onto the national debt directly harms children because they bear the burden of paying that debt back, either through prosperity-reducing future taxes, inflation-producing monetization via Federal Reserve money printing, or else perpetual refinancing. This amounts to picking the pockets of our children to temporarily relieve the problems of the present, while frequently failing to achieve even that short-term objective.

The "spending is investment" lie is particularly pernicious because while nearly all government spending consists of consumption expenditures and transfer payments that are consumed in the present, it crowds out real investment in the private sector that would grow the productive economy and raise incomes and standards of living in the future. The burden of debt this creates will fall upon children in the future.

The lie that all of this spending can be financed just by taxing the rich harms children by providing an alibi for big-spending politicians, who wave off any criticism of rising debt by blaming tax cuts and demagoguing against the rich. But this is a sideshow, as the chart above shows. This lie distracts from the fiscal burden placed on our children with a nonsolution proffered for political effect.

The lie that spending improves outcomes is the triumph of hope over experience. Ever-increasing spending on health care and education have not improved outcomes in those areas, but have dramatically inflated prices. The graph below shows that it is precisely the sectors with the most government spending and regulatory involvement that have had the largest price increases with the poorest outcomes, while sectors relatively untouched by government have seen falling prices and rising quality.

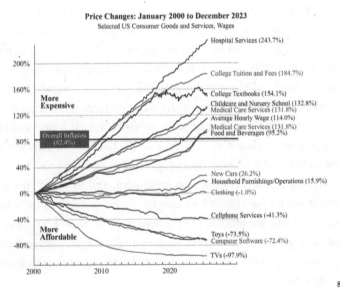

Price Changes: January 2000 to December 2023
Selected US Consumer Goods and Services, Wages

Economist Mark Perry—who created this chart and updates it regularly—noted: "Increases in College Tuition and Fees continue to far outpace increases in Average Wages and the Overall CPI. If College Tuition had increased at the rate of the Overall CPI since 2000, it would be 28% LESS expensive today vs. 2000 instead of 39% MORE expensive."[9]

Far from making college more affordable, the massive experiment in federal grants and loans has flowed through to higher tuitions, loading the next generation not just with their share of the national debt, but with outsized student loans as well.

The lie that spending cuts necessarily hurt the poor and the vulnerable keeps far too many children in the welfare trap, being raised in families dependent on federal benefits for food, housing, health care, and cash. This lie is often deployed as an argument against work requirements in federal programs, which is ironic given that they would actually benefit not just current and future taxpayers by reducing the burden of government spending and debt, but the families and children themselves by getting them off of welfare and into work. In the 1990s, welfare reform based on capping spending, work requirements, and block granting to the states was overwhelmingly successful. All federal welfare programs should follow this model.

Finally, the lie that Social Security is structurally sound and fair to all generations leaves our children on the hook for an increasingly untenable transfer scheme. The program is unlikely to provide them meaningful benefits at their own retirement, and its payroll tax will make it harder for children to save for their own retirement when they enter the workforce. They would be best served by reforms that keep promises to current seniors and workers while offering a modernized retirement system with better options for ensuing generations.

THE TRUTH ABOUT FEDERAL SPENDING AND DEBT

Truth #1: If we don't apply the brakes, debt disaster will visit our children.

Reinhart and Rogoff, in their pivotal study "Growth in a Time of Debt," found that as the debt burden reaches the level of 90 percent of a country's GDP, economic growth drops by 1 percent or more. That 1 percent is the difference between a strong economy and a mediocre one, or tipping a weak economy into recession.[10] There is academic debate over whether the 90 percent line is a tipping point, but the finding is a red flag for the United States, which blew past that mark a few years ago and is now moving into uncharted territory. The debt-to-GDP ratio is a ticking time bomb, set to explode from 97 percent in 2023 to a staggering 166 percent by 2054.[11]

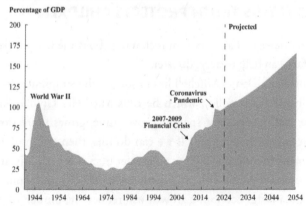

Federal Debt Held by the Public

Debt increases in relation to GDP, exceeding any previously recorded level in 2029 and continuing to soar through 2054. It is on track to increase even more thereafter.

Percentage of GDP

[12]

The Congressional Budget Office's long-term outlook paints a grim picture, with debt levels poised to throttle economic vitality and saddle future generations with a legacy of fiscal neglect.

Laden with this debt, a child born today faces diminished job prospects and a government too hamstrung by interest payments to effectively provide for the national defense, the administration of justice, and the other core functions of government.

As economist Herbert Stein famously said: "If something cannot go on forever, it will stop."[13] We can expect this astonishing debt path to be altered, possibly by a chaotic Greece-style debt crisis that forces a crash program of tax hikes and spending cuts.

Absent such a crisis, a significant erosion of American economic dynamism and opportunity will occur through some combination of higher taxes and chronic inflation. That would make the experience of COVID spending–fueled inflation in recent years not a singular episode but a chronic fact of American life, rendering every pursuit more challenging, every dream less attainable.

■ HOW THIS TRUTH PROTECTS CHILDREN

The good news is that an honest reckoning about the fiscal reckoning we face can help us avert disaster.

Economist Daniel Mitchell has produced the simplest guide to a sustainable fiscal policy, which he calls Mitchell's Golden Rule: "Ensure that government spending, over time, grows more slowly than the private economy."[14] If we can do this, then the burden of government spending will grow no greater than it is presently. If we combine that restraint with progrowth tax, regulatory, and monetary policy, then faster economic growth will reduce the burden of government spending and debt over time.

This chart from Mitchell shows that even modest spending restraint paired with revenue at currently projected levels can achieve a balanced budget:

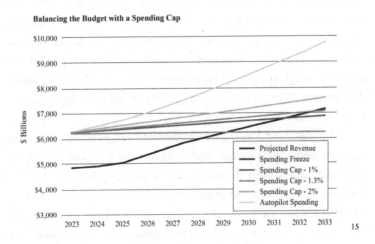

Balancing the Budget with a Spending Cap

By bringing spending in line with projected revenues, we can at least avoid leaving our children in worse debt than we are in today, and begin working toward reducing that massive albatross.

CHILD PROTECTION IN ACTION

The best model for spending limitation is the Swiss debt brake. This is a fiscal rule enshrined in the Swiss constitution designed to ensure responsible government spending and to limit national debt. The core principle is achieving a structural balance between government spending and revenue. This means excluding the effects of economic fluctuations to focus on long-term fiscal health. There is a ceiling on net debt, which is the total government debt minus financial assets. The limit is set as a percentage of GDP and can vary depending on the economic cycle.

The federal budget must be formulated within the framework of the debt brake. This means estimating revenue and planning expenditures to stay within the structural balance and debt ceiling. The Swiss parliament can authorize deviations from the debt brake only in extraordinary circumstances, requiring a supermajority vote. The debt brake allows for exceptions for capital expenditures like infrastructure projects. These are financed through special funds and don't directly impact the net debt ceiling.

The Swiss debt brake has fostered a culture of fiscal responsibility in Switzerland. It helps maintain a healthy balance sheet, promoting economic stability and investor confidence.

Even during the pandemic period, Switzerland exhibited far greater spending restraint than its European neighbors and the United States.[16]

Average Spending Growth
2003 - 2023: 4.9 Percent
2020 - 2023: 7.1 Percent

United States

Average Spending Growth
2003 - 2023: 2.2 Percent
2020 - 2023: 2.9 Percent

Switzerland

17

Living within spending caps would be a simple solution for the federal government's spending problem, but far from an easy one. It would require difficult decisions and major structural reforms, especially to Social Security and the federal health care programs that drive long-term federal spending and debt. With no structural framework forcing action on these challenges, Congress has repeatedly proven unwilling to do so.

Our children will pay the price. The current federal-debt trajectory is not just unsustainable; it is unethical, passing on a burden to our children that they did not create but will undoubtedly bear. Far too often, politicians of both parties choose the easy political path of borrowing funds today and deferring the bill to children who are too young to vote or have not even been born yet.

We must confront this crisis head-on, not with empty promises and more borrowing. We need spending reforms that prioritize core functions like national defense while eliminating large swaths of the federal leviathan that deal with fundamentally local issues like education and housing. We need to shrink the size and scope of government, eliminating wasteful programs and bureaucracies that serve principally to inhibit the growth of the private economy.

Most of all, we need to permanently defuse the debt bomb. We must demand that our policymakers take a leaf out of the Swiss playbook, implementing stringent fiscal rules to force the government to live within its means rather than burdening future generations.

Phil Kerpen, president of American Commitment

Phil Kerpen is the president of American Commitment and the Committee to Unleash Prosperity.

American Commitment is a 501(c)(4) advocacy group dedicated to restoring and protecting America's core commitment to free markets, economic growth, constitutionally-limited government, property rights, and individual freedom.

The Committee to Unleash Prosperity is a 501(c)(3) educational charity founded by supply-side icons Stephen Moore, Steve Forbes, and Art Laffer to promote faster economic growth through the key building blocks of low taxes, limited spending, less regulation, sound money, and free trade.

Mr. Kerpen has previously served as vice president for policy at Americans for Prosperity and as an analyst and researcher for the Free Enterprise Fund, the Club for Growth, and the Cato Institute.

A native of Brooklyn, N.Y., Mr. Kerpen lives in Washington, D.C., with his wife Joanna and their four children.

ENERGY

NEIL CHATTERJEE

I don't know many people who can say one of their relatives died of cholera. In the United States, cholera hasn't been a problem since the last major outbreak occurred in 1910. And yet my father's brother, just a baby, died of the disease during a strenuous overland trek from Burma to India as my family sought escape from World War II. No time could be spared for a funeral; his tiny body was gently committed to a nearby river and the journey to survive pressed on.

Poverty, disease, and death were a fact of life back then. Even in the best of years, the people of Bengal lived on the edge of subsistence. Simple amenities taken for granted in the West—sewage systems, running water, and electricity—were luxuries they would never know. The war never made it to southern Bengal, but in 1943, famine once again returned and a surging population coupled with dreadful economic policies created tragedy. Starvation, malaria, and other diseases caused by lack of sanitation and healthcare swept through the region's sixty million people. When it was over two years later, an estimated 2.3 million men, women, and children had died.

Thankfully, most of my family survived their flight to India. But when I think about my infant uncle, I see a frightful world fraught with hardships that the West has not known for centuries. The scale of human calamity that befell India in the middle of the twentieth century is incomprehensible to the average Western mind. Who among us has lived through a famine or even suffered hunger to a serious degree? Who has had family members die of cholera or malaria? The answer is almost no one. These things simply don't happen in the West, especially in the United States. But they could.

I am one generation removed from growing up in my grandparents' neighborhood in Calcutta, a place without running water or sewer systems, a place where children drew their water from wells and dumped their waste in open canals in the street. Even today, running water is a luxury and electricity is sporadic at best. India and other developing countries are working to overcome this adversity in the same way the West did more than a century ago—by building up industry, technology, and transportation. What they need most to emerge from poverty is *energy*—cheap, abundant, and consistent sources of energy required for food sufficiency, proper medical care, robust manufacturing and shipping, and everything else that lets a nation flourish.

Energy policy is of great consequence in the twenty-first century, playing a major role in relationships and conflicts both within and among nations. We in America have long enjoyed cheap and virtually unlimited energy, to the great benefit of our people. But now, the pressures of climate change, shifting geopolitical landscapes, and a growing reliance on cutting-edge technology command prudent action to avert a grim future. Weighed down by rank partisanship, America is failing to pursue measures needed to forestall fuel rationing, electricity shortages, skyrocketing energy prices, and other perils. Continued neglect could render our once cheap and bountiful energy a luxury item, risking broad economic disruption and geopolitical upheaval. And those who would be harmed the most are children.

▇ BIG LIES ABOUT ENERGY AND CLIMATE

Every day, we hear the hue and cry for climate protection at any cost, all in the name of saving the planet. Extremist climate advocates disrupt traffic, destroy property, and interrupt policymakers during official proceedings in relentless pursuit of their heavy-handed and onerous agenda. As elected leaders on the Left seek to appease this clamorous fringe of their base, realistic solutions for securing a clean and peaceful energy future are discounted or disregarded completely. The consequence is that the families and children who depend on sensible energy solutions are made to suffer. That said, let's turn to the big lies we are being told by climate extremists.

Lie #1: Climate Change Should Determine Energy Policy.

As important as climate science is, it isn't the only factor that should go into a sound energy policy. Fossil fuels such as coal, oil and gas are some of the most important natural resources we use every day. These fuels are composed of hydrogen and carbon. When burned in the presence of oxygen; their stored energy is converted to heat energy, producing carbon dioxide in the process. In the home, they are burned to produce heat. In large power stations, they are used to produce electricity. They are also used to power engines of all types—cars, trucks, industrial machinery, and much more.

Children need clean air and clean water, but they also need heat in the winter, air conditioning in the summer, and a flourishing economy in which their parents can find living-wage jobs. Fossil fuels today compose as much as 85 percent of the world's energy demand; if we simply choose to be "done" with them as soon as possible, then we also choose to be done with industry, manufacturing and production, and safety and security. In fact, under the wrong circumstances, we could see the collapse of global economies and a return to the more primitive kind of civilization we have worked so hard to overcome.

Lie #2: We Are Better Off Outsourcing Our Energy Decisions and Production.

The climate extremists inform us ceaselessly that our country does not need to produce its own energy. That is a lie. Blind reliance on others for our energy needs risks geopolitical subjugation of the kind that jeopardizes our national security, economic security, and individual freedoms. If we as Americans don't look out for our own best interests, then nobody else will.

Lie #3: Fossil Fuels Bad. Green Energy Good.

The goals of climate zealots are extreme, narrow minded, and authoritarian. Ineffective "command-and-control" policies—bans, mandates and subsidies—consistently produce worse results than innovation, competition, and regulatory reform. Indeed, the U.S. has already reduced emissions in the power sector significantly—without compromising reliability and affordability—by leveraging innovative natural-gas extraction methods, relicensing nuclear power plants, and lowering costs for renewables. Natural gas could be the backbone that allows renewables to flourish, temporarily providing consistent power as we scale up new battery-storage technology to offset the variability of solar and wind generation.

◼ HOW THESE LIES HARM CHILDREN

The Left's obsession with carbon reduction as a singular solution is ill-conceived. We cannot rush headlong toward a carbon-free future without considering what might happen before we get there. What climate activists can't admit is that failure to plan for adequate energy supplies will devastate the health and well-being of children, now and for generations to come. Two competing goals—climate protection and a stable energy supply—cannot be reconciled using extremist scare tactics. Instead, we need practical, realistic, and sustainable solutions conceived from an energy-first, people-always mindset—one that balances saving the earth against saving the earth *for people*—families and children who depend on reliable energy for their survival and quality of life.

This is not to trivialize harms associated with climate change. Much has been written about fossil-fuel pollution, rising temperatures, and the effects they can have on children—developmental problems, respiratory illnesses, heat- and water-related illnesses, food-system impacts, and mental-health issues, to name a few. The United Nations International Children's Emergency Fund (UNICEF) estimates that one billion children are already at extremely high risk of being impacted.[1] Left unchecked, climate change could lead to rising sea levels and serious coastal flooding, while causing water scarcity in arid regions where many of the world's poor live. We could also see increasingly severe weather events and greater incidence of vector-borne diseases like malaria and dengue fever.

But believing the energy lies—that all must be sacrificed to the god of climate change; that we should outsource our energy security to international bodies; and that fossil fuels are always the enemy—is harmful to everyone, especially the world's children, who are most vulnerable to the suffering that accompanies energy crises.

■ THE TRUTH ABOUT ENERGY AND CLIMATE

Truth #1: A "Climate-Only" Approach Doesn't Even Help the Climate.

On January 26, 2024, the Biden White House announced a temporary pause on decisions for export of liquified natural gas (LNG).[2] The reason given was to provide the Department of Energy time to evaluate impacts of LNG on energy costs; U.S. energy security; and climate change, which it called "the existential threat of our time." This order reflects a misapprehension of the issues that actually puts our children at great risk. LNG opponents cite concerns about emissions and argue that natural-gas exports undermine deployment of renewable energies. But delaying the permitting of new natural gas export terminals in the United States—even as gas shipments to Europe and Asia have soared since Russia's invasion of Ukraine—jeopardizes our economy and our allies' energy security.[3] Worse yet, it actually *increases* global greenhouse gas emissions. This is true because American LNG exports are less carbon intensive than the overseas alternatives they displace. And while affordable technologies for solar, wind, hydroelectric, and geothermal power look promising, transition to all-renewable energy is not possible overnight.

Demand for natural gas is increasing, and will continue to do so for the foreseeable future. Reducing American exports leads inevitably to their replacement by more pollutive exports from countries like Russia, where the natural gas today being exported to Europe produces 40 percent *more* greenhouse gas emissions than does American LNG. Other nations that do not share our concern for preventing increased global emissions will always be glad to fill the vacuum we leave behind.

Beyond misapprehending the environmental risks, the Biden administration's outsourcing of energy production threatens both U.S. national security and the safety and security of children around the world. Russia's invasion of Ukraine in 2022 spotlighted Europe's growing regional dependence on Russian natural gas. Russian president Vladimir Putin gambled that starving European countries of natural gas would weaken their resolve to support Ukraine. He lost that bet because LNG from America helped our allies wean themselves from dependence on Russian gas.

Japan furnishes another example of the dangers of depending on hostile powers for energy. Japan is still recovering from the earthquake that destroyed the Fukushima nuclear power plant in 2011. In the aftermath, the country shuttered or suspended operations at all nuclear plants and has been without nuclear-produced electricity since 2012. Now wholly dependent on imports of coal and gas from Russia and Australia, Japan is desperate to align with the U.S. for its future energy needs. Japan knows that if China invades Taiwan, one of its first strategic moves will be to cut off the energy pipeline running from Australia to Japan through the South China Sea. If faced with energy paralysis, without U.S. imports, Japan will have no choice but to acquiesce to Russian dominance.

Reducing or eliminating the supply of American LNG to the world weakens our strategic hand, limiting our ability to exploit global markets for the benefit of ourselves, our allies, and our economy. The result is an unstable, less safe world order for our children and for future generations.

Truth #2: Putting Climate Above All Else Deprives Children of Affordable Energy.

An outsized focus on green energy not only compromises national sovereignty, it undermines national prosperity. India is reckoning with this reality today. India's emergence from a millennium of abject poverty depends on the same fossil fuels that propelled Western growth. The Indian government is keenly aware of the need to mitigate carbon emissions, but must balance that need against the stark reality that large areas of the country still lack electricity. As its middle class grows, India's energy consumption will rise steeply, further stressing any commitment to carbon-neutral policies. Can we really blame India for prioritizing its children's quality of life above another country's climate goals? The answer is no. People in India, like us, are morally obligated to reject environmental measures that make the poorest children in the world even poorer.

Truth #3: Simple Solutions Are Always Wrong.

The Left's climate solution is perfectly simple: strip people of energy to save the earth. That is not a plan. No child should ever have to live on the edge of subsistence, without fresh food, sanitation, and adequate health care, for want of energy. Nor should they suffer the cruel hand of an ambitious authoritarian regime. Relinquishing America's global energy leadership role would bolster bad actors like Russia and China by pushing emerging nations to their side. If we care about protecting children, then America must lead the way. If we don't, then smaller nations will succumb to the pressure of energy-dominant nations ready to hold their futures hostage by denying them vital energy resources.

At home and abroad, energy policy will determine the future of the world's children. Energy security *is* national security, and children cannot thrive without it. Nations that craft their energy policy to serve their own families and children are *responsible*. Nations that produce their own energy are *secure*.

■ HOW THESE TRUTHS PROTECT CHILDREN

Energy touches every aspect of our daily lives. It enables our children (and one day, their children) to have running water, ample food, sanitary sewage systems, proper medical treatment, quality industrial production, good transportation, and exquisite technology. *Reliable* energy is necessary to keep life-saving hospital equipment and communications systems operating, keep buildings at safe temperatures with proper ventilation, and for virtually every other aspect of civilized life. *Affordable* energy drives economic development, fuels growth, enhances competitiveness, promotes international cooperation and investment, and fosters economic development around the world.

Prudent investment in energy infrastructure—consistent with free-market and limited-government principles—drives innovation, creates jobs, and enables the U.S. to maintain its competitive edge in the global economy. That edge provides a stable environment in which to form families and raise our children. A singular focus on reducing America's greenhouse gas emissions doesn't just marginalize energy policy options; it ignores the fact that reducing our emissions will have little effect on inaction by other countries. Even if America became entirely carbon-free, it wouldn't matter at all unless the rest of the world followed. To combat climate change effectively, we must bring the whole world together.

To keep our country secure, we must draw on principles deeply rooted in our national tradition. This includes a commitment to enhancing safety and well-being, fostering economic growth, and protecting national sovereignty for our families. These principles should guide our policy decisions and investment priorities, allowing us to better meet the needs of children everywhere.

Energy security takes long-range planning and investment, access to domestic resources, the capability to expand pipelines and export infrastructure, and an ability to foresee and respond to events affecting global energy supplies. These things can't happen when infrastructure projects languish in the quagmire of partisan gridlock. Initiatives that *should* yield pragmatic results for the common good become nothing more than battlegrounds for ideological debates and political point scoring.

The Infrastructure Investment and Jobs Act is a good example of such wrangling. The Act's passage was the result of highly politicized negotiations between Democrats and Republicans. Both parties advocated for investment in infrastructure, but they disagreed significantly about funding mechanisms and project priorities.

Democrats fought to include provisions addressing climate change and social equity; Republicans prioritized fiscal responsibility and regulatory reform.

CHILD PROTECTION IN ACTION

There is a better way. For the benefit of our children, policymakers should rethink how they view and authorize infrastructure projects. They should leverage the ingenuity and efficiency of the private sector, allowing private enterprise to drive infrastructure development by minimizing the regulatory burdens that hinder progress. Two areas ripe for reform are general permitting and eminent domain.

Today's land-use restrictions and environmental laws are significant obstacles to timely and cost-effective development of new energy projects. The tangled web of regulations and permitting requirements leads to lengthy approval processes, bureaucratic red tape, and exorbitant compliance costs that hinder progress and deter investment. The result is that much-needed upgrades get delayed or shelved, impeding economic growth and jeopardizing public welfare.

We owe it to ourselves and our children to change this burdensome regulatory framework. We must streamline regulatory processes and reduce bureaucratic hurdles to expedite project timelines, lower costs, and leave more room for robust environmental protections. Rather than allowing projects to be endlessly deferred due to environmental concerns and local stakeholder interests, Congress should find ways to shorten timelines for regulatory approval.

For example, the process for permitting electric generation and transmission projects is multilayered and arduous. One reason is that interstate transmission-line projects critical for U.S. national interests come with local costs that lead to frequent rejection of the plans by state authorities. To accelerate the process, Congress could place siting authority for interstate transmission lines under the jurisdiction of the Federal Energy Regulatory Commission, which already has similar sitting authority for gas pipelines and can issue permits with less delay.

Another area ripe for reform is eminent domain. The power of eminent domain derives from the Fifth Amendment's Takings Clause.[4] It allows a government (or a private party acting with permission from the government) to take private property for public use, as long as the owner of the property receives just compensation.

Today's eminent domain practices are largely contentious and fraught with legal challenges. Property owners who feel aggrieved by forced confiscation of their land engage in costly legal battles that impede the initiation and completion of new infrastructure projects. Reforms could be fashioned to increase respect for private property rights, ensuring that government agencies can exercise their eminent-domain powers only in pursuit of projects that serve a clear public purpose and benefit the community as a whole. Transparency and accountability could be increased by providing affected property owners more notice and opportunity for input. Solutions like these are sensible, and would help ensure that in the future, our children enjoy the same energy security that has enriched our lives.

Most of what we call energy infrastructure involves provision of fundamental energy services to our citizens. Because taxpayers, users, and voters pay for those services, the cost of delivery is always a political issue.

While cleanly decoupling politics from energy infrastructure might seem impossible, we *can* take steps to improve the dynamic. Policymakers should prioritize evidence-based decision making, create nonpolitical funding mechanisms, and aspire to independent decisions made with greater involvement from the private sector. An independent commission or agency could be established to evaluate and prioritize infrastructure investments based solely on objective criteria like economic impact, safety, and sustainability. Infrastructure funding can be insulated from political influence using dedicated funding streams, or through multiyear appropriations that reduce the risk of project delays or cancellations spurred by shifting political winds.

By respecting the true purpose of energy infrastructure, we can ensure that projects are driven by sound policy objectives, not by partisan agendas, to deliver the greatest benefit to the greatest number of families across the nation. We can then be assured that sound policy and sound politics will provide children of the future with *truly* sustainable energy to eradicate poverty, guarantee water and sanitation, ensure proper medical care, and most importantly, meet *their* global goals and aspirations.

Climate protection and secure energy do not have to be mutually exclusive. Common sense measures inspired by an "energy first, people always" mindset offer the best hope for our children's future. There is too much at stake for rancorous politics and political gamesmanship—our children and the generations that follow deserve better.

The Honorable Neil Chatterjee, former chairman of the Federal Energy Regulatory Commission

Neil Chatterjee is a former commissioner and chairman of the Federal Energy Regulatory Commission (FERC), and has deep ties in Washington and across the industry, with extensive experience across the energy landscape both domestically and internationally. He is respected for his ability to strike compromise and work with a wide variety of stakeholders.

In his time on the Hill and at FERC, Neil built a reputation as a bipartisan operator who builds alliances and cuts through red tape with an eye on always promoting innovation. Neil's significant knowledge and experience is derived from operating at the highest levels of government and as such, is able to provide clients valuable insights and counsel when navigating the highly regulated energy industry.

While at FERC, Neil championed several strategic initiatives, including streamlining and improving FERC's liquified natural gas application review and approval process, bolstering power grid reliability and resilience, and boosting renewable resources' ability to compete in regional power markets and for the reduction of carbon emissions.

Neil is a policy reformer who broke down market barriers for the entrance of new technologies, particularly for low-carbon technologies. He has been an advocate for harnessing technology to mitigate physical and cyber threats to critical energy infrastructure.

Prior to his time at the Commission, Neil served as an advisor to Senator Mitch McConnell (R-KY) where he aided in the passage of major energy, highway, and agriculture legislation. Neil also has experience working as a principal in government relations for the National Rural Electric Cooperative Association. He began his career as a staff member on the House Committee on Ways and Means.

ESG AND DEI

JUSTIN DANHOF

Shalomi sits on her mother's lap. The five-year-old's frail frame is held tight by her mother as the girl's big brown eyes peer straight ahead. She has just returned from the community kitchen in the village hall, run by a charitable organization to provide food in Sri Lanka's poorest regions.[1]

Shalomi is among the lucky ones. She has two parents, both of whom work in the tea fields to provide as best they can for their three girls. They often go hungry so that their children can eat.

Life in Sri Lanka wasn't always this hard. Not long ago, it was a solidly middle-income country. Its robust agricultural sector produced enough rice to feed the country and earn the nickname the "granary of the East." Children went to school. Milk, fish, rice, and eggs were plentiful. So were electricity and gas.

In 2021, that all changed. The culprit was a three-letter acronym few had heard of at the time: ESG, short for environmental, social and governance. The ESG movement is committed to using financial pressure to force countries and businesses to adopt the Left's environmental and social goals.

In Sri Lanka's case, the World Economic Forum—a major ESG proponent—urged the country to adopt "good environmental policies," including "high-productivity organic farming" that was "attuned to the cost of carbon and climate change."[2] So did BlackRock, the $10 trillion Wall Street behemoth that was one of Sri Lanka's largest private bondholders.

Sri Lanka's president heeded this call in 2021 when he banned the import of synthetic fertilizers, heralding the move at a UN climate change conference. Within six months, rice yields fell 20 percent.[3] One-third of farms shut down completely. The government scrambled to import nearly $500 million of rice. Inflation reached a punishing 90 percent.[4] Sri Lanka defaulted on its bonds. The economy collapsed. Fuel, food and other staples were suddenly in short supply.

As with most crises, children suffered most. "Sri Lanka's children go hungry as food prices soar," the BBC wrote. The article featured three-year-old Nitisha, who is losing weight and has leg pains due to malnutrition, while her infant sister was born underweight and lacks thyroxine, a growth hormone.[5]

Today, Sri Lankan children like Shalomi continue to feel the fallout, all so that the country's leadership can boast a near-perfect ESG score of 98.1.[6]

Sri Lanka provides a cautionary tale, and it's not an isolated case. ESG initiatives raise prices in all kinds of industries across the globe, including right here in the United States. ESG drives up the cost of food, gas, housing and more, draining Americans' bank accounts. If we let ESG advocates have their way, our own faces may soon look more similar to the grief-stricken faces of Sri Lankan parents struggling to provide for their children.

■ BIG LIES ABOUT ESG

Lie #1: ESG Helps Children.

ESG proponents regularly frame their causes as a means to protect children. The World Economic Forum claims "[t]he climate crisis is ... a child-rights crisis, affecting children first and worst."[7] UNICEF launched a "Tool for Investors on Integrating Children's Rights into ESG Analysis."[8] Even Sri Lanka's president claimed he was doing it for the children. He concluded his UN speech by intoning that "[a]ll of us alive today are custodians of this planet on behalf of future generations."[9]

These ploys amount to little more than marketing and political schemes to advance a globalist agenda and adjust investing dollars to back the same.

At the broadest level, ESG proponents argue that corporations exist not just to make profits for their owners and investors, but to serve all stakeholders, including the environment, employees, communities and children themselves. That means corporations must do everything in their power not just to provide goods and services in a legal, ethical and profitable way, but to affirmatively insert themselves into the political process in the name of child advocacy.

On *E* issues, proponents claim that organic farming helps children eat healthier food and that fighting climate change is necessary to preserve the world for the next generation. So they push corporations to adopt net-zero goals, even if it leads to food and energy shortages or surging prices.

On *S* issues, corporations push uniformly progressive policies on issues like education and abortion. They also use their products, like children's television programming, toys, or clothing, to foist similarly progressive diversity, equity, and inclusion (DEI) agendas on kids, promoting transgenderism and so-called antiracism.

On *G* issues, activists set quotas for racial and gender diversity on company boards, claiming to increase representation and show young girls and minorities that they too can reach the highest echelons of corporate America.

Lie #2: Corporations Should Serve Stakeholders, Not Shareholders.

All of this activism rests on a fundamental falsehood: that corporations do, or at least should, serve societal interests at large, rather than investors. But in American-style capitalism, that's not how things work. Corporations serve shareholders. They are engines of profitability that fuel our economy. A profitable company creates jobs, improves communities, and exports American goods, services, and values. It does all of those things *because* it focuses on the profits. The results are good not just for shareholders, but for all Americans.

Stakeholder capitalism is also an affront to democracy. Every November, Americans head to the polls, where each citizen's voice has equal weight. One person, one vote. The elected officials we vote into office then set public policy. At the corporate ballot box, things are different. It's one share, one vote. That means only investors can weigh in. And more shares mean more votes. That makes sense if shareholders are voting on issues related to corporate management, but it is abhorrent to our system of constitutional democracy if they're voting on matters of public policy. That's because activists that are unable to achieve their desired results at the political ballot box place their propositions on corporate ballots by way of shareholder proposals. You do not need to change a law to change culture. And when the Big Three asset managers, BlackRock, Vanguard, and State Street, back an ESG or DEI shareholder proposal, culture changes quickly.

Many of the specific policy prescriptions that ESG activists favor are also faulty.

E advocates claim their policies will save the environment, but they often merely shift emissions from Western companies that can be shamed into reducing their carbon footprint to Chinese, Russian, and Middle Eastern competitors that cannot. *S* and *G* proponents claim they want to promote diversity and inclusion, but their practice of handing out jobs, promotions, and board seats based on race and gender often fuels animus instead.

Examined closely, ESG policies are neither environmentally friendly, prosocial, or good governance.

■ HOW THESE LIES HARM CHILDREN

Children often shoulder the consequences of ESG folly. Take the *E* issues. Fossil-fuel phaseouts are a key plank in the ESG movement's environmental platform. Just like on Christmas morning, there's nothing more fearsome than a lump of coal. For years, the Big Three asset managers have pushed companies to reject fossil fuels and go green. In 2021, the Big Three supported a takeover of three of Exxon's board members by climate activists, after which Exxon slashed production targets by 25 percent.[10] That year, they also pushed Chevron to reduce emissions, essentially demanding production cuts. Sometimes, the result is that Western companies sell their fossil fuel projects to PetroChina and Russian companies, which will drill the same fields and refine the same oil. But other times, the pressure to reduce supply simply means less fossil fuel for U.S. customers to use.[11]

The result is higher energy prices, more blackouts, and more preventable deaths.

We've already begun to see the effects in places like renewables-obsessed California, where rolling blackouts are a regular occurrence.[12] When there's no electricity, people turn to gas-powered generators and cars for power and heat. The result is a 9.3

times greater risk of carbon monoxide poisoning for adults, and a 13.5 times greater risk for children.[13] A study showed that pediatric admissions for accidental injuries surge 30 percent during outages.[14] Yet ESG proponents never acknowledge these facts.

Instead, they dismiss any possible harm, claiming that failure to act will end human life itself. This isn't an exaggeration. Climate extremists such as Extinction Rebellion tell young children that the question isn't "what you want to be *when* you grow up," but "what you want to be *if* you grow up."[15] This fear mongering is scientifically unsound.[16] It's also dangerous. Children and teenagers are suffering alarming rates of anxiety, depression and suicide as they've internalized this climate misinformation. It's also causing people to have fewer kids. Morgan Stanley found that the "movement to not have children owing to fears over climate change is growing and impacting fertility rates quicker than any preceding trend in the field of fertility decline."[17] That means fewer little sisters and brothers for children to grow up with, learn from, and love. These extremists aren't working alone. They're amplifying their voice and credibility by partnering with businesses across the globe.[18]

The *S* and *G* in the ESG movement are just as dangerous. ESG-promoting asset managers have long touted diversity and inclusion as a key pillar of social responsibility and good governance, something they expect of all of the companies in which they invest.

BlackRock, for example, explicitly states that it "expect[s] companies in all countries" to create "long-term plans to improve diversity, equity and inclusion."[19] Vanguard supports companies that tie executive compensation to DEI goals. State Street does too, and has even launched index funds that choose which companies to invest in based on how many women those companies employ, rather than how the companies perform.

And again, they've somehow managed to marshal children for their cause. Vanguard claims that its DEI efforts include "promot[ing] equity in childcare and early education."[20] BlackRock laments that Black children are more likely to experience downward economic mobility, and promises that its ESG investing strategy will "address racial inequities."[21] And State Street famously commissioned the *Fearless Girl* statue—a literal four-foot-tall girl in a short-sleeved dress, ponytail swinging in the wind—to stare down the Wall Street Bull. Never mind that the statue was a PR ploy to deflect attention from the bank's gender-discrimination lawsuits.

Given Wall Street's outsized focus on DEI, it's no surprise that corporate America has followed suit. Frankly, they didn't have a choice. The Big Three control a staggering $20 trillion in capital. That makes them, collectively, the largest shareholder in almost 90 percent of S&P 500 companies.[22] They have the power to fire boards and set executive pay. When your largest shareholder tells you to do something, you do it. Even if it hurts the very children you supposedly serve.

THE TRUTH ABOUT ESG

Truth #1: ESG Targets Kids.

It has insidiously wormed its way into nearly every American company, including those that interact directly with children.

By now, most Americans know about Disney, as it has captured national headlines for proudly pushing a progressive DEI agenda on children.

In an all-hands meeting, one Disney executive boasted about putting "many, many, LGBTQIA characters" in its programming. Another executive bragged about implementing a "not-at-all-secret gay agenda" and was "adding queerness" to kid's shows.[23] That producer recently provoked a backlash for also promoting critical race theory to kids. She produces the Disney+ cartoon *Proud Family* that teaches children that the U.S. was founded on "systematic prejudice, racism and white supremacy."[24]

The company has also taken heat for casting a Black actress to play Ariel, featuring same-sex kisses in animated movies, and replacing Snow White and the seven dwarves with a Latina princess and seven multiracial, mixed-gender "magical creatures" instead.

Disney is not alone. Paramount, the parent company of Nickelodeon and MTV, issues its own ESG reports each year. According to its seventy-five-page missive, Paramount "driv[es] social impact through our content and brands," including in teen and children's programming.[25] MTV aired segments teaching teens "how to be an effective ally" and "what does it mean to defund the police."[26] It also "create[d] a program that helped 250 trans youth update their government IDs."[27] The report is silent on whether parents were ever consulted about the change.

Nickelodeon has been busy too. In 2021, the channel produced an episode of *Blue's Clues* featuring a pride parade. On the float is a beaver with—and I'm not kidding—scars from top surgery. The content activist who partnered with Nickelodeon said, "It's for sure the queerest thing I've ever seen happen in the preschool space."[28] As the father of two little girls, I agree.

But radical transgender ideology pushed by DEI harms kids. Ten-year-olds are receiving hormone blockers; twelve-year-olds are getting sex-change surgeries. Anyone who questions medical intervention is deemed a transphobe and silenced, even though research shows that between 80 percent and 95 percent of children who express gender dysphoria will ultimately identify with their bodily sex.[29]

Yet these are precisely the policies pushed by the ESG movement. On transgender issues, the biggest lobbyist is the Human Rights Campaign.[30] The advocacy group—which counts big banks like Goldman Sachs and JP Morgan among its sponsors—issues the Corporate Equality Index (CEI) each year, rating corporate America on how well they promote LGBTQ+ causes. Paramount and Disney, of course, hold perfect one hundred scores.[31]

ESG madness is everywhere. It's the reason Mattel launched a transgender Barbie, and Hasbro's Mr. Potato Head is no longer a "he." It's why Doritos partnered with a trans influencer who once tweeted heshe wanted to do "depraved things" with a "twelve-year-old girl,"[32] and The North Face grants discounts if you complete a racial inclusion course explaining why Black people can't enjoy the outdoors.[33]

Truth #2: ESG Is Poisoning All Areas of Our Culture.

ESG is the reason corporate America has adopted the Left's agenda not just on climate change and DEI, but on everything. From promoting abortion to illegal immigration to gun restrictions to vegan milk to online censorship to paper straws, ESG is about marshaling money to push social policies that Americans didn't vote for.

Sometimes the activism directly targets children; other times it doesn't. But the message gets through either way, because ESG works by changing the culture. When Dad has to endure corporate training telling him that punctuality and professionalism is a symptom of White supremacy, he will be less resistant when his child's public school says that math is racist too. When every company, regardless of its mission, is supposed to fight climate change, we don't blink when our children read books or watch movies preaching the same. It all becomes normalized. One transgender beaver at a time.

In other words, ESG is essentially upstream of every other chapter in this book. If there's a progressive social policy that harms children, the chances are good that there's an ESG money manager pushing it. Who do you think ranks among the top ten shareholders of Disney, Paramount, Hasbro, Mattel, Doritos, Exxon, Chevron, and every other company mentioned so far? The Big Three. Often, they're the largest shareholders of all. The surprise is there's no surprise. The Big Three speak, corporate America listens.

Truth #3: You're Funding ESG.

You may ask, if this is essentially a game of "follow the money," where do the Big Three get *their* money from? This time, the answer may surprise you: it's you. The $20 trillion in assets the Big Three manage is not their own. It's the money in your BlackRock 529 college savings account and Vanguard index funds, in your wife's State Street 401(k). It's your own money that's being conscripted into an ESG war on children.

HOW THESE TRUTHS PROTECT CHILDREN

Recognizing the truth about ESG means rejecting it to protect children's true interests. Our children do, in fact, need ESG—just not the kind its proponents favor today.

On the *E*, children need equality, not equity. They need to see that hard work pays off, and that they have an equal opportunity to thrive and succeed regardless of their race, ethnicity, sex, religion, class, or circumstances of their birth. They need to see themselves as agents with autonomy and free will, not as hapless victims, forever doomed to be "oppressors" or "oppressed." They deserve to grow up in a community with shared values, where what brings people together is more important than what breaks them apart.

On the *S*, children need safety. That means protecting their innocence from on-screen age-inappropriate displays of sexualized activities. It also means protecting children from climate catastrophizing, from anxiety-inducing falsehoods about the nature of global warming that children are ill equipped to understand and even less equipped to do anything about.

On the G, it means leaving governance to parents and government, not unelected corporate big shots more interested in shilling products and toasting themselves at Davos than helping children to learn, to be kind, and to reach their full potential.

At a minimum, helping our children means taking ESG, as it is defined today, out of corporate America.

▉ CHILD PROTECTION IN ACTION

Fortunately, child advocates can push back. States like Florida and Texas have already pulled funds from ESG-promoting asset managers. Everyday Americans can do so too. Starving these companies of our money will starve them of their power. That's why the company I work for, Strive Asset Management, was formed: to give Americans another choice, a way to invest their money purely to maximize returns, without political games. While it may be tempting to wield ESG's playbook against it—to use corporate money to steer child-focused policy, to convince corporations to use their financial clout to push the "right" policies—such an attempt would be misguided. Our children's well-being should not depend on which group of activist investors can marshal more money to buy corporate elections. Companies should stay far, far away.

Policymakers can also play a role, enacting legislation to prevent Wall Street from weaponizing assets to promote divisive social and political goals the owners of that money do not support.

We can also confront corporate America itself. To do so, we must identify and highlight how these policies are harming our kids. The concerned parents who spoke out about Target, for example, got this right. Target, of course, is enmeshed in all kinds of leftist nonsense: ESG reports, DEI initiatives, sustainability pledges, and the rest. But it never really had a reckoning until it released its Pride collection for children. Twitter users revolted at rainbow onesies,

T-shirts that read "Girls Gays Theys," and tuck-friendly swimsuits.[34] The backlash was swift. Customers boycotted. Its stock price plummeted as the company lost $15.7 billion in market cap.[35]

The company took note. It pulled the collection in some stores, relocated it in others. And months later, when sales were still down, the company's chief growth officer said that the "strong reaction to this year's Pride assortment" was "a signal for us to pause, adapt and learn."[36]

The learning will not be limited to Target, we hope. The lesson is simple enough, at least for those willing to listen: Children do best when they are raised by loving parents. Not by corporations. Not by Wall Street executives. When businesses lose sight of this basic principle, children suffer. A perfect CEI ranking cannot undo the damage inflicted by a surgeon's scalpel, and a high ESG score is not a nutritious meal. Just ask Shalomi. It's a lesson she understands all too well.

Justin Danhof, executive president and head of corporate governance at Strive Asset Management

Justin Danhof is the executive vice president and head of corporate governance at Strive Asset Management. Danhof is one the nation's leading corporate activists with vast experience in shareholder engagement and proxy voting.

Justin's work has been widely published and quoted in major newspapers, including the *Wall Street Journal*, the *New York Times*, *Politico*, *USA Today*, the *Los Angeles Times*, the *San Francisco Chronicle*, the *Boston Globe* and the *Washington Post*. He has also appeared on the Fox News Channel, Bloomberg, and the Fox Business Channel, among others.

Justin received his BS in economics and finance from Bentley University and his JD and LLM from the University of Miami School of Law. He lives in Ohio with his wife and two daughters.

NATIONAL

RELIGIOUS LIBERTY

ASHLEY MCGUIRE

We'll call him Doe Foster Child #1. We'll call him that, because that's what the courts called him when he found himself the victim of the Philadelphia Department of Human Services' political jihad against his foster-care agency, Catholic Social Services (CSS).

When Doe Foster Mother #1—as the courts dubbed her—brought him into her home, she didn't even know his age. He didn't either, as he came from a background of such abuse and neglect that he was nonverbal and struggled with basic bodily functions like eating. He was severely autistic and afraid of almost everyone and everything. Even bath time scared him.

Doe Foster Mother #1 had fostered fourteen children over eighteen years, many of whom had special needs and disabilities, two of whom she went on to adopt. She found the fortitude to do this noble work through the limitless support she received through her agency, Catholic Social Services. As she said in a sworn court declaration:

> I have been able to call social workers at any hour
> and receive an answer from someone I knew and
> trusted, and have always relied heavily on the
> social workers I interact with. These social workers

have always demonstrated the highest level of care and have shown great love and attention to my children. Although I am not Catholic, I am a religious person and I appreciate the spiritual environment at Catholic Social Services and the way that seems to motivate a dedication to children. My own religious beliefs inspire me to want to care for children in need.

Doe Foster Child #1 grew to feel safe and loved in her home, so much so that one day after returning from being taken to a dentist appointment by someone who was not his foster mother, he bolted from the car and ran to her happily repeating, "Hi, hi, hi" and clutching her. He began to develop a handful of words. He developed an affectionate bond with Doe Foster Mother's grandson. He even started to smile at bath time.

As is wont to happen in the world of foster care, Doe Foster Child was abruptly removed from the home where he had grown to feel secure and loved. Doe Foster Child repeatedly wriggled free from the arms of the social worker sent to retrieve him, and eventually, to the heartache of Doe Foster Mother, required multiple adults to remove him.

He began to regress. He stopped eating. He struggled to use the bathroom. His school reported he had stopped attending his special classes and therapy. Once on thriving trajectory, Doe Foster Child #1 had boomeranged and was rapidly failing.

An emergency effort went underway to return the child to Doe Foster Mother #1, who was eager to welcome him back and formally adopt him. But this time, she was informed, in her words, that "DHS denied the request to place Doe Foster Child #1 with me because I work with Catholic Social Services...I was devastated."

Unbeknownst to her, the city of Philadelphia had abruptly cut ties with Catholic Social Services because of the agency's long-standing religious beliefs about marriage. Despite declaring an emergency level of children in urgent and immediate need for foster homes, the city announced it was illegal to work with the agency that had been helping all children, regardless of their race, religion, ability, or sexual orientation, find safe and loving homes for over a century.

The announcement turned into a several years–long lawsuit, *Fulton v. Philadelphia*, that found its way to the Supreme Court. Eventually, the Court ruled that discriminating against religious adoption and foster-care agencies because of their religious tenets violated the Constitution. But not in time to save countless Doe Foster Children—already victims of severely destabilizing circumstances—from hellish limbo, passing from hotel to home to hotel, torn from the families and homes that were so desperate to love them.[1]

■ BIG LIES ABOUT RELIGIOUS LIBERTY

Lie #1: The Constitution Protects Only Freedom of Worship.

"Congress shall make no law prohibiting the freedom of worship." So reads the First Amendment of the Constitution.

Except that it doesn't.

The First Amendment protects the free exercise of religion, a broad concept of which freedom of worship is just one small slice. And yet beginning around a decade ago, the phrase "freedom of worship" appeared on the scene, put into play by no less than the then president of the United States, Barack Obama, and the Democratic nominee to replace him, Hillary Clinton.

Religious liberty proponents noticed right away because it happened to coincide with efforts at the federal level to require religious organizations like the Little Sisters of the Poor to cover things like abortion pills in their healthcare plans, an effort that resulted in four Supreme Court cases.

It was clearer than ever that religious liberty's detractors thought religion belonged in the four walls of a house of worship, and that once it escaped, it directly threatened other freedoms. The lie they spun—and spin still—is that religion and the free exercise thereof (as the Bill of Rights *does* state) work in competition with other rights and freedoms, especially the made-up ones found in the ever-elusive *emanating penumbras*, like *reproductive rights*.

Lie #2: Intolerance of Religion Must Be Tolerated.

Religious-liberty skeptics see a zero-sum game of rights in which religious liberty sucks up all the oxygen, and worse, becomes a weapon used to take away or whittle down other rights. Seeing religious liberty as a roadblock to their agenda, they strive to shrivel it down to a private right that one must check at the door of his school, workplace, business, or the public square.

"Keep your rosaries off our ovaries!" they shout. What they really mean is, "If you're a Lutheran, pro-life doctor, you must perform abortions." "If you're a Catholic pharmacist, you must prescribe abortion pills." "If you're a Mormon student, don't you dare pray on campus." "If you're Jewish, you can forget about that Kosher meal at a work conference."

The Left seeks a public square whitewashed of religion, while claiming the moral high ground on tolerance. They argue that religious liberty grants license to discriminate, while it is they that actively target and bully people of faith and religious organizations for beliefs that don't toe the progressive political line.

It's bad for women, men, and, yes, children.

■ HOW THESE LIES HARM CHILDREN

Religious institutions have long spearheaded essential services that serve the vulnerable and marginalized. The Catholic Church, for example, is the largest nongovernmental provider of healthcare, education, and charitable services to the poor.[2] Low-income children are arguably America's *most* vulnerable members, entirely reliant on others as they are.

Countless children every year are the direct beneficiary of American charitable giving, 73 percent of which flows through faith-based charities.[3] Charity and care for the poor is an essential feature of Judeo-Christian faiths, and thank goodness! The government couldn't possibly do it on its own. As one scholar put it in the *Oxford Research Encyclopedia of Religion*, "Religious charities also make up the largest percent of U.S. nonprofits. Beyond the numbers, however, religious charity and philanthropy has shaped America's religious and cultural contexts and served as a bedrock to American civil society."[4]

Be it foster and adoption agencies, soup kitchens, school scholarships, or health clinics, America's kids—one in six of whom live in poverty—need the aid that faith-based charities are eager to provide.[5]

But the adage that no good deed goes unpunished is all too real for America's religious charities, which have attracted the virulent scorn of left-wing ideologues. Just ask the Little Sisters of the Poor, a religious order of nuns that care for the indigent elderly, who had to spend more than a decade and three rounds at the Supreme Court fending off efforts by liberals to force them to use their healthcare plans to pay for and provide things like abortion pills. Were it not for the pro bono efforts of their lawyers at the Becket Fund for Religious Liberty, they would have been forced to close their doors, unable to pay the millions in fines the government threatened to levy against them for refusing to comply.

Left-wing attacks on these institutions directly affected kids. Countless adoption and foster agencies closed when local governments said they could not operate because of their religious beliefs about marriage. The government has robbed countless children of voucher and scholarship programs by blocking their use at affordable and high-performing parochial schools that happen to be religious. Charities have had to divert scarce time and resources away from helping vulnerable children and toward fighting off bigoted government attacks.

Perhaps worse still is the stigmatization of religion and shrinkage of religious liberty. Children of faith are raised to believe that an essential part of their identity renders them second-class citizens, enemies of freedom, and threats to their fellow man. This chills the innate human desire to ask big questions and pursue the Divine according to the dictates of their consciences.

Children raised with no religion are raised to be suspicious of their faith-oriented peers. They increasingly adopt a secular religion of wokeism that they perceive to be in direct competition with traditional religious belief. As attorney general Barr put it:

> The problem is not that religion is being forced on others. The problem is that irreligion and secular values are being forced on people of faith... Similarly, militant secularists today do not have a live and let live spirit—they are not content to leave religious people alone to practice their faith. Instead, they seem to take a delight in compelling people to violate their conscience.

This is antithetical to the American experiment, which espoused open and public religious pluralism as essential to a thriving democracy. Essential to freedom of religion is freedom of speech, which is why the two are paired together in the First Amendment. And freedom of speech is the foundation of freedom of thought. And so it's only natural that communist governments go right for the jugular by targeting religious liberty, it pulls the rug out from all the other rights. Look no further than Fidel Castro, who went so far as to "cancel" Christmas in Cuba.[6]

Or just look at my home county of Montgomery County, Maryland, where public school administrators told religious parents their children would be forced to read books featuring radical and explicit gender-ideology content.[7] After parents, most of whom had religious objections, organized a lawsuit, students were encouraged by left-wing activists and other parents to dox the children of these parents for a public shaming.[8] Naturally, the doxing included their religious affiliations. It was a secularist McCarthyism for minors, a training ground for a new generation of cultural Marxists.

This isn't just bad for America; it's bad for kids. Is it any wonder that America's youth are experiencing what social psychologist Jonathon Haidt referred to as "the largest epidemic of adolescent mental illness ever recorded?" America's youth, he argues, are being taught to "embrace" what he calls "harmful, depressogenic cognitive distortions," about the world.[9] Kids are being "supercharged" with "mutual hatred," he argues, which is resulting in soaring anxiety and depression among kids. Kids are being fed the big lies about religious liberty. These lies are teaching them to regard their own playmates with paranoid bigotry.

It's bad for kids, and it's bad for America.

THE TRUTH ABOUT RELIGIOUS LIBERTY

Truth #1: Religious Liberty Precedes the State.

The truth about religious liberty gets to the heart of the truth about what it means to be human.

As Seamus Hasson, the founder of the Becket Fund, wrote in his book, *The Right to be Wrong,* all of us are born "with our eyes fixed on the horizon." We are innately truth seekers. We want to know God, and we have the innate right to the freedom to pursue God according to the dictates of our conscience.

Religious freedom precedes the state; whether you believe we have inherent dignity endowed by God or that human dignity is self-evident without revelation, we can agree that it is the state's duty to protect it. As Pope Francis recently wrote in his recent papal declaration on human dignity, *Dignitas Infinita*, "Every human person possesses an infinite dignity, inalienably grounded in his or her very being, which prevails in and beyond every circumstance, state, or situation the person may ever encounter. This principle, which is fully recognizable even by reason alone, underlies the primary of the human person and the protection of human rights."[10]

Truth #2: The State Needs Religion and Religious Liberty.

As former attorney general William Barr said in a 2019 speech at the University of Notre Dame, "The imperative of protecting religious freedom was not just a nod in the direction of piety. It reflects the framers' belief that religion was indispensable to sustaining our free system of government."[11]

That's because religion inculcates the kind of virtue in a citizenry that is required for freedom to flourish. The founders called it our "First Freedom" because it was the vanguard of all others, and they made it the first order of business in the Bill of Rights.

Because conscience rights are the sacred source for religious liberty, it is consequently intertwined with religious tolerance. If every conscience is sacred, then the beliefs of every conscience must be respected. Religious liberty begets religious tolerance, and tolerant people make good citizens.

Truth #3: Freedom of Worship Is Not Enough.

But freedom of religion is so much more than freedom of worship. Freedom of worship is just one small slice of religious liberty, which also encapsulates the right to convert, the right to proselytize, the right to speak openly about one's faith and engage in the public square, the right to profess one's faith through religious symbols and attire, and the right to freely exercise one's faith. Religion is an all-permeating thing that we carry with us wherever we go. We do not stop being religious when we go to school, when we go to work, when we go to the grocery store, when we go to the doctor.

Any effort to whittle religious liberty down to just one of its many elements, especially when it reshapes religion into something private that we compartmentalize, strikes at the heart of what it means to be human.

HOW THESE TRUTHS PROTECT CHILDREN

Children benefit in tangible ways from the goods and services provided by the countless religious charities operating under the protections of the First Amendment. According to one study, three fourths of all charitable giving in the United States goes to religious charities. Forty of the top fifty charities in America are faith based.[12]

Further, religion nurtures a charitable mindset among youth. One study, for example, found that Christian millennials give three times more money to charity than their secular peers.[13] I see this firsthand in my own five children's lives. Their religious schools and programs constantly encourage them to participate in charitable giving and works of mercy. My six-year-old son's school just finished a baby-bottle fundraising drive for a crisis pregnancy center. He brought the bottle home on the first day and went straight to his piggy bank, where he happily took his own money and put it in the bottle.

We want to raise children who have learned this kind of altruism from a young age.

Religion also nurtures civic-minded citizens. According to the Philanthropy Roundtable, Americans who attend church weekly and pray daily are more than twice as likely than other Americans to have volunteered in the last week.[14] Not only does religion inculcate a strong sense of philanthropic duty, but it cultivates more positive, sociable behavior, something America's anxious, phone-based youth desperately need. The same study observes that "the capacity of religion to motivate pro-social behavior goes way beyond volunteering. Religious people are more involved in community groups. They have stronger links with their neighbors. They are more engaged with their own families."

We also want to raise children who regard others with a broadminded, tolerant attitude. Religious pluralism ensures that young people are exposed to myriad beliefs and learn to engage in a world of big ideas. We hear no end to the importance of "multiculturalism" and "diversity." Children raised in a world where religious diversity, flourishing under the protection of robust religious liberty, grow to be more compassionate and respectful toward others as well as better critical thinkers equipped to engage in the marketplace of ideas.

Religious liberty shapes children into confident, altruistic, and respectful adults that help their communities to thrive.

CHILD PROTECTION IN ACTION

Adrienne Cox went into foster care as a newborn. Her father beat her mother, who eventually felt she couldn't raise Adrienne in a safe environment. Catholic Social Services, the same organization that helped Doe Foster Child #1, placed her in the loving foster home of Winnie Perry, where she would stay for her entire childhood.[15]

The Perrys pushed Adrienne to do her best in all that she did. "My mom encouraged me to go to college, even though I did not want to go at the time," she said. She went on to not only graduate from college but earn a master's degree and build a successful career and a family of her own. Faith was an important part of the Perry home: "We were encouraged to do what is right and do right by others," she said.

For Adrienne, this meant emulating the generosity she experienced in her childhood home by becoming a foster mother herself.

Catholic Social Services "gave me a family," she said when the city of Philadelphia barred the agency from placing children into foster homes because of their religious beliefs. "Everyone needs a family."

In June of 2021, the Supreme Court held that discriminating against faith-based adoption and foster-care agencies because of their religious beliefs violates the Constitution. The decision was unanimous.[16] The decision enabled countless faith-based agencies to remain open to serve countless children in urgent need of loving homes.

The decision in *Fulton v. City of Philadelphia* was a welcome step, but attacks on religious charities and people of faith persist. We urgently need laws that protect the rights of parents, for example, to opt their children out of curricula that advance a radical agenda that directly conflicts with traditional religious beliefs about gender. Faith-based schools, havens of sanity and safety for children, face constant lawsuits for merely teaching basic religious beliefs and employing teachers who adhere to those beliefs. Children are steeped in the message that professing religious beliefs contrary to progressive dogma is hurtful and even hateful. Children must be taught at a young age to respect, not try to quash, religion in American society.

Adrienne's story shows what happens when religious liberty is protected. Guarding religious liberty benefits and protects children. Adrienne was placed into a loving home by an agency whose religious convictions motivated them to help vulnerable children thrive.

Adrienne went on to do just that, breaking a cycle of poverty and violence. Her personal experience of faith-based hospitality then led her to do the same for other children.

All of this happened under the broad umbrella of religious liberty, whose protection rightly extends to every child in this nation.

Ashley McGuire, senior fellow with the Catholic Association and the author of *Sex Scandal: The Drive to Abolish Male and Female*

Ashley McGuire is cohost of the nationally syndicated radio show, "Conversations with Consequences." She is an editor of the Institute for Family Studies blog, and her writing has appeared in the *Wall Street Journal,* the *Washington Post, USA TODAY, TIME, Newsweek, First Things, RealClearPolitics,* and the *New York Post,* among others. She has appeared on CNN, FOX, PBS, and most major television networks. Archbishop Charles Chaput of Philadelphia called Ashley "one of the most gifted young writers, cultural critics and lecturers in the United States." She is a veteran of the pro-bono, religious liberty law firm, Becket.

She lives in Kensington, Maryland, with her husband and five children.

EDUCATION

TIFFANY JUSTICE

I'll never forget hearing the story of Yaeli Martinez.

Abigail, Yaeli's mother, stood at the podium of the Heritage Foundation, bravely sharing her story for the first time. She recounted how her daughter, in her early teens, decided she didn't want to be a girl anymore. Prior to this revelation, Yaeli had never shown signs of gender confusion, but had struggled with depression.

Unbeknownst to her mom, Yaeli had been put into an experimental social gender-transition program at her California public school. When Abigail found out and expressed concerns, Yaeli's school counselor recommended that she would be better off living away from home. The state intervened and removed her from her family.[1] What followed was years of Abigail fighting the government for care and custody of her child.

Abigail shared that one day, after years of fighting to get her daughter back, Yaeli knelt down in front of an oncoming train and took her life. Audience members sobbed. I resolved to expose the cruelty of a government institution that separated a vulnerable teen from her mother—the only person truly willing to fight for her.

That institution is "public education."

▮ BIG LIES ABOUT EDUCATION

I wish this type of horrifying government overreach in the name of "schooling" only happened in "progressive" states like California. But public schools—or more accurately, government schools—in red states and blue states have been captured. They no longer prioritize education, but instead, indoctrination. This indoctrination is built upon falsehoods that harm children's mental and physical well-being, and tragically, sometimes lead to their untimely deaths. Yaeli is one of many such casualties of this system."

Lie #1 "They're All Our Children."

"They're all our children," President Biden announced at a White House event honoring the teacher of the year. "They are not somebody else's children. They're like yours when they're in the classroom."[2]

The first, and biggest, educational lie is that children don't belong to parents. They belong to "all of us."

The primary question that must be answered before you can critique education, or even determine what kind of educational system to establish in the first place is, "to whom do children belong?" The correct answer is "to their parents." However, Democrats, teachers unions, and #BigEducation take a different stance: "Your children belong to us."

That's why schools directly approach students with questions like those posed to January Littlejohn's daughter: "What name would you like to use at school? What name should we use when talking to your parents? What bathroom would you like to use on campus? What sex would you like to room with on field trips?"[3]

This occurred after January, a licensed mental-health counselor, informed the school of her daughter's gender confusion and opted not to "affirm" it. In response, administrators intentionally drove a wedge between this mother and her twelve-year-old child.

Beyond the woke math lesson here, co-ed sleeping arrangements there, pornographic library books everywhere, this agenda seeks to replace the parent in the child's life. That's the aim of initiatives like "community schools," the Whole School, Whole Child, and Whole Community model, which are championed by the Department of Health and Human Services, the CDC, and the Department of Education.[4] Community schools will transform public schools into community hubs, from clothing and food, to prom dresses and school-based health clinics. The federal government, supported by teachers unions, seeks to assume control over every aspect of our children's lives.

Community school expansion gives the federal government the opportunity to drastically expand their control in public education, and thus the lives of our children, by dangling federal money in exchange for compliance. Presently, the federal government contributes on average 9 percent of any state's funding. Imagine this proportion rising to 25 percent, 30 percent, or even 40 percent. We will never regain control of the education system if community schools are expanded and the important role of the parent is further disintegrated by our government system.

Answer the question of "to whom do children belong?" incorrectly, and you will botch every other educational priority too.

Lie #2 Schools Effectively Educate Our Kids.

Parents' expectations for our nation's schools have not changed—they want what they've always wanted, for their kids to get a quality, age-appropriate education that will help them thrive in their personal and professional lives beyond high school.

But the goal of public education *has* changed. Schools like to tout student achievement as a priority, but the facts tell another story. Also known as the "Nation's Report Card," 2022 National Assessment of Educational Progress (NAEP) scores revealed the worst academic performance by students in two decades. Math scores plummeted in fourth and eighth grades, and reading scores stagnated. Since 2004, scores remained flat until the pandemic hit, with only 34 percent of students proficient in reading and math. Minority students particularly struggle, with only 19 percent proficient in reading nationwide.[5]

Despite an annual investment exceeding $810 billion in federal, state, and local funds—equating to $16,390 per pupil—student performance continues to slip. The problem with American public education isn't a lack of funding—it's a twisted set of priorities, exposed by the obsession of radical "educational" ideologies like social and emotional learning (SEL), critical race theory (CRT), and diversity equity, and inclusion (DEI.) Contemporary schools focus chiefly on what Brazilian Marxist Paolo Freire termed "awakening a critical consciousness" in the child.[6] That is, turning kids into activists.

Materials introduced in the classroom are frequently followed by a politically charged question from teachers sporting T-shirts boldly proclaiming, "Educating is Activism." Progressive agendas seep into math lessons,[7] while English syllabi often eschew anything predating 2015, in the name of "decolonizing" the classroom.[8] History and social studies curricula foster hostility toward America and teach kids to hate one another. Need proof? Just ask Jewish college students who find themselves barricaded in libraries as classmates outside chant, "From the river to the sea, Palestine shall be free."[9]

School districts do two things well: celebrate themselves and protect themselves. And they often celebrate themselves in order to protect themselves. One need only scrutinize the disparity between record-high graduation rates and stagnant or declining eighth-grade reading proficiency to realize that much of the "success" lauded by public schools amounts to nothing more than graduation inflation. "Few who are paying close attention believe that rising graduation rates represent genuine academic progress. Test scores are stagnant or declining, so how are graduation rates up?"[10]

The harsh reality is that government schools are not primarily concerned with educating our kids. They are more interested in enlisting a new cadre of Red Guards to carry on the progressive revolution. Xi Van Fleet, author of *Mao's America: A Survivor's Warning*, knows Red Guards when she sees them:

> To launch a revolution, one needs revolutionaries...Mao had his revolutionaries, known as the Red Guards, tailor-made for him from his government schools. The American progressives have theirs from the same place: government schools. They are the social justice warriors, the American Red Guards.[11]

Lie #3 Trust the Experts. Teachers Are the Experts. Experts Are Trustworthy.

During the pandemic, parents witnessed teachers (often impressively credentialed ones) filling their children's minds with radical rhetoric. Despite evidence showing minimal risks to children from COVID, schools moved to remote learning on the pretext of "following the science."[12] Kids suffered, becoming bargaining chips for more funding, enduring prolonged closures and masks that hindered social interaction and learning.[13]

It wasn't just the teacher "expert" class wielding their professional clout against children. Parents scoffed when the American Academy of Pediatrics (AAP), in a bid to bolster masking mandates, suggested that babies didn't need to see their mothers' faces.[14] When it emerged that the AAP endorsed radical gender surgeries and harmful cross-sex hormones for children, we weren't surprised.[15]

Lie #4 Unions Care About Teachers and Kids.

> *"It has taken a pandemic for people to notice the effect of a union having veto power over a public service... In the private sector, unions organize against business owners and corporations. In the public sector, whom are they organized against?"*[16]
> —Mike Antonucci

Until COVID reared its head, few parents grasped the primary agenda of teacher unions—and it's not about supporting teachers or students. Over the past four years, the National Education Association (NEA) has spent more money on political activities and lobbying than on traditional "representational activities."[17] In 2021, the NEA and AFT gave approximately $30 million to left-wing issue advocacy groups; this is up from the $10 million given to these groups in 2005.[18]

I've seen firsthand how union bosses prioritize the interests of those at the bargaining table over the teachers in the classroom. Demands for increased funding from unions don't necessarily equate to better academic outcomes for our children or working conditions for teachers.

Take New York City, where a whopping $28,004 is spent per student—the highest among major US urban areas—yet student achievement continues to decline.[19] Alongside this downward trend, participation in parent conferences has dropped by 40 percent since the onset of COVID, as remote meetings became a fixture in the latest teachers union contract. Why would the union want to keep conferences virtual, despite realizing their negative impact on parent involvement? (Hint: because parental involvement is one of the greatest hindrances to their activist aims.)[20]

Education has become a jobs program that prioritizes adult wants over children's needs.

I vividly recall the moment on March 13, 2020, standing in the school district offices when news broke that schools would be closing due to COVID. It was a gut punch. School districts are like cruise ships—they don't power up or down swiftly. The notion of suddenly pivoting to virtual learning was wildly unrealistic. After the initial shutdown dragged on and on, parents saw exactly who was fighting to keep schools closed—the very unions that "champion fairness" and a "high quality education."[21] Randi Weingarten, head of the American Federation of Teachers boasted that the "Biden transition tea"' was "first to solicit the union's advice on schools reopening."[22] Spoiler—the union advised against it.

Beyond the disastrous COVID-era closures and mandates pushed by teachers unions, their leadership and policies have frequently obstructed educational progress and innovation. Former school-board member Erika Donalds recalled how the union blocked her attempts to offer targeted incentives for teachers to work at a high-poverty school on the outskirts of her district. It instead pushed for a blanket raise that did little to support struggling students. And, while they advocate for defunding the police, union bosses remain silent on violence and discipline issues affecting both teachers and students.

The union wields considerable power but often fails to prioritize the needs of students and, at times, teachers. Who truly benefits from this power? The "teachers unions" frequently appear to align against taxpayers, the very individuals they are meant to serve.

◼ HOW THESE LIES HARM CHILDREN

Simply pouring more money into education doesn't guarantee success, and can even produce the opposite effect.[23] Increased funding seems to support ideological agendas rather than educational initiatives, fostering activism over scholarly pursuits. Proposals for new levies and taxes under the guise of funding public education arise almost every election cycle. However, much of this money fails to enrich communities or the nation, instead funding what's essentially a corrupt jobs program for activists.

Children suffer the most. Many are deprived of instruction in real history and great literature. Essential subjects like mathematics get crowded out by SEL, which perpetuate feelings of student guilt or victimization.[24] Exposure to pornographic and sexually explicit content under the guise of inclusion and diversity further harms their mental health. Ideology supplants education, and our children pay the price.[25]

The family chapter in this book shows that children who become disconnected from their parents are vulnerable. Yet schools routinely encourage children to keep secrets from their parents.[26, 27] This is predatory behavior. While the #groomer tag was largely banned across social media in 2022,[28] the fact is that separation from one's parents is a predicate for abuse, sexual or otherwise. The U.S. education system is one of the largest institutional forces seeking to separate children from their parents emotionally and, sometimes, physically as well. That leaves children exposed to an array of dangers.

It's criminal that the education system is perverting our greatest national resource, the minds of our children. It's even more sickening that we have to pay for it.

■ THE TRUTH ABOUT EDUCATION

Truth #1: We Do Not Coparent with the Government.[29]

Children belong to their parents. Not the state. Not doctors. And certainly not the schools.

Children do not belong to "all of us." Children belong to their own mothers and fathers, the people who are statistically the safest, most connected to, most invested in, and most protective of them.[30] That natural reality supports the longstanding and universally recognized parental right to direct the upbringing of their own children, including but not limited to their education, medical care, morality, and religion.

Parental rights are not granted by the government and cannot be easily revoked. The Supreme Court has repeatedly recognized and upheld the preeminence of parental rights, viewing them as fundamental liberties safeguarded by the Constitution. These rights are protected under the Due Process Clause of the Fourteenth Amendment and the First Amendment's provisions for freedom of religion and association.[31]

Tina Descovich and I cofounded Moms for Liberty after serving on school boards in Florida from 2016 to 2020. We saw behind the education curtain and when COVID happened, all of America got to see behind the education curtain.[32] What exactly was behind that curtain? A massive, well-funded, coordinated effort to wrest control of children's minds, relationships, and even their bodies away from their parents. All of America got to see the cozy relationships among the teachers unions, the Biden administration, and the educational bureaucracy that undermines local control and our system of representative government. And they clearly understood that the very institution that has been charged with educating our children, was seeking to (effectively) parent our children. We like to call this

COVID Lemonade. Sour truths which have been stirred into a sweet parental rights movement.

As Tina has accurately noted, "If we don't have the fundamental right to direct the upbringing of our children, we have nothing."

Truth #2: Parents Are the Experts, Not the Enemy.

Not only do parents have a right to direct their children's upbringing, they know best how to do that. Just ask a mom of a child with special needs: odds are, she knows more about celiac disease or supraventricular tachycardia than the doctor. Antivax *or* provax, good luck arguing against a mother who has done her research.

It's precisely because we are the most connected to and invested in our children that we understand what our children need from schools. Maybe not all children, but certainly *our* children. So it's no surprise that parents are the number-one driver of student success.[33]

If schools really want children to succeed, they should roll out the red carpet for parents. But #BigEducation is doing the opposite. Within five days of the National School Boards Association requesting assistance to address parental concerns at school-board meetings, the Department of Justice labeled these parents domestic terrorists.[34] The FBI called parents at their homes who spoke up at school-board meetings.[35] Stephen Friend, an FBI whistleblower, testified that he was asked to write down license plate numbers at school-board meetings.[36] Parents speaking up for in-person schools, age-appropriate education, and refusing transgender interventions are treated as enemies of the state.

■ HOW THESE TRUTHS PROTECT CHILDREN

When parents know the truth, they fight for their kids.

For decades, many responsible Americans—busy living their lives, having babies, working, innovating, saving for college—considered holding elected office as someone else's job. And we handed over this critical vocation to radical activists.

No longer. A fresh wave of parents, recognizing that diversity officers with PhDs don't necessarily understand their children's third-grade needs better than they do, are now boldly stepping into the educational fray to safeguard their children.

Education is a local issue, not a federal issue. Parents should be the locus of control, then elected school boards, and only then the state. A D.C. bureaucrat who has never set foot in your state, let alone your child's school, doesn't know best. Lindsey Burke, director of the Center for Educational Policy at the Heritage Foundation, agrees: "Policymaking and funding should take place at the state and local level, closest to the affected families."[37]

Education freedom and school-choice expansion constitute an important part of reform and progress in American education. Years of activism are bearing fruit in the form of new school-choice legislation in over half a dozen states just this past year.[38] School choice forces public schools to compete for funding, improving their programs and increasing their willingness to heed parent feedback. We should "fund students, not systems."[39]

More parental control, more local control, and more school-board members who see it as their job to educate rather than indoctrinate students mean not only less financial waste, but better educational outcomes for kids, more educational choice, and a school system that reinforces the connection between parents and children rather than destroying it.

■ CHILD PROTECTION IN ACTION

No elected official has protected children in education better than Florida governor Ron DeSantis. "Because it's a war on truth," he declared, "I think we have no choice but to wage a war on the woke." What a war on the woke he hath waged.

DeSantis codified a "Parents' Bill of Rights," vastly expanded school choice, and advocated for new workforce education while placing "key allies in statewide posts."[40] He emphasizes child protection, stating that "[i]n Florida, we let kids be kids, and we protect children from those who seek to harm them." His recent signing of SB 1264 strengthens education standards by emphasizing the dangers of Communism.[41]

DeSantis has also acted against union power and has increased parental involvement in education. He endorsed conservative school-board candidates in the 2022 elections, leading to conservative majorities in several localities.[42] He's also supported legislation that limits union power by ending paycheck deductions for specific public-sector union dues and increasing membership requirements.[43]

DeSantis' comprehensive approach to reform involves litigating, promoting legislation, reforming public academic institutions, appointing allies to key positions, endorsing strong school-board candidates, and holding abusive labor unions accountable. These efforts signify a proactive and successful overhaul of Florida's educational system, resulting in better protection of parental rights and improved student outcomes.[44]

Florida isn't the only state making progress.[45] Oklahoma state superintendent Ryan Walters has a waged a relentless fight against woke,[46] while Arkansas and South Carolina[47] are working to reverse the literacy crisis. Governor Huckabee Sanders is improving working conditions for teachers,[48] and Cade Brumley, state superintendent of Louisiana, is overhauling the state's social-studies standards.[49]

Successful efforts to reform public education have one thing in common: ground game. They enlist an army of parents, who are hands down *the most* effective advocates to hold leaders accountable, spread awareness, oppose government overreach, promote liberty, engage on key issues and activate citizens to public service.

It's also a *local* ground game. While national legislation does matter, pro-child advocates' top goal should be building relationships with state and county decision-makers. The parents in our Moms for Liberty movement have been doing this for the past three years. And it's working.

These moms will tell you that they didn't ask for this fight. But they saw the schools coming for their kids, so they rolled up their sleeves, laced up their boots, and got to work, not just for their children, but for everybody's children.

Americans must always pay attention to the decision-makers closest to them in their communities. Encouraging people to run for and serve on school boards across the country is essential for protecting local control of education. But it's not enough to get people elected. We must build a grassroots army to support those candidates once elected. We must rally together as parents to defend our fundamental right to direct the upbringing of our children.

We must put kids first in America. It's up to parents to make that happen.

Tiffany M. Justice, cofounder of Moms for Liberty

Tiffany is a wife and mom of four school-aged children. In 2016 she stepped up to serve for four years on the school district of Indian River County, FL, school board. She believes that kids in public school deserve innovation, and parents have the right to know the union interference and government bureaucracy that is keeping that innovation from happening in their children's district.

DIGITAL TECHNOLOGY

MARIA BAER

When ten-year-old Kyle Lyons' school shifted online at the start of the COVID-19 pandemic, his class was just beginning to learn long division. Carrying ones and tallying remainders are challenging enough for a fourth-grader, but remote school made it even harder: now Kyle had to find all these new mathematical symbols on a *keyboard*.

"At the computer, you have to click all these buttons," he told Buzzfeed News. "I eventually got it, but it was still quite hard."[1]

By the fall of 2020, Kyle's Catholic school in the Bronx was still nowhere close to reopening. His mom watched him become more and more discouraged with "online" school, frustrated when his teachers would zip through the material, oblivious when he or his classmates were struggling to keep up.

Nevertheless, schools across the country remained committed to "remote learning." A few months earlier and a few states away, the city of Columbus, Ohio, had recently bought twenty thousand laptops for $7 million, promising a Chromebook to every single kid in the district. Columbus classrooms would remain empty for another year, but superintendent Dr. Talisa Dixon made a bold claim: these Chromebooks meant school was back in session.

"Having that Chromebook is like having a textbook," she told the media in July 2020.[2] School districts nationwide made similar promises and purchases. That May, Los Angeles school officials claimed to "solve" the problem of lockdown education by devoting $100 million to procuring devices and internet access for every public-school student.[3]

Back in the Bronx, Kyle's mom said her son was losing interest in things he used to love. He said he didn't care about dressing up for Halloween that fall. He wasn't sure he wanted to play basketball anymore. Kyle was a "hands-on" learner, his mom said. Remote learning was not working for him.

What if *every* kid is a hands-on learner?

Calling a glorified video chat "remote learning" made some big assumptions about what constitutes *learning* and what kids need to achieve it. Those assumptions were mostly wrong.[4] But they weren't new.

In 2016, tech companies sold and shipped nearly thirteen million mobile devices to K-12 schools in the United States.[5] In 2017, the *New York Times* reported that more than half of all American elementary schoolers were using Google education apps in the classroom.[6] The digital revolution had reached the school building.

By then, of course, America's kids were hooked on digital technology outside of school. In 2015, 72 percent of Apple's most popular for-purchase digital apps were in the toddler category.[7] That same year, 73 percent of teens reported having a smartphone.[8] The Centers for Disease Control estimate that kids between eight and ten years old spend an average of six hours a day in front of a screen.[9] Why shouldn't they, if adults spend six to eight hours a day on screens themselves?[10]

Digital tech holds a powerful allure for children (and their parents). The devices are slick, tech companies promise they are at least potentially "educational," and the glowing screens soothe and occupy even the most hyperactive kids.

But digital tech also has incredible power to shape our habits, our desires, and even our conception of who we are and what kind of world this is. That power is exponentially stronger for children. This means it is adults' responsibility to be thoughtful and deliberate about what digital tech we give to kids, and when. It also means seeing through the lies about what the tech is really doing, and how it is changing *us*, too.

▉ BIG LIES ABOUT DIGITAL TECHNOLOGY

Lie #1: The Only Thing Dangerous About Digital Technology for Kids Is Harmful Content.

In 2013, "Internet Gaming Disorder" was added to the *Diagnostic and Statistical Manual of Mental Disorders*.[11] Psychiatrists were increasingly encountering young adults addicted to video games. In severe cases, they would stay up all night, urinate in bottles next to their screens to save time, and even neglect to eat.[12]

This was just what digital game designers hoped for. Big tech companies routinely hire neuroscientists to help them craft their games, adding addictive features meant to keep players playing. They know what colors and sounds to use, how frequently to reward players, and how to design challenges that are *just* difficult enough.

By 2013, the problem wasn't just the deliberately hypnotic elements of the games themselves, or even the fact that exposure to violent and explicit video games can desensitize players to actual violence.[13] Video games were changing the way players saw the *real* world. Psychologists saw more and more gamers suffering from psychiatric "derealization"—they had lost the ability to distinguish between their games and reality.[14]

Most adults know the risks of dangerous digital *content*. There's bullying on social media. Predatory pornography companies target kids online. There's exploitative data mining, hacking, digital surveillance, the dark web, deep fakes, and artificial intelligence–powered "companions." These threats aren't insubstantial, but they're not the *only* dangers digital tech poses for kids.

Social psychologist Jonathan Haidt believes digital technology is changing *"the nature of childhood"* itself.[15] The more digital tech embeds itself in our everyday lives, the more we start to believe we can substitute a virtual world for the physical one. This makes it harder for kids to become healthy, empathetic, resilient, discerning adults.

Lie #2: Digital Technology Can Educate.

In 2014, researchers at the nonprofit Joan Ganz Cooney Center called the market of "educational" apps the "digital wild west."[16] While federal legislation bars the creators of these apps from collecting or selling student data, there is no meaningful gatekeeping over which apps and games get to call themselves educational in the first place.[17]

A deeper, more fundamental question lurks: can digital technology really educate at all?

When American public schools went remote in the spring of 2020, not everyone was as optimistic as the teachers unions or the tech companies. Some in the media worried over what they called the "digital divide," prophesying that poor kids would struggle most with online school because they had fewer devices, spottier internet access, and lived in less stable homes.

In May of 2020, one reporter lamented that "perhaps as many as one-third of the Los Angeles Unified School District's students [lack] both a personal computer and broadband internet at home — a major problem if the best way to deliver lessons is online."[18]

"If" it's the best way? Wasn't anyone going to ask?

Maybe no one questioned digital learning in 2020 because the cat was already out of the bag (and down the street). Most American public schools were already using tablets, online communications, digital academic testing platforms, and even social media in the classroom. In 2014, Google announced the launch of "Google Classroom," an online platform for schools.[19] Google project manager Zach Yeskel waxed poetic about the precious time this would save teachers. They could take attendance, assign papers (using Google Docs, of course) communicate with students (using Gmail, obviously) and grade papers (on Google Drive). Google Classroom, Yeskel said, would "improve class communications" by allowing teachers to "make announcements, ask questions, and comment with students in real time."

It's a classic marketing strategy: create a problem and then promise to solve it. But all the trumped-up enthusiasm and slick language just distracted from the truth that there already existed an easy, simple way for teachers to make announcements, ask questions, and "comment with students in real time": *showing up to class.*

Tech companies that market their devices for children exploit the cultural assumption that shiny, new things are the best things. Anyone who disagrees is consigned to history's embarrassing club of technophobes, alongside the fusty old philosophers who thought the automobile would ruin the world.[20]

There's a fundamental difference between adopting new technology that eases drudgery and enhances the human experience in the real world, and seeking to meaningfully *replicate* or even *replace* the human experience in the real world.

In 2016, the director of Google's education apps group, Jonathan Rochelle, gave a speech at an education conference. Talking about his own kids, he said:

> I cannot answer for them what they are going to do with the quadratic equation. I don't know why they are learning it…And I don't know why they can't ask Google for the answer if the answer is right there.[21]

If the very designers of the tech that is revolutionizing our kids' lives can't remember why it's *good to know things*, then we have every reason to be skeptical that their inventions can truly "educate."

Lie #3: If We Can Do Something, We Should Do It.

In 1972, the first scientific calculator hit the American market.[22] The HP-35, invented by Hewlett-Packard, could perform complicated trigonometry and even calculus. By 1980, America's National Council of Teachers of Mathematics had recommended that calculators become standard in every classroom "at all grade levels."[23] By 1994, the College Board announced that high schoolers could use a calculator during the SAT, and the very next year, students were *required* to use graphing calculators on the standardized Advanced Placement calculus exams.[24]

The speed with which the calculator went from brand-new to standard to required was dizzying. It was an easy sell: calculators turn arduous equations into a few keystrokes. They still require a certain amount of skill and conceptual understanding—users have to know *which* keystrokes and in *what* order. But calculators, like all digital tech, had free PR: they capitalized on Western culture's idolization of efficiency.

It's an unwritten rule for us that if something difficult can be done easier or faster, it should be. There's a problem, though. Efficiency is *not* always what's best, especially when it comes to the needs and development of children. In 1986—just six years after the calculator became "standard" in all classrooms—the country's top mathematicians gathered for a conference at Tulane University. They were worried. Their students were learning how to perform equations on calculators, but they weren't grasping the mathematical concepts behind them. In a paper collectively published after the conference, the professors launched the calculus reform movement:

> The availability of handheld calculators... removes the necessity for covering many of the techniques and for much of the drill which now form such a large part of the calculus... Calculus instruction should make use of the latest technology but the goals of the calculus *must extend far beyond facility with either calculators or computers.* [emphasis added].[25]

In 2008, researchers at Vanderbilt's College of education and human development put it more simply: "Calculators [are] ok in math class, if students know the facts first."[26]

If a sixteen-year-old can pass the AP Calculus exam with a TI-83 but can't explain how mass influences velocity, it's worth asking what they've actually *learned,* other than a sophisticated shortcut. Shortcuts are meant for people who've learned the long way first. They are not the same as progress.

■ HOW THESE LIES HARM CHILDREN

Using digital tech as a substitute for a teacher, parent, or friend isn't just an existential threat to kids. It also imperils them physically. Research shows exposure to digital screens may shorten kids' attention spans, dampen their ability to focus, put them at higher risk of obesity and mental-health problems, and make it harder for them to sleep at night.[27] The fast pace of digital games and apps make the pace of real life seem slower—hampering kids' cultivation of patience. Kids who use digital tech for more than an hour a day tend to have more behavioral problems and smaller vocabularies.[28]

Other research suggests too much digital technology too early can stunt the growth of gray matter in young children's brains, impeding the development of the neural connections that allow them to speak, move, learn, and develop into functioning social creatures.[29] More than forty years ago, German researchers found that digital technology was shrinking young people's capacity to notice varying shades of color or differentiate sounds—that even the *Flintstones*-age tech of 1980 was overstimulating young people to the point of sensory numbness.[30]

Other studies have suggested that prolonged or premature exposure to digital tech negatively impacts kids' ability to learn social skills (including empathy), read nonverbal communication cues, and regulate their own emotions.[31]

All this is old news to the world's tech gurus. In 2010, Apple cofounder Steve Jobs infamously revealed he didn't let his kids use iPads.[32] Other Silicon Valley executives, including Google CEO Sundar Pichai and Microsoft founder Bill Gates, admitted a similar aversion to their own products.[33]

Behind the smoke screens of clever marketing, cultural pressure to embrace progress for progress's sake, and false promises about the "educational value" and "safety" of digital devices for kids, tech designers and CEOs saw their products as a net negative for kids.

They were right.

■ THE TRUTH ABOUT DIGITAL TECHNOLOGY

Truth #1: Digital Technology Can't Match the Benefits of an Embodied Childhood.

Some of the brightest points in human history have been the development of some technology that mitigated suffering or enhanced our ability to learn about the world.

Digital technology holds similar promise. It can eliminate drudgery, foster relationships between people who are physically distant from each other, and dramatically ease many of the burdens on people living with disabilities. It can help us more efficiently and more exactly study the physical world around us (and the universe far beyond us). But maximizing digital technology's salutary effects requires understanding what it *can't* do as well as what it can.

Research shows that digital technology cannot meaningfully replicate, replace, or improve upon a child's physical experience in the real world. To be human isn't merely an inner experience. Being human means being a soul *and a body*. That means human children need to learn about the world with their minds *and their bodies*. Not even the most sophisticated simulation will ever match a human-to-human, hands-on learning environment—whether inside or outside of the classroom.

Studies routinely show that kids understand and remember information much better when they physically write it down on paper than when they take notes electronically.[34] Readers of all ages comprehend and remember much more when they read a physical book compared to a blue-lit digital version.[35]

Even if digital tech can "help" kids write an essay, solve an equation, or find answers on a search engine, a machine will never be able to teach them the value of that information itself, or the dignifying, humanizing, irreplaceable experience of finding it on their own.

Truth #2: Helping Kids Use Digital Technology "Well" Requires Asking a Few Key Questions First.

Does this digital technology offer something we lack? Say, a digital translator that allows us to speak to a friend, or a hearing aid. Or is it promising to give us something we "didn't know" we wanted or needed—distraction, titillation, or numbness?

Second, do we use this digital tech, or does *it* use *us*? Dr. Katie Davis, director of the University of Washington's Digital Youth Lab, says digital tech that "helps" and doesn't "hurt" kids will respect their agency—the apps won't try to hook them with bells, whistles, and rewards, but instead will require substantial, thoughtful interaction from their young users.[36]

Third, is the digital tech making false promises that it can somehow replicate, effectively mimic, or "improve upon" the human experience? Fourth, what might this technology change about life in the real world, and will that change be a *good* one—will it lead to health, or merely to "efficiency" or a quick hit of dopamine? We should be suspicious of anyone proffering a new digital technology to our kids (or us) who can't satisfactorily answer these questions.

▪ HOW THESE TRUTHS PROTECT CHILDREN

A healthy embrace of digital tech for kids would respect them as both bodies and souls, which means it wouldn't exploit their physiological vulnerabilities or cause them to neglect their natural physical and emotional needs. It would be meticulously risk averse, considering at each point (development and design, regulation, integration in schools) who kids are, at what stage of development they are, and what they need most to flourish at that stage. When we prioritize the needs of kids over adults' desires for efficiency, ease, "progress," profit, or quiet, we'll protect kids from tech that threatens their mental, emotional, spiritual, and physical health.

The multibillion-dollar tech industry makes a lot of promises. It promises parents it can help soothe their anxious or rowdy kids, that it can educate them, and that it can foster their "social connections." In practice, when digital tech is used too much or given to kids too early, it not only fails to deliver these goods, but actively impedes them. Adults who want to foster kids' healthy development should be willing to shoulder the very burdens that digital tech claims it can lift off of them. It's parents' job to shepherd kids into becoming empathetic, resilient, discerning adults. Often, that will mean protecting them from the false promises of a virtual replacement for the real world. It will mean letting them learn about the world the hard, slow way instead of the glowing shortcut way. Doing the work to regulate kids' screen exposure may be arduous because it has become so countercultural, but it will redound to their benefit.

"Remote school" proved to be an oxymoron. So is "virtual reality." Technology may enhance the experience of being human, but it can never give kids a more beautiful, meaningful world than the real one.

CHILD PROTECTION IN ACTION

Even for digital tech that is content appropriate for children, tech designers, regulators, educators and parents should take further steps. They should consider introducing screens later in school, if at all. In 2003, investigative reporter Todd Oppenheimer found a directly inverse relationship between the amount of digital tech used in a classroom and kids' academic achievement.[37] So-called "low-tech" schools, such as Waldorf academies and Montessori schools, are among the academically best performing in the country.[38]

Parent and pro-child advocates have every right to compel their public schools to delay the use of digital tech in the classroom until kids are older; to urge state officials to stop administering state exams digitally; and to lobby schools to stop using digital tech exclusively to communicate with students and families. Tell them to send that classroom newsletter, field-trip announcement, or sports team sign-up on actual paper!

Parents, pediatricians, regulators, teachers, and caregivers should also stop giving screens to kids under age two. The data is conclusive—it's simply too dangerous.[39] Regulators should dramatically tighten the definition of "educational" for apps, games, devices and online learning platforms. They should also mandate that tech devices come out of the box in their safest, most locked-down versions. The factory settings of most big tech devices tend to be as open and permissive as possible, placing the burden on parents to tinker with complicated and hard-to-find settings to turn "on" parental controls. It should work the other way around.

In 2022, the public middle school in Maple Grove, Minnesota, banned smartphones. That meant that from 8:10 am to 2:40 pm every day, students' phones sat dormant in their lockers. A year later, principal Patrick Smith said kids were fighting less, bullying had decreased, and students were more engaged in class and with each other. Not a single parent had complained about the policy—in fact, many reported their kids were doing better in school than ever before. Smith told CBS News the change was "night and day."[40]

Had the digital revolution only just begun, it would be easier to protect kids from its false promises and pitfalls. There's no doubt that resisting the pull toward virtual reality becomes a little bit harder with each shiny new technological development. But adults are meant to do hard things for our kids. And protecting their embodied childhoods in the real world will always be worth it.

Maria Baer, reporter and cohost of *Breakpoint This Week* **with The Colson Center for Christian Worldview**

Maria Baer is a writer, reporter and podcast host. She has been published at The Colson Center for Christian Worldview, WORLD, The Gospel Coalition, *Christianity Today*, and elsewhere. In 2023, Maria won an Evangelical Press Association award for her coverage of prison conditions for pregnant women in *Christianity Today*. Maria's work can be found at www.mariaebaer.com and in her Substack newsletter, *It Is As If*.

Maria lives in Ohio with her husband and two daughters.

THE ENVIRONMENT

CHRIS BARNARD

It was an ordinary Tuesday. Fourteen-year-old Trevor had just eaten breakfast. While his grandmother Debra headed out to drop off his four younger siblings at Happy Camp Elementary School, Trevor logged on to his distance-learning program.

His grandmother came home and told him there was a wild-fire nearby. Debra threw some things in a bag on the off chance they needed to evacuate. Trevor didn't think much of it. Wildfires had become routine in California over the last couple years. So he just put his headphones back on and kept working.

When it was time to pick his siblings up from school, Debra said, "Why don't you grab the dogs and come with me?"

He did. Thank God.

By the time all five kids were in the car headed back home, the fire had spread and the road was blocked. Within a couple hours, Trevor's house was gone.

In September of 2020, Happy Camp Elementary School in Northern California was one of the first schools in the state to start classes again, following the COVID-19 pandemic lockdowns. A week later, the school and the town went up in flames. A devastating wildfire tore through the community, destroying 150 homes, more than a quarter of the entire town.[1] Of the 109 children at the school, half were made homeless including Trevor's family. Two people died, as the fire burned one hundred fifty-seven thousand acres and caused $54 million in economic damage.[2]

The threat of wildfires, especially in the western United States, has grown in recent decades due to bad environmental policymaking that disproportionately harms young children. Historically, proactive forest management prevented or rapidly snuffed out wildfires. This entailed removing excessive underbrush, carrying out prescribed burns in overgrown areas, and implementing responsible logging practices. Forests were saved by strategically removing parts of the ecosystem that act as fuel for wildfires. Indigenous communities across the world have pioneered this practice for millennia, understanding that proactive human management of the land can actually be *good* for the environment.

Unfortunately, forest management has fallen out of favor with modern environmentalist orthodoxy. For some, the idea that humans would preventatively burn underbrush or log overgrown parts of the forest is nothing short of eco-blasphemy: meddling with nature in this way is disruptive and unjustifiable. This mindset has yielded rules and stipulations that make genuine forest management very difficult in many parts of the country. Decades worth of wildfire tinder has built up across the West. Political inertia has prevented solutions from emerging.

The consequences have been dire. In 2022 alone, 7.5 million acres of land burned in wildfires across America, releasing millions of tons of particulate pollution into the air. Four and a half million U.S. homes are at risk from wildfires, as are thousands of schools and hospitals, while wildfire occurrences have increased 223 percent since 1983.[3] Our "environmentalist" approach to wildfires and forest management has destroyed schools, forced evacuations from hospitals, and made countless families with children homeless. Perhaps most damning are recent studies detailing the effect these wildfires are having on young children. One study finds that as many as 7.4 million children in the U.S. are affected by wildfire smoke annually; it accounts for 20 percent of particulate matter pollution they are exposed to. Smoke causes asthma and other respiratory diseases that disproportionately harm the youngest people.[4] While most wildfires are started by humans, climate change only exacerbates the problem, as warmer temperatures prime even more forests for going up in flames. Between 2000 and 2021, the number of dangerous air quality days in the American West grew by nearly 400 percent. Research projects that PM2.5 air pollution (fine particulate matter often caused by wildfires) will grow by as much as 50 percent in the next thirty years.[5]

Our failure to act on adequate environmental protection hurts children first and foremost. From wildfires to pollution to climate change, we need better answers than the mainstream orthodoxy.

BIG LIES ABOUT THE ENVIRONMENT

The cautionary tale of wildfires in the U.S. is symptomatic of a broader, modern approach to environmental issues that finds its roots more in ideology and emotion than in science and reason. This approach rests on two main lies.

Lie #1: Conservationism Means Radical Environmentalism.

This idea wilts before a brief look at history. Once upon a time, environmental protection was the domain of farmers and ranchers, hunters and anglers. These are the people who spend most of their lives outdoors, and their lifestyles directly depend on a healthy environment that they can pass down to future generations. They are the natural conservationists. President Teddy Roosevelt, a Republican with a penchant for ranching himself, founded the modern conservation movement, setting aside more than two hundred million acres of forest and laying the foundation for the National Park Service. Millions of Americans gained access to the great outdoors, and children were exposed to the extraordinary natural beauty we have inherited. Roosevelt always argued that *conservation* is distinct from *preservation*—protecting the environment is not about removing all human interaction with the outdoors, but enjoying and living in harmony with nature. While we must avoid exploitation, we can responsibly use natural resources. Proactive human conservation efforts can actually *improve* environmental outcomes for the benefit of future generations. This approach to environmentalism was mainstream, and actively embodied by rural conservatives nationwide.

Everything changed in the 1970s. With the original Earth Day and the mass demonstrations associated with it, the conservationism of farmers and hunters gave place to the brand of environmentalism championed by activist groups like Greenpeace and PETA. As I've written in an essay for The American Conservative:

> On a macro level, this change signified a larger shift within the environmental movement toward a more emotional and political message. Rather than the salt-of-the-earth image of country folks as environmentalists, the modern movement came to be dominated by mostly metropolitan voices that valued idealistic notions of "natural" preservation over pragmatic conservation. The image of the polar bear surfaced, conveying Rousseauian notions of fuzzy natural beauty untainted by humans, as opposed to those meddlesome farmers and sportsmen.[6]

Hunting, farming, and other rural lifestyles were alien to a movement led by urban, college-educated elites. Forest management, natural-resource development, and sportsmanship were all seen as antienvironmental.

Today, these activists' misplaced idealism has evolved into full-blown eco-alarmism, advanced by people who claim to be rescuing the planet from imminent extinction. The crunchy environmentalism of well-meaning tree huggers has mutated into a gigantic political movement that wields great influence over policy decisions and electoral outcomes.

Understandably, conservatives are uncomfortable with this modern manifestation of environmentalism. They have increasingly disassociated themselves from climate and environmental activism, sometimes going as far as denying climate change or other environmental challenges altogether. A pernicious narrative has consequently taken hold that conservatives don't care about the environment, and that left-wing environmentalists are the ones looking out for children and the planet they will inherit.

Both in the United States and abroad, large majorities believe in climate change and want politicians to pass measures to reduce pollution and protect the environment. Research shows that the Democratic Party has gained the trust of both independents and young people in huge numbers on climate issues.[7]

The Left declares that we must stop climate change and protect the environment for the sake of future generations. Activists have effectively humanized and emotionalized environmental issues, conveying a deep concern for the well-being of humans and the planet we inhabit. They elevate stories of how pollution affects marginalized communities; they highlight the ways climate change affects the vulnerable. The Left has convinced vast swathes of voters that only they can be trusted to solve the environmental challenges of our time—as opposed to the evil conservatives who are owned by fossil fuel interests.

Lie #2: Humans Are the Problem: Caring for the Environment Means Leaving It Untouched.

This naïve idea of natural purity has a religious dimension. In an increasingly secular world, many are searching for a sense of belonging and spiritual meaning. Climate change is portrayed as an existential battle between good and evil, sin and redemption. Fossil fuels and capitalism are the demons we must conquer, while climate activists are the twenty-first-century crusaders waging a holy war. This worldview sees what is "natural" as good, and what's "human" as bad. We ought, for example, to leave forests alone entirely rather than removing trees that might lead to wildfires. Wind and solar energy are natural; nuclear energy is unnatural. Eating plants is acceptable; eating animals is immoral.

Some environmental extremists even take an overtly antihuman, antichild stand. So-called degrowthers believe we must halt and reverse economic growth to stop climate change. They assert that population control, whether through expanding abortion access in the developing world or simply discouraging people from having children, is a legitimate environmental solution. Even Senator Bernie Sanders has echoed these arguments.[8] In their eyes, fewer humans existing is better for the planet.

▨ HOW THESE LIES HARM CHILDREN

Modern political environmentalism traffics in idealism and emotion in ways that ultimately hurt children more than anyone else. Across the world, progressive activists have campaigned to shut down nuclear plants—a clean source of electricity—leading to higher energy costs and increased reliance on dirtier coal and natural gas. If it were up to them, they would also shut down fossil fuel production overnight. Poorer communities and children would feel the resultant energy poverty and higher electricity bills most painfully.

The dangers of environmental utopianism aren't hypothetical. In Sri Lanka, environmentalists experimented with phasing out synthetic fertilizers virtually overnight, leading to wide-scale hunger and poverty.[9] In Africa, Western NGOs have lobbied governments to prevent the use of biotechnology that would increase the nutritional value of the limited food that is available to severely vitamin-deficient children.[10] In America, politicians fund programs to administer birth control to excessive deer populations rather than expanding hunter access.[11] California has banned internal combustion engines by 2035 while asking electric-vehicle owners to avoid charging their cars due to a strained grid.[12] We've made it nearly impossible to mine resources like critical minerals in the U.S.—required for everything from military and medical equipment to clean energy technologies—making us reliant on imports from countries like China and Congo that have been found guilty of child and slave labor.[13] Rolling blackouts, higher energy costs, more wildfires, greater pollution, and malnutrition are all avoidable problems with dramatic consequences for the youngest and most vulnerable in society. Unfortunately, the ascendant naturalist ideology only exacerbates them.

As we discussed, some extreme environmentalists even argue that we must stop and reverse economic growth to protect the environment. These degrowthers would wreck our modern standards of living, plunging billions of people into poverty and denying the developing world the opportunity to attain prosperity. Ironically, they wouldn't even address the very problem they claim to address: tackling climate change is a thorny technological problem that requires constant innovation and creativity, which flow forth only from economic growth and resource abundance. The degrowth narrative would keep us in a perpetual limbo of both poverty and environmental failure.

The extremism and alarmism of progressive climate activists leads not only to bad policy, but to severe psychological neglect too. In Britain, birthplace of the infamous Extinction Rebellion climate protests, one in five children report having nightmares about climate change.[14] The concept of "climate anxiety" has become a legitimate field of psychological research across the West, with far-reaching implications for the mental and emotional well-being of young children. Many women have been emotionally abused into believing that motherhood is somehow selfish and environmentally reckless. A recent study shows that nearly 40 percent of young people aged sixteen to twenty-five across ten major countries, including the U.S., said they were reluctant to have children due to climate change.[15] One in four childless adults say climate change has already factored into their decision to not have children.[16]

Sincere concern for the environment has devolved into alarmism, ideology, and, in some cases, disdain for human life. The mainstream approach to environmentalism is clearly broken. How can we do better?

▮ THE TRUTH ABOUT THE ENVIRONMENT

Truth #1: We Have a Duty to Conserve Our Natural Inheritance.

There are many bad solutions on offer, but our environmental challenges are very real. Unfortunately, in reacting to their progressive counterparts, conservatives have often ignored the problems altogether. Saying the Green New Deal sucks and then burying one's head in the sand is not a compelling vision. There needs to be a reckoning with the scientific and on-the-ground reality behind issues like climate change, plastic pollution, and other forms of environmental degradation.

Edmund Burke wrote eloquently about the partnership "between those who are living, those who are dead, and those who are to be born."[17] This vertical relationship across generations and time should impel us to conserve what is good and beautiful about the world, and pass it on to our children and grandchildren. From our faith to our community institutions to our national pride, we inherit timeless gifts worth preserving. The same is true of the natural world we inhabit. We have an obligation to conserve our natural heritage, the vast and beautiful lands of the American wilderness that our forefathers traversed and tamed. Polluting or exploiting this inheritance is an insult to past generations and a disservice to future ones.

For most of American history, farmers, ranchers, hunters, and anglers dutifully strove to pass on a healthier environment to their children than they received. Conservatives pursued the same task in politics. Ulysses Grant founded the first National Park (Yellowstone). Theodore Roosevelt protected more acres of land than any other president. Richard Nixon founded the Environmental Protection Agency. Ronald Reagan signed the Montreal Protocol to phase out ozone-damaging pollutants. George H. W. Bush strengthened the Clear Air Act. These decisions all moved to steward the next generation's inheritance, and were all guided by scientific fact and common sense. We must recover this legacy for the twenty-first century.

Truth #2: A Free Economy Produces a Clean Environment.

Bottom-up technological innovation, free enterprise, private-property rights, community leadership, and strategic public-private partnerships protect the environment—and children by extension—better than does economic centralization.

The Conservative Coalition for Climate Solutions (C3 Solutions) publishes an annual report titled *Free Economies Are Clean Economies*.[18] It finds that economically free countries are almost twice as clean as economically unfree countries, due to something called the Environmental Kuznets Curve. As countries industrialize and grow richer, their environmental footprint initially grows due to increased energy and resource consumption, but at a certain GDP level, this trend halts and even reverses. Competitive and entrepreneurial economies unlock additional resources that help them naturally become more sustainable over time. This happens because capitalism drives greater efficiency and innovation, but also because populations in advanced economies reach a level of disposable income and time that they can dedicate to better environmental outcomes.

By contrast, top-down, centralized economies produce worse environmental outcomes. The Soviet Union turned Lake Baikal into an open-air sewer, shrunk the Aral Sea by nearly half, and chopped down entire forests in implementing its five-year plans. In the late 1980s, particulate air pollution was thirteen times higher in Eastern Europe than Western Europe, while the Soviet economy doubled America's carbon emissions in proportion to its GDP.[19] Socialist economies generally require three times more steel and energy inputs per unit of GDP compared to market economies, as economist Mikhail Bernstam has argued.[20]

This is not to deny that there is space for limited and effective government action, like R&D funding for promising technologies, or strategic enforcement of laws and regulations surrounding public health and pollution. Nonetheless, we should prioritize innovation over regulation, and the local over the federal.

Truth #3: Bottom-Up Solutions and Human Stewardship Are Best.

In her book *Governing the Commons*, Nobel Prize–winning economist Elinor Ostrom showed the power of local collaboration and knowledge in tackling the so-called tragedy of the commons.[21] She detailed numerous case studies across the world where local communities, not bureaucrats, remedied severe environmental challenges like coastal overfishing and farmland degradation. Other research demonstrates a strong correlation between private-property rights and environmental protection.[22] Empowering communities and individuals puts responsibility for environmental protection in the hands of those who have the greatest knowledge and greatest stake in the places they will pass on to their children.

■ HOW THESE TRUTHS PROTECT CHILDREN

Mainstream emotional environmentalism pits human prosperity against environmental protection. But denunciation isn't enough. To protect children from the consequences of this lie will require presenting a positive agenda paired with a sincere concern for the next generation. We can't win the policy battle if we don't win the emotional battle first.

There is much that can be done in pursuit of a cleaner, safer, more prosperous world for our children. We can embrace an all-of-the-above energy strategy to ensure reliable and affordable energy for all. We can unleash nuclear energy to meaningfully reduce carbon emissions. We can bring manufacturing back to the U.S., compete with China, and unleash innovation to reduce electricity costs and pollution. We can implement proper forest-management practices to fight wildfires, work with communities to restore natural ecosystems, conserve areas of natural beauty, and ensure access to outdoor recreation. We can empower farmers to implement technology and sustainable practices to make their land more productive and resilient. We can cut government red tape that impedes all of these things. The alternative is a poorer, more polluted world that's reliant on countries like China as it struggles with the harms of climate change.

These truths make for a cleaner, more prosperous world in which to raise children. In their book *Superabundance*, Marian Tupy and Gale Pooley show a positive correlation between population growth and resource abundance. This means that "[o]n average, every additional human being create[s] more value than he or she consume[s]."[23] Their argument is that human ingenuity, innovation and entrepreneurialism allow us to overcome our resource and environmental challenges, but only if we allow them to. We can create a virtuous cycle where having more children leads to more creativity, which produces an economic climate (and literal climate) friendlier to future children.

▎ CHILD PROTECTION IN ACTION

There are many examples of successful environmental child-protection in action; one in particular stands out for its outcomes and its effective messaging. As have so many progressive states, California embarked on a journey to shut down all of its nuclear plants. In 2016, amid longstanding pressure from environmental groups, the Pacific Gas & Electric Company (PG&E) announced plans to shut down the state's last remaining nuclear reactors at Diablo Canyon by 2025.[24] Contrary to all evidence, these activist groups claimed that Diablo was an unacceptable hazard to the local human and wildlife populations.

That same year, two moms who were employees at the nuclear plant formed an organization called Mothers for Nuclear to help save Diablo Canyon from a premature closure that would increase energy costs and blackouts across California. It would also increase pollution, since clean nuclear electricity would give way to fossil fuels. The tagline on the Mothers for Nuclear website reads: "As mothers, we feel a responsibility to protect our children and the planet they'll inherit."[25]

In 2023, after years of education, campaigning, and grassroots advocacy, Mothers for Nuclear was successful in overturning the decision to shut down the reactors and extending the lifeline of Diablo Canyon through at least 2030. By leaning into the human message—mothers standing up for the plant where they worked to give their kids a better life—they altered the public perception of nuclear energy as dangerous and antihuman. A similar—though separate—messaging campaign featured a picture of Madison Hilly, a prominent nuclear advocate, posing alongside a nuclear waste container while pregnant also went viral on social media.[26]

Framing the nuclear plants as critical to the future of their children's lives, these mothers were able to change not only hearts, but also political outcomes. Conservative environmentalists would do well to learn from their example and reframe all environmental issues as child-protection issues.

Christopher Barnard, president of the American Conservation Coalition

Chris Barnard is the president of the American Conservation Coalition (ACC), the largest conservative environmental organization in the United States. He also serves on the RNC Youth Advisory Council.

Chris has a master's degree from the London School of Economics, and speaks Dutch, French, and English fluently. He has been published in the *Wall Street Journal*, the *Independent*, the *Daily Telegraph*, *National Review*, the *Washington Examiner*, and more. Chris has also spoken at conferences in more than ten countries. He currently lives in Arlington, Virginia, with his wife Hayley.

FOREIGN POLICY

DAN CALDWELL

In the early morning of December 6, 2010, Kait Wyatt heard a knock on her door at her home in Camp Pendleton, California. Upon opening the door, Kait was greeted by two Marines in their dress blue uniforms who informed her that her husband, Corporal Derek Wyatt, was killed in action in Sangin, Afghanistan. Derek was a member of 3rd Battalion, 5th Marines—a unit deployed as part of President Obama's "surge" of U.S. forces to Afghanistan. The 3rd Battalion, 5th Marines would suffer the heaviest casualties of any marine unit during the Afghanistan War, losing twenty-five Marines and suffering over two hundred wounded, including many amputees.[1]

When that knock came, Kait was nine months pregnant. That afternoon, she went to the hospital with her mother. Once there, doctors made the decision to induce delivery. On December 7, 2010—the day after her husband Derek was killed in Afghanistan—Kait gave birth to a son named Michael.[2]

Like thousands of other children born to military families in the post-9/11 era, Michael will grow up having lost a parent in service of a foreign policy that is increasingly disconnected from America's national interest and fails to adequately ensure a safe and prosperous future for its children.

▣ BIG LIES ABOUT AMERICAN FOREIGN POLICY

Lie #1: The United States Needs to Be the World's Policeman.

After the United States victory in the Cold War, our foreign policy elites sold the American people the myth that securing their safety and prosperity would require pursuing a foreign policy of primacy. This meant that the U.S. would seek to be the world's dominant power in order to uphold a liberal, "rules-based" international order. Essentially, this foreign policy commits the U.S. to be the world's policeman and impose liberal hegemony—forcing it to intervene in foreign crises in places that matter little or not at all to American security.

This foreign policy approach—advanced by the establishments of *both* political parties—has done everything but make America safer and more prosperous. Instead, it led the U.S. into a series of costly wars in places like Iraq and Afghanistan where America's military focused on imposing liberal democracy instead of deterring true threats to its national interests. Success in these wars was often not measured in terrorist attacks prevented or enemies killed, but by the number of girls' schools built in the deserts of Afghanistan and Iraq or the number of Pride flags flying over U.S. outposts.[3]

The cost of these brushfire wars in strategic backwaters have proven immense. Thousands of America's sons and daughters lost their lives along with hundreds of thousands more who suffered life-altering injuries. Suicide rates for veterans and active service members more than double that of the civilian population.[4] Tens of thousands of families were forever altered by the loss of a loved one or by having to reorient their lives to care for a grievously injured veteran.

America's interventions have incurred steep financial costs as well. Over $8 trillion and counting were added to the national debt by the post-9/11 wars, threatening the financial security of future generations.[5]

Twenty years of fighting the global war on terror have also degraded the U.S. military's ability to fight and win major wars. Important strategic assets like the B-1 bomber fleet were worn down, and massive amounts of money were wasted on platforms like the Littoral Combat Ship that are not suited for combat against adversaries like China. Meanwhile, the navy and air force were cut to build an army designed for counterinsurgency conflicts.[6] Concurrently, the U.S. expanded its security umbrella to more countries, particularly in Europe through the expansion of NATO, enabling wealthy European welfare states to neglect their own militaries.

Despite all the evidence to the contrary, America's foreign policy elites continue to advance the lie that the pursuit of global liberal hegemony is essential for the safety and prosperity of the U.S.

Lie #2: We Don't Need a Strong Military.

While America's foreign policy elites have utilized armed intervention far too often since the end of the Cold War, that does not negate the need for a strong U.S. military. Even if the U.S. pursues a more restrained foreign policy, it should still maintain a peerless military that can project power globally against real threats to America's security.

The last twenty years have seen an erosion of American military strength. The pursuit of objectives not tied to our national interest has diminished our ability to deter real threats, and our leaders have undermined America's military's readiness by using those in uniform as lab rats for social engineering experiments or indoctrinating them in divisive ideologies like critical race theory (CRT). This must stop.

Lie #3: Realism and Restraint Mean Isolationism.

America's failed foreign policy elites reflexively tar anyone who questions America's role in the world as an isolationist, in an attempt to invoke similar attacks made against those who opposed America's entry into World War II.

But pursuing a more restrained and realist foreign policy is not the same as pursuing an isolationist or pacifist foreign policy. Instead, it is a recognition that the U.S. has limited resources and must prioritize them toward the threats that pose the gravest risks to America's safety.

■ HOW THESE LIES HARM CHILDREN

Our foreign policy elites often use children—American and non-American alike—as props to justify an interventionist foreign policy. Hawks have used the fates of children in places like Iraq, Syria, and Afghanistan to garner support for entanglement in conflicts with little relation to American security. For example, the risks to girls' education under Taliban rule in Afghanistan was often used as a justification to keep U.S. troops in that country indefinitely.

However, it is American children more than any other group in the U.S. who will have to bear the burden of America's failed foreign policy.

American children who belong to military families have suffered the most. In addition to children like Michael Wyatt who must grow up without one of their parents due to their deaths in combat, millions more military kids have had to suffer the consequences of America's endless wars. The high operation tempos needed to sustain the wars in Iraq and Syria, along with servicing America's expanded security commitments in Europe, have meant even longer periods where military families have one or even both parents deployed abroad. This trend has continued even with the end of the war in Afghanistan and contributes to the U.S. military having the highest divorce rate of any career field.[7]

When these high operation tempos are combined with the introduction of divisive ideologies like CRT into military training and a declining standard of living for service members due to inflation, it's no surprise that military family members are discouraging their children from joining the armed services. According to Blue Star Families, a military family advocacy group, only 32 percent of active-duty military family members would recommend the military as a career to their children—a drop of over 20 percent since 2016.[8] Given that military families were one of the largest sources of recruits in the post-9/11 era, this trend helps explain why the military is missing its annual recruiting goals by over forty thousand personnel.[9]

The children of military families aren't the only children harmed by America's failed foreign policy. All American children will pay some price for the hubris of America's foreign policy elites.

First, the massive cost of America's endless wars abroad has driven the growth of the national debt to over $35 trillion. This debt—unless radical action is taken soon to reduce it—will inhibit economic opportunity and prosperity for future generations (see this book's chapter about debt). As Admiral Mike Mullen, former chairman of the Joint Chiefs of Staff, warned in the early 2010s, the national debt is arguably one of the greatest long-term national security threats for the U.S.

In addition, the military's focus on nation building and counterinsurgency has left it unprepared for a conflict with a peer or near-peer adversary like China. Unlike the remnants of Al-Qaeda or ISIS in the Middle East or Russia in eastern Ukraine, China can truly threaten American safety and economic prosperity. While the U.S. was sacrificing dozens of troops and spending tens of billions of dollars every year to prop up a corrupt Afghan government, China was massively expanding its defense industrial base. While the U.S. was enabling wealthy European states like Germany to free ride off its defense umbrella and shirk its responsibility to deter Russia, China was preparing for a war over Taiwan.

A war with China would be catastrophic, threatening the safety and prosperity of future generations in a way that no other national-security challenge currently does. Our foreign policy elites' refusal to properly prepare for this challenge has left America and its children vulnerable.

THE TRUTH ABOUT AMERICAN FOREIGN POLICY

Truth #1: We Need Realism and Restraint.

Contrary to the assertions of America's foreign policy elites—who often talk like America's foreign policy traditions began in 1939—America's founding fathers never intended for the U.S. to be the world's policeman. Rather, they warned against America becoming overly involved in the affairs of other nations.

In his 1796 Farewell Address, George Washington went out of his way to alert the American people to the dangers of foreign entanglements. He specifically warned against maintaining "permanent alliances with any portion of the foreign world" and that "a passionate attachment of one nation for another produces a variety of evils." Washington stated that "foreign influence is one of the most baneful foes of republican government" and exhorted Americans to constant vigilance against attempts by foreign powers to influence domestic and foreign policy.[10]

John Quincy Adams, the sixth president and son of the second, used his Fourth of July speech to Congress in 1821 to articulate a foreign policy vision of restraint. The U.S. should stand as a beacon of freedom, he said, but should "[go] not abroad, in search of monsters to destroy. She is the well-wisher to the freedom and independence of all. She is the champion and vindicator only of her own."[11]

The founding fathers rightly observed that it was not in America's interest to get embroiled in the chaos engulfing Europe in the eighteenth and nineteenth centuries. Doing so would have distracted the young nation from growing into an unrivaled power.

Our founding fathers and most presidents up to the twentieth century understood that the United States has unique advantages that shield it from foreign threats and chaos. The U.S. is bordered by two oceans that serve as a kind of insulation, since long-distance amphibious assaults are difficult to pull off even in the modern age. In the North and South, the U.S. is bordered by two weak neighbors—Canada and Mexico—who could not successfully invade the American mainland.

While the world has changed significantly since America's founding, there is still much wisdom in the founders' foreign policy vision.

Instead of continuing to pursue primacy—where America commits itself to serve as the world's policeman, and to settle disputes that aren't connected to our security—the U.S. should pursue a foreign policy of realism and restraint. Realism means recognizing the world as it is, that the U.S. has limited ability to shape it outside of its own borders, and that balances of power are constantly shifting between nations. Restraint means accepting that American power is limited, must be used judiciously, and that military force should always be a last resort.

Truth #2: We Need a Stronger Military in Fewer Places.

A foreign policy of realism and restraint recognizes real threats to America's safety and economic prosperity. While maintaining a military that is second to none, we must only use it when direct threats to American security arise. This means no more delusional nation-building wars or regime-change operations in the Middle East or Africa.

A foreign policy of realism and restraint requires a reckoning with the hard constraints on America's current power position. The U.S. has a $35 trillion national debt, a military worn down by two decades of combat, and a withered defense industrial base that cannot sustain Ukraine in its fight against Russia, much less backfill U.S. stockpiles or adequately support partners like Israel and Taiwan. After Hamas's brutal attack against Israel in October 2023, the U.S. redirected an artillery shipment from Ukraine to Israel because American industry couldn't produce enough artillery shells for both Ukraine and Israel at the same time.[12] What's worse, this occurred ten months after the U.S. withdrew three hundred thousand artillery shells from an emergency stockpile for Israel to support Ukraine's failed counteroffensive against Russia.[13]

These constraints can't be overcome by inauthentic optimism and sheer willpower. They necessitate a serious prioritization of American defense resources toward the biggest threats to U.S. national interests while ending other commitments that are disconnected from what is required to keep America safe.

This means pulling back most U.S. troops from Europe, and forcing wealthy European welfare states to take the lead in securing their own continent—including in Ukraine. Europe has nearly ten times the GDP and four times the population of Russia; it's more than capable of deterring Russia and supporting Ukraine without significant American backing. Restraint also means recognizing that the question of who controls the Donbas or Crimea is not worth risking nuclear war with Russia, much less undermining the U.S.'s ability to deal with other national security priorities.

The United States should also significantly draw down its military presence in the Middle East, particularly from the ongoing wars in Iraq and Syria. The U.S. should maintain a naval presence only at its longstanding base in Bahrain along with a regional counterterrorism force with long-range strike capabilities to deal with terrorist threats that could harm American interests. The U.S. should also lean more on the coalition between Israel and Gulf Arab states created by the Abraham Accords to contain Iran.

Truth #3: Realism and Restraint Mean Focusing on Real Threats While Not Getting Distracted.

There are real U.S. interests at stake that we must defend—particularly in the Pacific. This region should be the primary focus of U.S. defense and foreign policy. China poses threats that America's foreign policy elites refused to take seriously until lately. Resources freed up from deprioritizing the Middle East and Europe should be devoted to hardening allies in East Asia and further developing military capabilities to effectively deter China. Future defense budgets should prioritize funding for the air force and navy over other branches since these two services would be at the forefront of any potential conflict in the Pacific. Additionally, the U.S. intelligence community should confront China's malign economic and military espionage activities more aggressively.

The U.S. should not, however, overinflate the threat. China has its own constraints that may hinder its ability to threaten the U.S. or dominate large parts of the world. Policymakers should deal with the China challenge without resurrecting a Cold War outlook or barreling toward a direct conflict.

We must also remember that American economic strength underwrites American military strength. Neglecting the former will weaken the latter. We must couple a strong foreign policy with an economic and fiscal policy that enables growth.

HOW THESE TRUTHS PROTECT CHILDREN

An American foreign policy firmly rooted in what actually matters for American safety will better protect American children. The pursuit of global primacy and the enforcement of liberal hegemony are not necessary to guard the security and prosperity of America's children.

First, a more restrained and realist American foreign policy will benefit America's children by better protecting them from actual threats to their well-being. Not getting distracted by every crisis in every corner of the world will allow the U.S. to husband its limited military and financial resources more effectively and better prepare for the national security challenges that threaten its safety and the conditions of its economic prosperity—China above all.

This approach will also prevent the U.S. from racking up trillions more in debt in the Middle East, or getting itself on the hook for a blank check to Ukraine while wealthy Europeans abdicate security responsibility for their own continent. Combined with reforms to domestic spending programs (see this book's chapter on debt), this approach would help reduce the threat the national debt poses to America's economy.

CHILD PROTECTION IN ACTION

How does this approach to foreign policy look in practice? The presidencies of Ronald Reagan and Donald Trump provide examples.

In 1982, President Reagan sent U.S. marines into Lebanon during its civil war as part of a peacekeeping force intended to the stabilize the country. The marines' mission became increasingly confused and disconnected from American interests the longer they stayed in Lebanon, as factional loyalties constantly shifted and regional powers like Syria and Israel sought advantage over one another in the country. Tragically, in October 1983, 241 U.S. Marines, sailors, and soldiers were killed in a truck-bomb attack against an American barracks.

Instead of doubling down on a war where there were no vital national interests at stake and needlessly sacrificing more American lives, President Reagan withdrew American troops from Lebanon. This was the right call not only because of the lack of a clear mission and connection to American safety, but also because pouring more military resources into Lebanon would have distracted away from the real threat: the Soviet Union.

Similarly in 2020, after decisively ordering the killing of Iranian general Qasem Soleimani, President Trump decided not to escalate further against Iran, rightly recognizing that another major Middle East war was not in America's interest—especially with the growing threat posed by China.

Neither Reagan nor Trump were pacifists or isolationists. They believed in American strength. But they also understood the dangers of getting bogged down in conflicts that are disconnected from America's core national interests.

A U.S. foreign policy based on the principles of realism and restraint would benefit all Americans while securing a prosperous and safe future for America's children. It would particularly benefit the children of military families.

It would mean more time at home for parents who wear the nation's uniform, since they wouldn't be frequently deployed in support of missions that aren't in the nation's interest. More time at home for America's service members would likely bring down the military divorce rate, leading to fewer broken families.

Most importantly, a more prudent American foreign policy would mean fewer early morning knocks on the door bringing news that a loved one has died in a faraway land whose connection to

American security is anything but clear. It would mean that fewer children like Michael Wyatt have to grow up without a father or mother. That is a blessing whose value cannot be measured.

Dan Caldwell, public policy advisor for Defense Priorities

Dan Caldwell is a public policy advisor for Defense Priorities. Previously, he was the vice president of foreign policy for Stand Together and the vice president of the Center for Renewing America. Dan also served as the executive director of Concerned Veterans for America.

Dan is a veteran of the United States Marine Corps and the Iraq War. Following his initial training, Dan first served at the presidential retreat at Camp David and then deployed to Iraq with 2nd Battalion, 1st Marines.

Following his service in the Marines, Dan worked for Representative David Schweikert, focusing on veterans and defense issues.

POLICING

ARI HOFFMAN

On January 15, 2022, twelve-year-old Immaculee Goldade and her best friend Kathleen Olson were walking home hand in hand from a sleepover near Midland Elementary School in Tacoma, Washington.

As they walked, a stolen landscaping truck came barreling down the street. The driver, Terry Kohl, was high on methamphetamine. He struck the two girls with the truck, instantly killing Immaculee and severely injuring Kathleen. Kohl did not realize he had even hit the girls until two days later.

"Children should be able to walk home," said deputy prosecutor Elizabeth Dasse at the trial, during which Kohl was sentenced to forty years in prison. "Children should be able to walk in their neighborhoods without worrying if somebody is going to hit them with a truck."

This tragedy was predictable and preventable, and a direct result of the Defund the Police movement.

▓ BIG LIES ABOUT POLICING

Lie #1: Cops Shoot Black Men Disproportionately.

Following the death of Michael Brown in 2014, which gave rise to the Black Lives Matter movement, the Left used the false narrative that police officers disproportionately kill unarmed Black men. However, the numbers don't bear out that conclusion. Study after study has shown that not only are police less likely to shoot and kill minorities, but that unarmed White men are shot much more often by police than Black men.[1]

The majority of the mainstream media pushes an agenda and omits anything that doesn't conform to their narrative. A study authored by John Lott and Carlisle Moody of the Crime Prevention Research Center not only debunked the narrative that cops disproportionately shoot unarmed Black men, but also stated, "For the estimates where we know the race of the officer who killed the suspect, the ratio of the rate that blacks are killed by black versus white officers is large — ranging from three to five times larger."[2]

Lie #2: We Need to Defund the Police.

Following the rise of the Black Lives Matter (BLM) movement in 2016 and the death of George Floyd in 2020, Democrats across America embraced the Defund the Police movement, with some calling to abolish departments outright.

George Stephanopoulos asked then senator Kamala Harris if she agreed with Los Angeles mayor Eric Garcetti's plan to take $150 million from the LAPD. "I applaud Eric Garcetti for doing what he's done," our current vice president replied. On Twitter, she promoted a bail fund for releasing BLM rioters.

"When they're saying defund the police, what are they saying?" asked New York Democratic governor Andrew Cuomo. "They're saying we want fundamental, basic change when it comes to policing. Uh, and they're right."

Missouri congresswoman Cori Bush spoke out more aggressively: "Suck it up. Defunding the police has to happen. We need to defund the police." (Years later, it came out that Bush spent hundreds of thousands of dollars on private security.)

Congresswoman Ilhan Omar (D-MN) went further: "Not only do we need to disinvest in police, but we need to completely dismantle the Minneapolis Police Department." She would later add, "The police department here in Minneapolis needs to be dismantled and we need to start anew." Her ally Rashida Tlaib (D-MI) voiced agreement: "No more policing, incarceration and militarization. It can't be reformed."

Lie #3: We Need Social Workers, Not Police.

Most even of these radical politicians realized that *someone* needed to step into the gap left by defunded police. Who would get that reallocated money? New York Democrat mayor Bill DeBlasio spoke for many: "We will be moving funding from the NYPD to youth initiatives and social services." Then Speaker of the House Nancy Pelosi gestured at the same solution. "There's some issues that we ask police to do, like mental health issues or policing in schools and all the rest, that perhaps we can, uh, shuffle some of that money around."

HOW THESE LIES HARM CHILDREN

Without police, children and young people die. Washington state has become the poster child of failed antipolice policies put into action without any regard for the consequences. In June 2020, following almost two weeks of BLM and antipolice riots in Emerald City, Seattle, police were ordered to abandon the department's East Precinct in the Capitol Hill neighborhood and turn it over to the community.

The rioters quickly blockaded an area which they called the Capitol Hill Autonomous Zone (CHAZ), later renamed the Capitol Hill Occupied Protest (CHOP).

Ironically, one of the first things anticop activists did was establish their own security force to enforce their rules. Armed antifa and BLM activists patrolled the streets, and self-proclaimed "warlord" Raz Simone handed out AR-15s from his trunk to his makeshift police squad.

Local officials played along, providing water and lavatory facilities and giving the activists the run of city hall. Mayor Jenny Durkan explained her actions by saying that "we have a system that was built on systemic racism, and we have to dismantle that system piece by piece."

The CHAZ rapidly became a death zone for Black teens. On June 20, nineteen-year-old Horace Lorenzo Anderson Jr. was gunned down in the zone. The rioters who controlled the CHAZ prevented first responders from reaching the scene in time to save Anderson. The next day, a seventeen-year-old boy was shot.

On June 29, sixteen-year-old Antonio Mays, Jr. and fourteen-year-old Robert West were shot while driving in the zone. Mays Jr. was killed, and West lost an eye and part of his skull.[3] West said he was "lured" to the zone by the mayor's "positive statements about the area on television" and went there "with the intention of participating in what we thought to be a peaceful protest in support of the Black Lives Matter movement."[4] Rapes, robberies, and murders rose 250 percent during the month the zone existed.[5]

The CHAZ was broken up only when activists vandalized the mayor's home in July.

Despite all this death and destruction, the Seattle City Council still voted to defund the police department in August 2020, prompting a massive exodus of police officers.[6] Over seven hundred officers quit the force, leaving the department well below minimum staffing levels. Crime and 911 response times spiked. By 2023, Seattle had broken its all-time homicide record, leaving kids dead and children without parents.

Beyond the radical step of defunding, Washington has knee-capped police in other ways—causing loss of child life. During Washington's 2021 legislative session, Democrats voted to restrict police pursuits and not allow officers to pursue suspects in the majority of circumstances, despite being cautioned that the new restrictions would embolden criminals.[7]

As a result of the new restrictions, suspects fleeing police climbed by the thousands. One kidnapper even called 911[8] to complain that police were not allowed to chase him under the new law.

This new law led directly to the death of children. Remember Immaculee Goldade, the twelve-year-old girl who was hit by a methhead's truck? Two weeks before Immaculee was killed, the driver Kohl and his accomplices stole the truck from a landscaping company. The police initially gave chase but then had to let them go because of the pursuit law. Kohl was a repeat offender who had missed a court date for a prior offense. He had two DUIs and a felony, and the arrest would have likely led to a harsh sentence. Had he been in jail, had the stolen truck not been out on the road driven by a career criminal high on methamphetamine, the Goldade family would still have their child.

Another preventable tragedy happened in March 2023, when eight-year-old Delilah Minshew and her six-year-old brother Timothy Escamilla were in a car that was hit head-on by a driver named Keith Goings.[9] Under the influence of intoxicants, he was going the wrong way on the interstate. Delilah and Timothy were killed, and their five-year-old sister and the driver were rushed to the hospital. They were foster children, headed to a supervised visit with their parents.

An hour before the crash, Washington State Patrol troopers in Ellensburg attempted to stop Goings, who was speeding at 111 miles per hour, but the pursuit law prevented the troopers from tracking him down. This was just one of the multiple times[10] he was spotted that day, and various law enforcement agencies were not allowed to pursue him.

During the 2023 legislative session, a bipartisan fix for the flawed legislation was passed in the Washington House, but Democratic senator Manka Dhingra refused to let the bill advance, citing faulty data to claim the original legislation saved lives.[11] The legislature ended up passing a watered-down fix which still prevented police from pursuing in many cases, including, most notably, pursuing stolen cars.[12] The final product was legislation that still would not have protected Immaculee.

THE TRUTH ABOUT POLICE

Truth #1: Cops Make Kids Safe.

We need more, not fewer, officers.

On November 2, 2021, a thirteen-year-old boy did exactly what he was supposed to do when his father William Yurek was having chest pains and difficulty breathing: he called 911.

The boy can be heard on 911 tapes saying, "My dad, I don't know, he can't breathe or something. He's not okay." Unfortunately for Yurek, his address was on an outdated blacklist of residents with hostility to police responders. The city's policy is that police are required to enter a blacklisted domicile to secure the scene for other first responders before they can enter. Medics arrived quickly to the scene but weren't able to enter because police had not yet arrived. Less police meant slower response times.

Fourteen minutes after the first 911 call, Yurek's son called again. Medics decided to enter without an escort, but it was too late. The child had watched his father die from cardiac arrest while medics were forced to wait outside. He and his two siblings were left without a father.

The family sued Seattle for failing to keep an accurate and updated list, and for continuing to require police escorts for medics even though it was known that the Seattle Police Department was understaffed and could not meet the demand.[13] Because of the Seattle City Council's defunding of the police and the mass exodus that followed, response times were slower because the department was understaffed. Following the incident, a whistleblower came forward and said that he had specifically warned the city about the problems in 911 response times in light of this understaffing.[14]

The city of Seattle ended up settling the case with the family for $1.86 million.

Truth #2: Social Workers Are No Substitute.

Unarmed social workers are no substitute for police. On November 23, 2020, while the Seattle City Council was voting to defund the police and reallocate funding to hire social workers, Kristin Benson, a social worker at Plymouth Housing, a homeless agency in Seattle, was stabbed to death by one of her homeless clients.[15] During the riots in the summer of 2020, Plymouth Housing had advocated for defunding the police to fund more social workers. The tragedy put a spotlight on the flawed policy. Public safety advocates had long cautioned against sending out social workers to potentially dangerous situations without protection and instead recommended augmenting police departments with social workers to handle mental health crises and other situations. However, Seattle leaders ignored those suggestions and chose instead to defund specialized units that had a combination of police and social workers.[16]

HOW THESE TRUTHS PROTECT CHILDREN

We owe it to all American children to fund a well-manned police force, and to empower it to protect public safety and personal security. Underfunding and undermining police departments causes crime waves, but robust policing reduces murder rates.[17] It saves lives like that of William Yurek, and saves children like his from fatherlessness. It allows kids like Immaculee Goldade to walk home without being killed.

Policing also makes schools, and the children in them, much safer. We typically protect the things we value most with armed security and police: our money, our politicians, our airports, even our celebrities and sporting events. Yet we repeatedly fail to protect our children the same way. In 2020, Seattle Public Schools banned school resource officers from its campuses. The district had previously partnered with the Seattle Police Department to have these officers on campus. Violence immediately spiked on campuses when kids returned to in-person learning following the COVID-19 pandemic.

In October 2021, the staff at Ingraham High School called 911 because there were no officers on campus when several students were threatened by two people with an AR-15. In June, a video of a vicious gang-related fight between students at the school went viral on social media. In November 2022, police responded to a report of shots fired at Ingraham High. After arriving and entering the building, officers located a student with a gunshot wound and provided aid until medics arrived. The student died. Seattle police chief Adrian Diaz said at the time that no school resource officers were at the school when the shooting occurred.

The following day was Election Day, and Paul Franklin-Bihary, a teacher at the school, posted a photo to social media of his students in lockdown during the shooting. His caption was: "If you didn't vote blue today, f*ck you."[18] Voting Democrat will solve the violence that Democratic policies helped cause! There are clearly people who care more about pushing antipolice policies than about protecting kids.

In response to the increase in violence, parents demanded police back on Seattle public school campuses. One parent told the *Post Millennial*, "Seattle Public Schools has become less and less about education and more about what's the daily 'popular' political view. The same taxpayer-funded 'for the people' institution that banned police because of false BLM narratives, had to call the police after armed trespassers entered school property at least twice."[19]

Perhaps instead of "reimagining" police as many on the Left have suggested, we need to look at what is working now and what worked in previous generations. I grew up in Jewish day schools and synagogues. We always had security guards and police on campus because we were always targets for antisemitic attacks. The guards became our protectors, friends, and confidants. As a result, I and many of my peers grew up with a deep appreciation, even reverence, for police officers. Jewish schools have similar measures in place today. My son and his friends regularly have lunch with the security guard at their Jewish high school and always greet him with a high five when they see him working security at local events and synagogues.

■ CHILD PROTECTION IN ACTION

The Defund the Police movement bore appalling fruit. Murder rates increased by double digits in many cities.[20] According to the FBI's *Quarterly Uniform Crime Report*, during the final three months of 2020, homicides jumped by 32.2 percent in U.S. cities with a population of at least one million.

Literally mugged by reality, many cities have recovered sanity and reversed course. CNN reported that Los Angeles, New York,

Seattle, and Austin are among the cities that began refunding their police departments after a massive exodus of officers was followed by spiking crime.[21] Voters in New York and Seattle elected more moderate candidates specifically because of public-safety concerns. During a meeting of the Major Cities Chiefs Association, police chiefs discussed "the increase in gun violence, the increase in younger shooters who see guns as tools for conflict resolution, as well as the defund the police movement." According to the *Wall Street Journal,* "[i]n the nation's twenty largest local law-enforcement agencies, city and county leaders want funding increases for nine of the twelve departments where next year's budgets already have been proposed. The increases range from 1% to nearly 6%."[22]

As dangerous policies fail and reason is restored, the professionals have returned to the truth instead of clinging to political narratives. This is good news. Even more hope lies in the fact that rational citizens, when they step up, can make an enormous difference.

After a series of threats against schools in Bellevue Public Schools, the district ended up hiring a private security firm that primarily employs off-duty and retired police officers.[23]

Following the shooting of a seventeen-year-old girl at a bus stop outside Seattle's Garfield High School, the community demanded that police emphasize patrols at school campuses.

In 2023, fed-up Washingtonians collected enough signatures to qualify Initiative 2113 for the ballot to restore police pursuits. This was one of six initiatives championed by the citizen action group Let's Go Washington to undo disastrous Democratic policies.

Citizens were racing the clock to prevent more deaths. A week before the legislature took up the initiative, prolific offender Pedro Garcia, thirty-two, crashed a stolen truck into a car driven by Oscar Morales Saucedo in SeaTac, Washington, then fled on foot, leaving behind a sawed-off shotgun. The forty-two-year-old father and his five-year-old son were taken to Harborview Medical Center, where the dad was pronounced dead. The five-year-old suffered multiple skull fractures that required surgery. Garcia had been spotted earlier by police but could not be pursued because of the restrictions placed on officers.

Thanks to the massive public pressure campaign, the legislature passed the initiative, even with many Democrats still voting against it.[24] But it did pass.

It's time for every municipality to take action and restore law and order by funding and empowering the police to actually... police. The lives of our nation's children depend on it.

Ari Hoffman, host of *The Ari Hoffman Show* **and**
West Coast editor of the *Post Millennial*

Ari Hoffman is the host of *The Ari Hoffman Show* on Talk Radio 570 KVI and the West Coast editor of the *Post Millennial*. He is a frequent guest on Fox News and Newsmax and has been featured on various shows and podcasts across the U.S. and around the world, including *60 Minutes* with Anderson Cooper, *The Dr. Drew Show*, *The Glenn Beck Show*, and the KOMO News documentary *Seattle Is Dying*.

Originally from New York, Ari now lives with his family in Seattle, Washington.

BORDER SECURITY AND IMMIGRATION

LORA RIES

Yolanda, a fifteen-year-old girl from El Salvador, finally reached the U.S.-Mexico border after weeks of travel by pickup truck, bus, and foot. After leaving her mother in her small Salvadoran village to go to America for a job, Yolanda had been passed along multiple smugglers, some of whom kept their hands to themselves, others of whom did not.

Now that she was entering the United States, however, she could put her nightmare travel behind her. Or so she thought.

Her Mexican smuggler instructed her to walk across the border among a large group of migrants and wait for the U.S. Border Patrol to show up and process her into America. She and the dozens of others waited in the early morning for Border Patrol agents to arrive. When an agent finally approached Yolanda, he asked her in Spanish if she was with anyone in the group. "No, I am by myself," she replied. The agent asked a number of questions while filling out official-looking forms. He gave her a piece of paper and instructed her toward a bus, which would take her to a shelter where an agency would find her a sponsor with whom she could live.

The bus delivered Yolanda to a camp made up of several trailers. She saw many other teenagers among the "buildings," some walking with manilla envelopes, others just passing time, talking to others at picnic tables, looking at their cell phones, or kicking a soccer ball around on the grass.

Yolanda spent four days at the camp before a Health and Human Services contractor informed her they had found an aunt in Virginia who would sponsor her. After riding another bus to Virginia, Yolanda was met by her "Aunt" Christina. Yolanda had never met her before.

Christina took Yolanda to a neighborhood with several tall apartment buildings. Christina's apartment in one of the buildings was small. It had two bedrooms, one with a set of bunk beds and a third bed crammed in it, where Yolanda would sleep. Christina told her two other girls were also staying there, but were at work. Christina told Yolanda how important it was for her to start working right away to pay off her smuggling debt. When Yolanda asked where she should look for a job, Christina told her not to worry—her friend José already had a food-delivery job for her. She could start the next day.

The next morning, José came to Christina's apartment to meet Yolanda and take her to her new job. They walked to a nearby apartment building with a small restaurant on the first floor. José explained that she would start out by delivering food to customers in the apartment complex. If she was a good worker, she could work her way up to being a waitress in the restaurant, which paid more money. Yolanda noticed another teenage girl cleaning up a table after customers left, and a third girl, about her age, waiting for an order to be bagged up for delivery.

When Yolanda's first food delivery order came in, José accompanied her to an apartment in another building while explaining the layout of the complex to her. He emphasized that she should get to the customer quickly so the food would still be hot and the customer would be satisfied and would order from the restaurant again.

A large man in his forties wearing a T-shirt and shorts answered the door. He knew José, but he stared at Yolanda as he spoke. He told her to put the food on a small table in the kitchen while he checked her out from behind. He handed José a wad of twenty-dollar bills and told Yolanda to join him for lunch. José said he'd see her back at the restaurant and left the apartment.

Yolanda came to the U.S. as an unaccompanied alien child (UAC), and she is just one among thousands whom U.S. Customs and Border Protection agents encounter each month. Like Yolanda, too many of these children are subjected to sex trafficking once in the U.S.

BIG LIES ABOUT IMMIGRATION

The Left has become radical regarding U.S. border security and immigration in recent years. Politicians such as then president Bill Clinton,[1] then senator Joe Biden,[2] and then senator Barack Obama[3] used to support border security, the border wall, and immigration enforcement. Now, the Left opposes such measures and has implemented open-border policies. Rather than admit its open border policy stance, however, the Left lies about why it supports such an agenda. Here are three frequent lies that the Left uses.

Lie #1: We Need More Immigration to Support the Economy.

The Left makes simplistic arguments that more workers generate more goods and services and a larger number of people earning paychecks results in more consumer spending, which fuels the U.S. economy.[4] In turn, the Left says, there are more people paying income tax on earnings increases tax revenues when the U.S. has a growing budget deficit, and props up welfare programs such as Social Security and Medicare, which are facing shortfalls.[5]

The Left notes that native-born U.S. households are having fewer children, and the baby boom generation is rapidly retiring. More immigration is needed, they argue, to increase the population.[6] Never mind that the Left pushes for more abortions and works against marriage, families, and having more children. More immigration is their solution to the problems created by their depopulation policies.[7]

Lie #2: Border Security and Immigration Enforcement Are Racist.

To perpetuate its open-border agenda, the Left now opposes proven policies that secure the border or enforce immigration laws, particularly immigration detention and deportations. Similar to the Defund the Police movement, the Left advocates to abolish, defund, or fundamentally transform Immigration and Customs Enforcement (ICE), the Department of Homeland Security (DHS) agency responsible for detention, deportations, and other immigration enforcement functions.

Opponents of immigration enforcement argue that America's immigration system is rooted in xenophobia and racism.[8] They state that immigration detention and deportations disproportionately affect Blacks and Latinos.[9]

Beyond enforcement policies, the Left continues to label any person who advocates for real border security and immigration enforcement as racist. They have not given up their Saul Alinsky tactic of "pick the target, freeze it, personalize it, and polarize it" in this context.[10]

Lie #3: The Biden Administration Has Created Safe, Orderly, and Lawful Pathways for Migrants to Come to the United States.

From day one, the Biden administration has sought to erase the line between legal and illegal immigration. Corrupting the language is a favored tactic of the Left.[11] The administration directed federal agencies to stop using terms such as "alien" and "illegal alien."[12] Instead, the administration replaced those words with "noncitizen."[13] The administration ignored the fact that "alien" is the term used throughout the Immigration and Nationality Act. It also disregarded that by making a one-for-one substitution of "noncitizen" for "illegal alien," the administration was erroneously including lawful temporary visitors and lawful permanent residents (green card holders) in its "noncitizen" net.[14] Their purpose was to erase illegality and group all aliens together as "lawful."

In addition, the Biden administration has also intentionally violated immigration laws and given millions of illegal aliens immigration benefits ("pathways") such as humanitarian parole into the U.S. (a temporary form of entry that is to be rarely used when an alien does not have time to apply for a visa)[15] and renewable, two-year work authorization to provide them the patina of being here "lawfully."[16] The Biden administration labels this a "safe, orderly, and lawful pathway" because illegal aliens do not have to make the dangerous journey to the U.S. border from Mexico and beyond using dangerous cartels and smugglers to transport them.[17] Instead, the U.S. government does it for them.

■ HOW THESE LIES HARM CHILDREN

As with so many issues in this book, advocates of open borders claim they have the moral high ground regarding children crossing our borders—whether lawfully or unlawfully, unaccompanied or accompanied. They justify open border and immigration policies as a means of "protecting vulnerable children." In reality, however, their irresponsible approach endangers children while advancing the interests of activist adults.

In 2000, California senator Dianne Feinstein and congresswoman Zoe Lofgren introduced legislation called the Unaccompanied Alien Child Protection Act, "[t]o protect the children."[18] The legislation eventually became law in the Trafficking Victims Protection Reauthorization Act of 2008 (TVPRA)[19]—and negatively changed the course of U.S. immigration.

Section 235 of the TVPRA, under the heading "Enhancing Efforts to Combat the Trafficking of Children," begins by stating:

> [T]o enhance the efforts of the United States to prevent trafficking in persons, the Secretar[ies] of Homeland Security, ... State, [Health and Human Services, and] the Attorney General ... shall develop policies and procedures to ensure that unaccompanied alien children in the United States are safely repatriated to their country of nationality or of last habitual residence.[20]

However, the remainder of section 235, and the implementation of it, have had the opposite effect.

Section 235 requires unaccompanied children from countries other than Canada and Mexico to be brought into the U.S.;[21] turned over to the Department of Health and Human Services (HHS); and provided legal counsel, child advocates, and eligibility for expanded and expedited immigration benefits, including the otherwise rarely used special-immigrant juvenile status,[22] green cards, and asylum protection.[23] Anyone who read the bill easily understood that it would entice parents to send their children across the border unaccompanied to gain entry, receive immigration benefits, and to establish a family foothold in the U.S. for subsequent family reunification in this country.

Predictably, the number of unaccompanied children coming to the U.S. skyrocketed after the TVPRA was enacted. In 2010, the U.S. Border Patrol apprehended less than twenty thousand UACs.[24] By 2013, the number doubled to nearly forty thousand.[25] In 2014, almost seventy thousand UACs were apprehended.[26] In 2019, the number of UACs was over seventy-six thousand.[27] The number that CBP encountered rose to almost one hundred forty-eight thousand in 2021 and over one hundred fifty-two thousand in 2022.[28] While Joe Biden has been in the White House, CBP agents have encountered over four hundred ninety thousand unaccompanied children nationwide, a historic number.[29] Yet, it was by design.

Since becoming secretary of Homeland Security in 2021, Alejandro Mayorkas repeatedly stated that unaccompanied children would be allowed entry into the U.S.[30] His words amounted to free advertising for the Mexican trafficking cartels. Mayorkas frequently describes his open-border policies and operations as "safe, orderly, and humane,"[31] including for unaccompanied children. Yet, there is nothing safe or humane about enticing parents to separate from their children or placing them unaccompanied in the hands of vicious cartels, which regularly rape girls and abandon toddlers near the border, or drop them over the border wall.[32] In one particular video, a smuggler left a one-year-old at the river's edge where he could easily have drowned.[33]

Smugglers also "recycle" young children to make single adult aliens appear as a family unit for easier catch and release into the U.S.[34] These children are often drugged to make them unresponsive to border agents questioning their family "relationship."[35] Separated from their real family, these children can be forever traumatized by smugglers' physical and mental abuse. As in Yolanda's case, their circumstances often do not improve once they enter the U.S.

With the historic numbers of unaccompanied children released into the U.S. during the Biden administration, HHS lowered its standards for required sponsors who take the children into their homes.[36] HHS secretary Xavier Becerra has viewed these children as widgets on an assembly line, rushing to get the children out of HHS shelters and matched to sponsors as fast as possible, without vetting the sponsors.[37]

The results have been neither humane nor legal. In June 2022, Florida governor Ron DeSantis petitioned the Florida Supreme Court to impanel a statewide grand jury to examine alien smuggling across the U.S. southern border.[38] The grand jury released a report detailing disturbing findings regarding unaccompanied children, including lack of HHS background checks on the sponsors, human trafficking, and child abuse.[39] According to the grand jury, "ORR is facilitating the forced migration, sale, and abuse of foreign children…This process exposes children to horrifying health conditions, constant criminal threat, labor and sex trafficking, robbery, rape and other experiences not done justice by mere words."[40] In addition, the Biden administration's HHS has lost track of at least eighty-five thousand unaccompanied children in the U.S.[41]

Section 235 of the TVPRA, erroneously called "Enhancing Efforts to Combat the Trafficking of Children," has been an abject failure at protecting children and at combating trafficking.[42] Yet the Left can see the historic numbers of unaccompanied children, read the *New York Times* articles detailing the dangerous child-labor violations, and knows HHS has lost track of tens of thousands of children. Why, then, doesn't the Left repeal section 235 of the TVPRA and stop enticing unaccompanied child border crossers with easy immigration benefits? Because adults are exploiting kids for their own purposes, be it for money, open borders, political power, sex, or cheap labor.[43]

THE TRUTH ABOUT IMMIGRATION

Truth #1: Unlimited Immigration Hurts America's Economy.

What the Left omits from its simplistic economic arguments for more immigration is the cost to U.S. taxpayers. As Nobel Prize–winning economist Milton Friedman stated, "You can't have free immigration and a welfare state."[44] America is living this in real time under the Biden administration, and it is unsustainable. For example, the administration continues to pour billions of dollars into sanctuary cities such as New York, Chicago, Denver, and Los Angeles for sheltering, feeding, and giving legal and social services to the millions of illegal aliens Biden has released into the country.[45] Because the Biden administration does not turn off the pipeline of illegal aliens entering the U.S., the money disbursements are never enough. The sanctuary cities and the nongovernmental organizations (NGOs) that transport and facilitate the mass migration drain their funds and demand more.[46] In turn, the administration keeps coming back to Congress requesting more money.

The results of this fiscal bottomless pit are dire for American communities. Homelessness has increased; veterans and other U.S. citizens lose resources to illegal aliens; schools, parks, recreation centers, even portions of airports are used to shelter Biden's mass migration;[47] crime and drug use have increased; and sanctuary politicians shift money from police and first responder budgets to pay for the services provided to those here illegally.[48]

The downstream welfare and benefits that aliens receive cost U.S. taxpayers additional billions. Social security, Medicare, Medicaid, Supplemental Security Income, Temporary Assistance to Needy Families, public education, and other benefits result in illegal aliens receiving $84 billion to $94 billion more in government benefits and services than they pay in total taxes per year, according to The Heritage Foundation's Senior Research Fellow Robert Rector.[49] Mass illegal immigration and welfare benefits compound America's debt, which is already at the eye-popping level of over $34.6 trillion.[50]

Truth #2: There Is Nothing Racist About Border Security or Immigration Enforcement.

To come to the U.S., the Immigration and Nationality Act (INA) lays out purposes for which an alien may receive a visa, including business, pleasure, study, and work. The INA lists the reasons why a visa applicant would be ineligible for the visa, including health issues, crimes, national security and terrorism grounds, lack of documentation, and fraud.[51] Race is not a basis to be granted or denied a visa. By extension, race is also not a basis for CBP to admit or deny an alien's entry into the U.S.

With respect to immigration enforcement, the INA lists how an alien already in the U.S. becomes deportable. Similar to the grounds of inadmissibility mentioned above, the grounds of deportability include illegal entry into the U.S., overstaying a visa, crimes, national security, terrorism, and fraud.[52] Race is nowhere among these grounds.

Yet, the Left continues to mindlessly label as racist any suggestion to deport aliens who are deportable, including the millions who the Biden administration has unlawfully released into the U.S. It is important to note that CBP has encountered aliens from over 180 countries around the world during the Biden administration.[53] That is over 93 percent of the globe's 193 countries. This defies the Left's trope that enforcing the law against the Biden illegal alien population is somehow racist.

Truth #3: The Biden Administration's Policies Create Dangerous, Chaotic, and Unlawful Pathways for Aliens to Come to the United States.

During a 2020 presidential primary debate, then candidate Joe Biden called on future illegal aliens to surge the border.[54] Biden's words rang the dinner bell for Mexican cartel traffickers and smugglers. Then, starting his first day in office, President Biden ushered in the most lucrative business years for cartels by halting border wall system construction and rescinding effective border security and enforcement measures. Cartels increased their human trafficking business and saw their profits rise to $30 million per day, or $1 billion per month, according to the House Budget Committee.[55] The cartels' wealth and power grew so significantly that they took operational control of our U.S. border. Anyone crossing that border must go through the vicious hands of a cartel.

Among the several destructive records President Biden has achieved from his open border policies are migrant deaths and CBP rescues. The International Organization for Migration reported 686 deaths and disappearances on the U.S.-Mexico border in 2022, the deadliest land route for migrants worldwide on record.[56] In fiscal year (FY) 2020, CBP rescued 5,336 people.[57] In FY21, that number rose to 12,857, and to 22,075 in FY22.[58]

■ HOW THESE TRUTHS PROTECT CHILDREN

America has always provided a generous immigration system. But as long as it's easier and faster to come to the U.S. illegally than legally, without consequences, then rational human beings will take the illegal path. To return America's immigration system to a lawful, orderly, and affordable one, the U.S. must begin by shutting down illegal avenues and applying consequences to illegal immigration. This will change the risk calculus of would-be illegal aliens. They will not risk their lives or their life savings if chances are low that they will be able to enter, stay, or work in the U.S.

Fully securing our borders not only encourages legal rather than illegal immigration, it also keeps American and migrants safe, especially children. Migrants would no longer be subjected to brutal cartel treatment or risk the elements or drowning trying to illegally enter the U.S.

Preventing unaccompanied child border crossings likewise protects children from abandonment, drugging, rape, recruitment into gangs, and other trauma while still in Mexico. Inside the U.S., unaccompanied children would be spared from having to pay off smuggling debts, child labor, dangerous work conditions, sex trafficking, and sponsor abuse.

If we change the incentives for unaccompanied child border crossings, we can save hundreds of thousands of children from needless suffering. This requires removing the pull factors for such children to come to the U.S., namely terminating the TVPRA's offer of easy immigration benefits to minors simply because they illegally entered the U.S. unaccompanied.

Children should be with their parents and siblings, as a family. It is better for children's health, safety, and well-being to remain with their families in their home country, even if that country is poorer than the United States, than to knowingly separate a family to exploit current bad law for entry into the U.S.

▩ CHILD PROTECTION IN ACTION

The 2023 film *Sound of Freedom* is a true story of former DHS agent Tim Ballard rescuing children in and outside the U.S. from sex trafficking. Such brave agents are essential to remove children who are already in the sex and labor trafficking pipeline.

Facing the current Biden unaccompanied child crisis, state officials are making common sense requests. Virginia attorney general Jason Miyares proposed that HHS secretary Becerra change Office of Refugee Resettlement (ORR) policies to immediately notify local governments of unaccompanied child placements.[59] Miyares explained that such notification would make local law enforcement aware of the presence of these minors and allow law enforcement to alert ORR to known unsafe placement locations.[60]

In Florida, Governor DeSantis signed border crisis legislation that, among other things, made the smuggling of a minor a second-degree felony, subject to a $10,000 fine and up to fifteen years in prison.[61]

While these state responses are necessary, they are addressing downstream effects. To prevent child trafficking in the first place requires removing the incentives for unaccompanied child border crossings.

Sixteen years is too long for this pipeline of child exploitation to operate. It is past time for Congress to stop enticing unaccompanied child border crossings with the promise of easy immigration benefits here in the U.S. That means members of Congress must stand up to spurious attacks and false cries of compassion from open-borders activists.

Pro-parent and pro-child advocates have made real headway in the last few years against radicalism on the issues of school closures, masks, indoctrination, and gender ideology. In standing up for sound immigration policy, members of Congress need to emulate the brave parents who have staunchly fought for child protections. Congress should repeal section 235 of the TVPRA to end this ongoing child exploitation.

Lora Ries, director, Border Security and Immigration Center at The Heritage Foundation

Lora Ries is director of the Border Security and Immigration Center at The Heritage Foundation. She has nearly thirty years' experience in the immigration and homeland security arena. Ries twice worked at the Department of Homeland Security, most recently as the acting deputy chief of staff.

She worked in the private sector as a homeland security strategist and in government relations.

Ries previously worked for the U.S. House of Representatives Judiciary Committee. She started her career at the Department of Justice's Board of Immigration Appeals and the Immigration and Naturalization Service.

Ries has done numerous print, radio, and TV interviews and has testified before Congress.

Ries earned her law and bachelor of arts degrees at Valparaiso University in Indiana.

CONCLUSION

JOSH WOOD

Back before the pandemic, my wife and I visited a friend who had recently become a foster parent. Not long after he and his wife had been vetted and approved by the state, they had a little girl placed with them who, in very short order, stole their hearts. This sweet child had come from a difficult situation, but in her new home surrounded by a new family, she was thriving. After a few days observing her discovering new toys, performing dance routines, and easily charming the whole house with her smile, I asked my friend about her future.

Was she going to be able to stay with them long term?

"No, the plan was reunification with her mother."

How long might that take?

"It could be months, it could be years, it could be next week."

What if you get attached to her, won't that be hard?

"It will absolutely break our hearts."

After a long pause in the conversation, I remember telling my friend that I was happy for him, but I could never willingly subject myself to such pain. It would just be too hard to love and lose someone like that.

I will never forget his response. He turned to me and said, "It is too hard on us, but it isn't about us. If we only have her for a few short months, or years, those will all be days that we know she was loved. And that is enough."

My friend spoke a great truth that day. He was crystal clear that the pro-child position is costly, but it is worth it. Being truly pro-child means centering children in every decision we make. Of all groups of people, children are the most vulnerable, the least powerful, and the most affected by our selfishness. When we mess with someone's childhood, we mess with his or her whole life. This is why Jesus reserved his harshest threat of punishment for those who harmed or led children astray: *"If anyone causes one of these little ones—those who believe in me—to stumble, it would be better for them to have a large millstone hung around their neck and to be drowned in the depths of the sea."* Matthew 18:6

You've just read 266 pages on nineteen issues where we regularly put children's interests last, nineteen issues where adult comfort and ideology win out at the price of victimizing and sacrificing children. Now you have a choice. Will you continue to prioritize your own interests, or will you choose to put them before us?

The contents of this book may have left you feeling empowered, angry, or just overwhelmed. Here are some steps to help you turn those feelings into action.

STEP 1: STAY INFORMED

Maybe you're not ready to run for office or start a podcast. But you can become an expert in child-centric truth.

Become informed on the issues and remain vigilant about our society's "adults-first" mentality. To this end, diversify the voices to which you expose yourself to daily, starting with the authors of this book. Find them on social media, subscribe to their newsletters, order their books. Especially seek out those whose topics you feel most uninformed about. Make yourself a student of these authors and investigate the topics their colleagues are covering.

Read a few in-depth articles weekly on a topic that interests you, or seek out informative documentaries and long-form podcasts. As you read, keep foremost in mind: "Who will this policy affect most?" and "Who is being asked or forced to sacrifice in this situation?"

Be mindful of the people you follow and sources you watch, read, and listen to every day. Take stock of where you spend your time and who you give your attention to. Whether we realize it or not, the media we consume influences our thoughts, desires, and actions. Regular culling of unhelpful voices will guard against an us-before-them mentality. Be careful to retain challenging perspectives to avoid the pitfall of confirmation bias. The point is to be conscious of what you are consuming.

▇ STEP 2: GET TO NEUTRAL

Remember when the wave of "fair trade" products hit the shelves several years back? Suddenly, with every purchase, every subscription, every click, you joined either the oppressors or the liberation fighters. As analysis paralysis predictably set in, the easiest approach was to ignore everything and go about your business.

To avoid being paralyzed by information inflow, here's an achievable second step. If you feel responsible for solving all of the world's problems, you will become overwhelmed. Instead, focus on getting to neutral.

This means ceasing to pursue or passively support harmful policies that do not center the child. You can't fight back everywhere on everything, but you can stop the me-before-them choices and behaviors in your own life. In what ways are your thoughts and actions out of step with the child-centric worldview presented in *Pro-Child Politics*?

Have you gotten caught up in the career-advancement and material-accumulation rat race to the detriment of your present or future children? If so, getting to neutral looks like reordering your goals and priorities to ensure family stands at the forefront. The notion that there are more important things than a little more money or influence will strike the world as strange, but it is true. And prioritizing your family might push others to reconsider their choices too.

Are you living a life of fiscal irresponsibility and debt? Getting to neutral means modeling the virtues of hard work, responsibility, and honesty for children. It's easier to run up credit card bills, clamor for student-loan forgiveness, or use bankruptcy as a fiscal strategy instead of a last resort, but these behaviors force others to pay for our mistakes. A neutral mindset strives to be financially healthy and dependable to avoid passing on a burden of debt to the next generation. A person who lives like this will have credibility to expect the same from our politicians.

Have you promoted a "live and let live" philosophy that may signal acceptance but results in children bearing the cost? Maybe you have developed an agnostic attitude toward transgenderism that fails to acknowledge the dangers inherent in child transitions and men invading women's spaces. Neutral means rejecting this libertine attitude and protecting all children's interests when it comes to their lives, families, minds, bodies, and futures. This won't require you to run for office, but it will mean speaking the truth and refusing to go along to get along. Bad ideas often metastasize amid silence from the masses. While guarding against the mental exhaustion of the fair-trade phenomenon, consider redirecting your spending power away from outlets that promote dangerous ideas.

Have you outsourced your role as a parent to digital technology for education and entertainment? Getting neutral means cutting down on your screen time, not only for your well-being, but to model healthy technology use for your children. It means avoiding reliance on technology to teach, train, or even babysit your children. There is no substitute for human interaction, and that's especially true in the limited, early window of child development. Rejecting our culture's transition to a virtual reality is vital for your children's maturation and flourishing.

Have you supported unjust immigration policies that make you sound virtuous but victimize the most vulnerable? Neutral means refusing to back policies that encourage human trafficking and drain resources from the citizens our nation has a duty to protect.

▰ STEP 3: PICK YOUR BATTLES

Becoming informed and getting to neutral is the foundation of a pro-child mindset. But we need to get beyond "do no harm" and actively protect children.

When you're ready to engage in the fight, identify a pro-child issue where your advocacy can make a difference. The following formula can help:

1. **Find your calling.** We have assembled a diverse set of topics in this book, and in the fight for the next generation, we cannot ignore any of them. That said, it is impossible for one person to do it all. As you read through the chapters, which lingered with you the most? Which stories of children harmed, which lie, struck you as particularly egregious? Where did you say out loud, "Oh, that's not right"? You may be called to get involved in that arena.

2. **Craft your plan.** As you consider your calling, engage in a self-inventory to assess what exactly you can bring to table. Consider your strengths and abilities. Take into account what finances, connections, or platforms you possess. Most importantly, think about what activities or actions energize you. An honest self-assessment will help you determine your next steps.

3. **Get to work.** Chart a course of action. For those low on time but high on resources, consider supporting organizations already making change in your chosen area. This may occur via real cash or by spending social currency to leverage your networks. If your portfolio is small but the gaps in your calendar are big, consider volunteering with a group or institution to help it gain ground in your area of interest. Finally, for highly motivated individuals with both the gifts and resources necessary for moving mountains, consider starting an organization aimed specifically at impacting your area of calling. Or run for an office that would empower you to tackle your issue directly. These actions—in addition to voting and lobbying your local community—are great ways to make real change and advance a pro-child agenda.

▮ STEP 4: GROW YOUR TEAM

Even the most dynamic individuals cannot do it alone. Use this book to walk others through a journey from awareness to action.

- **Start at home.** Remember the importance of having kids, and then raising them to assume a responsible worldview. Change begins with those closest to us.

- **Educate your friends.** This can be as simple as hosting a book club, inviting friends to a fundraiser for an organization doing great work, or sending this book to a friend with your endorsement.

- **Expand your network.** As you meet leaders deep in the trenches of pro-child work, host dinner parties and activities where you can introduce your community to these leaders. Share the stories and testimonials of victimized children—these are the most powerful agents for awareness and education.

There is no more important fight than the pro-child battle. The philosophical shift from *us* before *them* to *them* before *us* goes far beyond preference. It's a mentality required for a thriving national future, and it harkens back to our national origins.

From the very beginning, America's revolutionary spirit has led adults to voluntarily assume the burden of sacrifice in the hopes that the union their children inherit might be a little "more perfect" than when they started. Adults like this welcomed the stranger from all corners of the world, ended slavery, advocated for suffrage, gave up their lives on foreign battlefields, fought for civil rights, took us to the moon, and defeated communism. They set aside their comfort, reputation, possessions, and sometimes their lives to plant trees whose shade they would never enjoy.

Today's adults are called to the same spirit of sacrifice for the next generation. Together we can put them before us and build the just society our children deserve.

Josh Wood, executive director of Them Before Us

Josh Wood is the executive director at Them Before Us. He holds a master's degree in humanitarian and disaster leadership from Wheaton College and a bachelor's degree in cross-cultural ministry from Messiah University.

Josh has spent his career in nonprofit leadership and church ministry, focused on serving others and solving problems. He lives in Charlotte, North Carolina, with his wife, Corinne, and three kids: Savannah, Lincoln, and Gideon.

ACKNOWLEDGMENTS

From contract to copy, this book was assembled in less than six months, a feat accomplished solely due to the commitment and flexibility of everyone at Post Hill Press. Unending thanks to project manager Amy Parrish, who managed to corral every contribution, attribution, and allocation, and to Evan Myers and Howe Wittman for their dogged editing. Thanks to the team at Them Before Us—Josh, Jenn, Mary, Patience—who filled in the gaps during my frenzied book work, for Katie B's research help and for Stacy's always-perfect wordsmithing. This collaboration would not have been possible without the help of a certain champion couple who financially got it off the ground. And supreme thanks to my husband, Ryan, for holding down the fort while I move from adventure to adventure.

ENDNOTES

INTRODUCTION

[1] Lee, Benjamin, and William V. Raszka. 2020. "COVID-19 Transmission and Children: The Child Is Not to Blame." *Pediatrics* 146 (2). https://doi.org/10.1542/peds.2020-004879.

[2] Jenssen, Brian P., Mary Kate Kelly, Maura Powell, Zoe Bouchelle, Stephanie L. Mayne, and Alexander G. Fiks. 2021. "COVID-19 and Changes in Child Obesity." *Pediatrics* 147 (5). https://doi.org/10.1542/peds.2021-050123.

[3] Hedderson, Monique M., Traci A. Bekelman, Mingyi Li, Emily A. Knapp, Meredith Palmore, Yanan Dong, Amy J. Elliott et al. 2023. "Trends in Screen Time Use Among Children During the COVID-19 Pandemic, July 2019 through August 2021." *JAMA Network Open* 6 (2): e2256157. https://doi.org/10.1001/jamanetworkopen.2022.56157.

[4] Guzman, Susanna. 2023. "What Is Anxiety? Symptoms, Causes, Diagnosis and Treatment." *Forbes Health*. https://www.forbes.com/health/mind/what-is-anxiety.

[5] Beer, Tommy. n.d. "Self-Harm Claims Among U.S. Teenagers Increased 99% During Pandemic, Study Finds." *Forbes*. Accessed April 11, 2024. https://www.forbes.com/sites/tommybeer/2021/03/03/self-harm-claims-among-us-teenagers-increased-99-during-pandemic-study-finds/?sh=6e8d3d5233e0.

[6] Will, Madeline. 2020. "Teachers Are Scared to Go Back to School. Will They Strike?" *Education Week*. https://www.edweek.org/leadership/teachers-are-scared-to-go-back-to-school-will-they-strike/2020/07.

[7] Will, Madeline. 2023. "How Teachers' Unions Are Influencing Decisions on School Reopenings." *Education Week*. https://www.edweek.org/teaching-learning/how-teachers-unions-are-influencing-decisions-on-school-reopenings/2020/12.

[8] Antonucci, Mike. 2021. Review of *Teacher Union Resistance to Reopening Schools: An Examination of the Largest U.S. School Districts*. Defense of Freedom

Institute. https://dfipolicy.org/wp-content/uploads/2021/10/DFI_Teachers-Union-Resistance-to-Reopening-Schools-Report.pdf.

9   Schwalbach, Jude. n.d. "Outsized and Opaque: K–12 Pandemic Education Spending." The Heritage Foundation. https://www.heritage.org/education/report/outsized-and-opaque-k-12-pandemic-education-spending.

10   PAHO TV. 2020. "Keep Grandma Safe, Stay at Home #BeatCOVID19." You-Tube video. https://www.youtube.com/watch?v=wrN2_ABccPk.

11   Leonhardt, David. 2022. "No Way to Grow Up." *The New York Times*, https://www.nytimes.com/2022/01/04/briefing/american-children-crisis-pandemic.html.

LIFE

1   "Pro-Choice Quotes Archives." 2023. ClinicQuotes. https://clinicquotes.com/category/quotes/pro-choice-quotes/.

2   Paulson, Richard J. 2022. "It Is Worth Repeating: 'Life Begins at Conception' Is a Religious, Not Scientific, Concept." *F&S Reports* 3 (3): 177. https://doi.org/10.1016/j.xfre.2022.08.005.

3   "World-Famous Supermodel Gracefully Obliterates Every Pro-Choice Argument." 2017. Save the Storks. https://savethestorks.com/2017/11/world-famous-supermodel-gracefully-obliterates-every-pro-choice-argument/.

4   Waters, Emma. n.d. "Why the IVF Industry Must Be Regulated." The Heritage Foundation. Accessed April 27, 2024. https://www.heritage.org/life/report/why-the-ivf-industry-must-be-regulated. https://www.heritage.org/life/report/why-the-ivf-industry-must-be-regulated.

5   Austin, Stephen. 2022. "IVF: A Second Front in the Cause for Life." *Public Discourse*. https://www.google.com/url?q=https://www.thepublicdiscourse.com/2022/07/83359/&sa=D&source=docs&ust=1714265225592225&usg=AOvVaw1RIhd35o83yOYj_KO9nWj8.

6   Reda, Natasha. 2019. "Twenty-Five Celebrities Who Are Pro-Choice." *Pop Crush*.

7   Oh, Reginald. "Black Citizenship, Dehumanization, and the Fourteenth Amendment." https://ideaexchange.uakron.edu/cgi/viewcontent.cgi?article=1122&context=conlawnow.

8   Maddow-Zimet, Isaac, and Candace Gibson. 2024. "Despite Bans, Number of Abortions in the United States Increased in 2023 | Guttmacher Institute." https://www.guttmacher.org/2024/03/despite-bans-number-abortions-united-states-increased-2023.

9   Sivak, David. 2018. "FACT CHECK: Have There Really Been 60 Million Abortions since Roe v. Wade?" Check Your Fact. https://checkyourfact.com/2018/07/03/fact-check-60-million-abortions/.

[10] Letterie, Gerard. 2022. "In Re: The Disposition of Frozen Embryos: 2022." *Fertility and Sterility*, February. https://doi.org/10.1016/j.fertnstert.2022.01.001.

[11] Dalzell, Julia. 2018. "The Enforcement of Selective Reduction Clauses in Surrogacy Contracts." *Law Student Scholarship* 7. https://digital.sandiego.edu/law_stu_schol/7.

[12] See this book's chapter on family for the risks and struggles donor-conceived children face.

[13] "Fetal Surgery Photo Still Making an Impact." 2011. *The Catholic Spirit*. https://thecatholicspirit.com/news/local-news/fetal-surgery-photo-still-making-an-impact/.

[14] Condic, Maureen. 2014. "A Scientific View of When Life Begins | Charlotte Lozier Institute." Lozier Institute. https://lozierinstitute.org/a-scientific-view-of-when-life-begins/.

MASCULINITY

[1] David J. Handelsman et. al. 2018. "Circulating Testosterone as the Hormonal Basis of Sex Differences in Athletic Performance." *Endocrine Reviews* 39 (5). https://www.ncbi.nlm.nih.gov/pmc/articles/PMC6391653/#:~:text=This%20indicates%20that%20androgen%20action,of%20males%20compared%20with%20females.

[2] Roy F. Baumeister et. al. 2001. "Is There a Gender Difference in Strength of Sex Drive? Theoretical Views, Conceptual Distinctions, and a Review of Relevant Evidence." *Personality and Social Psychology Review.* 5 (3). https://journals.sagepub.com/doi/abs/10.1207/S15327957PSPR0503_5.

[3] Walters, Suzanna Danuta. 2018. "Why Can't We Hate Men?" *Washington Post.* https://www.washingtonpost.com/opinions/why-cant-we-hate-men/2018/06/08/f1a3a8e0-6451-11e8-a69c-b944de66d9e7_story.html.

[4] Stoltenberg, John. 2021. "Why Talking About "Healthy Masculinity" Is Like Talking About "Healthy Cancer.'" *Medium.* https://johnstoltenberg.medium.com/why-talking-about-healthy-masculinity-is-like-talking-about-healthy-cancer-96610e4b50c0.

[5] Garibaldi, Gerry. 2006. "How the Schools Shortchange Boys." *City Journal.* https://www.city-journal.org/article/how-the-schools-shortchange-boys.

[6] Cox, Daniel A. 2023. "Why Young Men Are Turning Against Feminism." *American Survey Center.* https://www.americansurveycenter.org/newsletter/why-young-men-are-turning-against-feminism/.

[7] Sommers, Christina Hoff. 2013. "The Boys at the Back." *New York Times.* https://archive.nytimes.com/opinionator.blogs.nytimes.com/2013/02/02/the-boys-at-the-back/.

8 Wedge, Marilyn. 2015. "Are We Medicating the True Selves of Boys?" *Psychology Today*. https://www.psychologytoday.com/us/blog/suffer-the-children/201504/are-we-medicating-the-true-selves-boys.

9 Garibaldi, Gerry. 2006. "How the Schools Shortchange Boys." *City Journal*. https://www.city-journal.org/article/how-the-schools-shortchange-boys.

10 Wedge, Marilyn. 2015. "Are We Medicating the True Selves of Boys?" *Psychology Today*. https://www.psychologytoday.com/us/blog/suffer-the-children/201504/are-we-medicating-the-true-selves-boys; Mark Olfson, et. al. 2023. "Treatment of US Children with Attention-Deficit/Hyperactivity Disorder in the Adolescent Brain Cognitive Development Study." *JAMA Network* 6 (4). https://www.ncbi.nlm.nih.gov/pmc/articles/PMC10148191/#:~:text=Children%20receiving%20ADHD%20medications%20included,of%20parents%20with%20a%20bachelor's.

11 Myers, Evan, and Howe Whitman III, "Men's Realism." *American Compass*. https://americancompass.org/mens-realism/.

12 Rosenberg, Jeffrey, and W. Bradford Wilcox. 2006. "The Importance of Fathers in the Healthy Development of Children." U.S. Department of Health and Human Services. https://cantasd.acf.hhs.gov/wp-content/uploads/Importance-of-Fathers-Healthy-Development.pdf.

13 Proverbs 25:28, ESV.

14 Gewertz, Ken. 2003. "'Manliness,' An Obsolete Concept? Discuss." *The Harvard Gazette*. https://news.harvard.edu/gazette/story/2003/04/manliness-an-obsolete-concept-discuss/.

15 Lindner, Jannik. 2023. "Must-Know Fatherless Homes Statistics [Latest Report]." *Gitnux*. https://gitnux.org/fatherless-homes-statistics/.

16 Lindner, Jannik. 2023. "Must-Know Fatherless Homes Statistics [Latest Report]." *Gitnux*. https://gitnux.org/fatherless-homes-statistics/.

17 Walkabouts. Last accessed May 30, 2024. https://www.walkabouts.com/.

FEMININITY

1 Scorah. Amber. 2015. "A Baby Dies at Day Care, and a Mother Asks Why She Had to Leave Him So Soon." *New York Times*. https://archive.nytimes.com/parenting.blogs.nytimes.com/2015/11/15/a-baby-dies-at-day-care-and-a-mother-asks-why-she-had-to-leave-him-so-soon/.

2 "Does Amount of Time Spent in Child Care Predict Socioemotional Adjustment During the Transition to Kindergarten?" 2003. *Child Development* 74 (4). https://pubmed.ncbi.nlm.nih.gov/12938694/.

3 Munrof Blum, Hfather, Michaei H. Boyle, and David R. Offord. 1988. "Single-Parent Families: Child Psychiatric Disorder and School

Performance." *Journal of the American Academy of Child & Adolescent Psychiatry* 27 (2). https://www.sciencedirect.com/science/article/abs/pii/S0890856709655520.

[4]   Stulpin, Caitlyn. 2024. "US's STD epidemic worsened again in 2023." Infection Disease News. https://www.healio.com/news/infectious-disease/20231222/uss-std-epidemic-worsened-again-in-2023.

[5]   Planned Parenthood. 2024. "What Happens the First Time You Have Sex? | Planned Parenthood Video." YouTube video. https://www.youtube.com/watch?v=EXEJzWChqB4&t=11s.

[6]   Planned Parenthood. 2024. "What Is Virginity? |Planned Parenthood Video." YouTube video. https://www.youtube.com/watch?v=ozhO62z2nag&t=19s.

[7]   Keenan, Peachy. 2023. *Domestic Extremist: A Practical Guide to Winning the Culture War.* Regnery.

[8]   T. Johansson et al. "Population-Based Cohort Study of Oral Contraceptive Use and Risk of Depression." *Epidemiology and Psychiatric Sciences* 32. https://www.cambridge.org/core/journals/epidemiology-and-psychiatric-sciences/article/populationbased-cohort-study-of-oral-contraceptive-use-and-risk-of-depression/B3C611DD318D7DC536B4BD439343A5BD.

[9]   Kaminski, Pawel, Monika Szpotanska-Sikorska, and Miroslaw Wielgos. 2013. "Cardiovascular Risk and the Use of Oral Contraceptives." *Neuroendocrinology Letters* 34 (7). https://pubmed.ncbi.nlm.nih.gov/24464000/.

[10] Gupta, Alisha Haridasani. 2024. "The Link Between Birth Control Pills and Sex Drive." *New York Times.* https://www.nytimes.com/2024/01/23/well/live/birth-control-sex-drive-libido.html.

[11] Morrison, Cassidy. 2022. "Can Birth Control Make You a LESBIAN? As a Number of Women Say Their Homosexuality Was 'Woken Up' After Starting or Coming Off the Pill, Studies Suggest There Might Be Some Truth About the Unlikely Side Effect." *Daily Mail.* https://www.dailymail.co.uk/health/article-11457347/Can-Pill-turn-GAY-Growing-number-women-report-bizarre-symptom.html.

[12] Bendix, Aria. 2019. "Birth-Control Pills Could Add 10 Million Doses of Hormones to Our Wastewater Every Day. Some of That Estrogen May Wind Up in Our Taps." *Business Insider.* https://www.businessinsider.com/birth-control-pills-hormones-estrogen-drinking-water-health-effects-2019-10.

[13] "Does Amount of Time Spent in Child Care Predict Socioemotional Adjustment During the Transition to Kindergarten?" 2003. *Child Development* 74 (4). https://pubmed.ncbi.nlm.nih.gov/12938694/.

[14] Erikson, Jenet, and Jay Belsky. "Another Perspective on the Latest Research on Early Child Care." *Institute for Family Studies.* https://ifstudies.org/blog/another-perspective-on-the-latest-research-on-early-child-care#:~:text=By%20third%20grade%2C%20children%20who,been%20in%20day%20care%20centers.

15 Keenan, Peachy. 2023. *Domestic Extremist: A Practical Guide to Winning the Culture War*. Regnery.
16 Keenan, Peachy. 2023. *Domestic Extremist: A Practical Guide to Winning the Culture War*. Regnery.

FAMILY

1 Gettleman, Susan, and Janet Markowitz. 1974. *The Courage to Divorce*. Simon and Schuster.
2 Freed, Meghan. 2023. "What's Better for the Kids: Staying in an Unhappy Marriage or Divorce?" *Freed Marcroft Divorce and Family Law*. https://freedmarcroft.com/whats-better-for-kids-staying-in-an-unhappy-marriage-or-divorce/.
3 BLM has since scrubbed that language from its website, but until recently it was still used in BLM's classroom curriculum.
4 In #BigFertility, no one is "donating" anything. Everyone is buying and selling.
5 Alfred Blumstein et al. 1998. "What Can the Federal Government Do to Decrease Crime and Revitalize Communities?" U.S. Department of Justice. https://www.ojp.gov/pdffiles/172210.pdf.
6 Alfred Blumstein et al. 1998. "What Can the Federal Government Do to Decrease Crime and Revitalize Communities?" U.S. Department of Justice. https://www.ojp.gov/pdffiles/172210.pdf.
7 Teachman, Jay D. 2004. "The Childhood Living Arrangements of Children and the Characteristics of Their Marriages." *Journal of Family Issues* 25 (1). https://doi.org/10.1177/0192513X03255346.
8 Alfred Blumstein et al. 1998. "What Can the Federal Government Do to Decrease Crime and Revitalize Communities?" U.S. Department of Justice. https://www.ojp.gov/pdffiles/172210.pdf.
9 Alfred Blumstein et al. 1998. "What Can the Federal Government Do to Decrease Crime and Revitalize Communities?" U.S. Department of Justice. https://www.ojp.gov/pdffiles/172210.pdf.
10 Alfred Blumstein et al. 1998. "What Can the Federal Government Do to Decrease Crime and Revitalize Communities?" U.S. Department of Justice. https://www.ojp.gov/pdffiles/172210.pdf.
11 Alfred Blumstein et al. 1998. "What Can the Federal Government Do to Decrease Crime and Revitalize Communities?" U.S. Department of Justice. https://www.ojp.gov/pdffiles/172210.pdf.
12 Alfred Blumstein et al. 1998. "What Can the Federal Government Do to Decrease Crime and Revitalize Communities?" U.S. Department of Justice. https://www.ojp.gov/pdffiles/172210.pdf.
13 Herbert, Wray. 1985. "Dousing the Kindlers." *Psychology Today* 19 (1).

14   Makhijani, Pooja. 2017. "At the Cellular Level, a Child's Loss of a Father Is Associated with Increased Stress." *Princeton University.* https://www.princeton.edu/news/2017/07/18/cellular-level-childs-loss-father-associated-increased-stress.

15   Anne Gaml-Sørensen et al. 2021. "Father Absence in Pregnancy or During Childhood and Pubertal Development in Girls and Boys: A Population-Based Cohort Study." *Child Development* 92 (4). https://doi.org/10.1111/cdev.13488; Julianna Deardorff et al. 2011. "Father Absence, Body Mass Index, and Pubertal Timing in Girls: Differential Effects by Family Income and Ethnicity." *Journal of Adolescent Health* 48 (5). https://doi.org/10.1016/j.jadohealth.2010.07.032.

16   Cohabiting relationships last, on average, eighteen months. Manning, Wendy D. 2015. "Cohabitation and Child Wellbeing." *Future Child* 25 (2).

17   Duursma, Anna E. "The Effects of Fathers' and Mothers' Reading to Their Children on Language Outcomes of Children Participating in Early Head Start in the United States." *Fathering: A Journal of Theory, Research, and Practice about Men as Fathers* 12 (3).

18   Wilcox, Brad. 2023. "The Distinct, Positive Impact of a Good Dad," *The Atlantic.* https://www.theatlantic.com/sexes/archive/2013/06/the-distinct-positive-impact-of-a-good-dad/276874/.

19   Amato, Paul R., and Joan Gilbreth. 1999. "Non-Resident Fathers and Children's Wellbeing," *Journal of Marriage and Family* 61 (3).

20   "Among adults who have both a grown biological child and a grown step-child, the biological child exerts a stronger pull. Nearly eight-in-ten (78%) of these parents say they would feel very obligated to provide assistance to a grown child. Closer to six-in-ten (62%) say they would feel equally obligated to their grown stepchild." "A Portrait of Stepfamilies." 2011. *Pew Research Center's Social & Demographic Trends Project.* https://www.pewresearch.org/social-trends/2011/01/13/a-portrait-of-stepfamilies/.

21   Case, Anne, and Christina Paxson. 2001. "Mothers and Others: Who Invests in Children's Health?" *Journal of Health Economics* 20.

22   Wilcox, W. Bradford. 2011. "Suffer the Little Children: Cohabitation and the Abuse of America's Children." *Public Discourse.* https://www.thepublicdiscourse.com/2011/04/3181/.

23   Daly, Martin, and Margo Wilson. 2005. "The 'Cinderella Effect' Is No Fairy Tale." *Trends in Cognitive Sciences* 9 (11). https://doi.org/10.1016/j.tics.2005.09.007.

24   2010. "Family Structure and Children's Health in the United States: Findings from the National Health Interview Survey, 2001–2007." *Centers for Disease Control and Prevention.* www.cdc.gov/nchs/data/series/sr_10/sr10_246.pdf.

25   Fourth National Incidence Study of Child Abuse and Neglect, https://www.acf.hhs.gov/sites/default/files/documents/opre/nis4_report_congress_full_pdf_jan2010.pdf.

26 "Reform Myths." American Adoption Congress. https://www.americanad optioncongress.org/reform_myths.php.

27 Clark, Karen, and Elizabeth Marquardt. 2010. "My Daddy's Name Is Donor." Institute for American Values. https://thembeforeus.com/wp-content/ uploads/2023/02/My-Daddys-Name-is-Donor-Full-Study.pdf.

RACE

1 KHOU.com staff. 2019. "Sheila Jackson Lee Defends Calling Jazmine Barnes Murder a Hate Crime." *KHOU* https://www.khou.com/article/news/ local/sheila-jackson-lee-defends-calling-jazmine-barnes-murder-a-hate-crime/285-626751344; Merritt, Lee. @MerrittForTexas. 2018. X post. https:// twitter.com/MeritLaw/status/1079880803600027649; 2019. "$100,000 Reward Offered for Information in Death of 7-Year-Old Girl Shot and Killed While Leaving Houston-Area Walmart with Mother." *ABC11*. https://abc11. com/jazmine-barnes-justiceforjazmine-shaun-king-murdered/5009366/.

2 Be A King. @BerniceKing. 2019. X post. https://twitter.com/BerniceKing/ status/1080868659021651972.

3 Lockhart, P.R. 2019. "Why the Death of a 7-Year-Old Black Girl Became a National Story About Race and Violence." *Vox.* https://www.vox.com/ identities/2019/1/5/18168865/jazmine-barnes-shooting-manhunt-texas-race.

4 2019. "Inmate Once Wrongfully Accused of Killing 7-Year-Old Jazmine Barnes Killed Himself Behind Bars." *ABC13*. https://abc13.com/robert-paul-cantrell-jazmine-barnes-shooting-threatening-comments/5428054/.

5 Davis, F. James. 1991. "Who Is Black? One Nation's Definition." *PBS.* https:// www.pbs.org/wgbh/pages/frontline/shows/jefferson/mixed/onedrop.html.

6 Cartright, Samuel. 1851. ""Diseases and Peculiarities of the Negro Race." *De Bow's Review (Southern and Western States* XI. https://www.pbs.org/wgbh/aia/ part4/4h3106t.html.

7 Parks, Kristine. 2023. "Fed-Up Staff Seethe Over Boston U's Antiracist Center: 'Colossal Waste of Millions of Dol-lars.'" *Fox News.* https://www.foxnews.com/media/ fed-up-staff-seethe-boston-us-antiracist-center-colossal-waste-millions-dollars.

8 Kendi, Ibram X. "Pass an Anti-Racist Constitutional Amendment." *Politico.* https://www.politico.com/interactives/2019/how-to-fix-politics-in-america/ inequality/pass-an-anti-racist-constitutional-amendment/.

9 "How to Be an Antiracist." ibramxkendi.com.

10 Ibram X. Kendi, "Ibram X. Kendi Defines What It Means to Be an Antirac-ist," Penguin, June 9, 2020. https://www.penguin.co.uk/articles/2020/06/ ibram-x-kendi-definition-of-antiracist.

11   "2023. Proficiency Rates for NYC Students in Math & ELA." 2023 Math and ELA Results. *NYC Public Schools.* https://infohub.nyced.org/docs/default-source/default-document-library/2023-math-ela---website.pdf.

12   McGee, Kate. 2017. "What Really Happened at Ballou, the D.C. High School Where Every Senior Got into College." *WAMU 88.5.* https://wamu.org/story/17/11/28/really-happened-ballou-d-c-high-school-every-senior-got-college/.

13   Rufo, Christopher F. 2021. "Failure Factory." *City Journal.* https://www.city-journal.org/article/failure-factory.

14   "Buffalo City School District Grades 3-8 ELA Assessment Data." https://data.nysed.gov/assessment38.php?instid=800000052968&year=2019&-subject=ELA&grades%5B%5D=8&prof24=0.

15   Watts, Marina. 2020. "In Smithsonian Race Guidelines, Rational Thinking and Hard Work Are White Values." *Newsweek.* https://www.newsweek.com/smithsonian-race-guidelines-rational-thinking-hard-work-are-white-values-1518333.

16   Rufo, Christopher F. 2021. "Gone Crazy." *City Journal.* https://www.city-journal.org/article/gone-crazy; Algar, Selim. 2019. "DOE-Sponsored Group Said Asians Benefit from White Privilege: Parent." *New York Post.* https://nypost.com/2019/05/26/doe-may-have-claimed-asian-students-benefit-from-white-supremacy/.

17   "*Brown v. Board* and 'The Doll Test.'" Legal Defense Fund. https://www.naacpldf.org/brown-vs-board/significance-doll-test/.

18   2010. "Study: White and Black Children Biased Toward Lighter Skin." *CNN.* https://www.cnn.com/2010/US/05/13/doll.study/index.html.

19   Wilcox, Brad, Wendy Wang, and Ian Rowe. 2021. "Less Poverty, Less Prison, More College: What Two Parents Mean for Black and White Children," Institute for Family Studies. https://ifstudies.org/blog/less-poverty-less-prison-more-college-what-two-parents-mean-for-black-and-white-children.

20   "13 Guiding Principles." https://www.blacklivesmatteratschool.com/13-guiding-principles.html.

21   2023. "Births: Final Data for 2021." National Vital Statistics Reports. https://www.cdc.gov/nchs/data/nvsr/nvsr72/nvsr72-01.pdf.

22   Wang, Wendy, and Brad Wilcox. 2022. "The Power of the Success Sequence for Disadvantaged Young Adults," *American Enterprise Institute and the Institute for Family Studies.* https://www.aei.org/wp-content/uploads/2022/05/successsequencedisadvantagedya-final.pdf?x85095.

23   Terry, Eva. 2023. "Educator Ian Rowe at Wheatley: 'There Are No Victims in Our School, Only Architects of Their Own Lives.'" *Deseret News.* https://www.deseret.com/2023/10/26/23932615/ian-rowe-at-wheatley-no-victims-only-architects-of-our-own-lives/.

24   Post Editorial Board. 2023. "Success Academy Smashes Regents and Lefty Lies on Standardized Testing." *New York Post.* https://nypost.com/2023/07/02/success-academy-excels-on-standardized-tests-despite-democrats-claims/.

25 "New York State Assessment Results Comparison of All Success Academy Charter Schools to Their Districts of Location." https://www.suny.edu/about/leadership/board-of-trustees/meetings/webcastdocs/D_Success%20-%20Appendix%20A%20-%20School%20Performance.pdf.

GENDER IDEOLOGY

1 Independent Women's Forum. 2022. "Identity Crisis: Detransitioner Betrayed by Health Professionals Who Left Her 'Mutilated.'" YouTube video. https://www.youtube.com/watch?v=CFaAW0z50iQ.

2 Mosley, Prisha. 2023. "I Began 'Gender Transition' at 16. I Was Lied to in a Terrible Way. Now I Am Seeking Justice." *Independent Women's Forum.* https://www.iwf.org/2023/07/27/i-began-gender-transition-at-16-i-was-lied-to-in-a-terrible-way-now-i-am-seeking-justice/.

3 Green, Richard. 2010. "Robert Stoller's *Sex and Gender*: 40 Years On." *Archives of Sexual Behavior* 39 (6). https://doi.org/10.1007/s10508-010-9665-5.

4 The Associated Press. 2006. "Dr. John Money, Pioneer in Sexual Identity, Dies." *NBC News.* https://www.nbcnews.com/health/health-news/dr-john-money-pioneer-sexual-identity-dies-flna1c9439208.

5 2023. "Berkeley Philosopher Judith Butler's Theory of Gender for the 21st Century." *Big Think.* July 28, 2023. https://bigthink.com/thinking/judith-butler-theory-gender-21st-century/.

6 2022. "Gonadotropin-Releasing Hormone (GnRH)." *Cleveland Clinic.* https://my.clevelandclinic.org/health/body/22525-gonadotropin-releasing-hormone.

7 Savchenko, Marina. 2020. "Puberty Blockers: How Hormone Blockers Suppress Sexual Characteristics in Teens." *Flo Health.* https://flo.health/menstrual-cycle/teens/your-body/puberty-blockers.

8 Varshini Murugesh et al. 2024. "Puberty Blocker and Aging Impact on Testicular Cell States and Function." bioRxiv (Cold Spring Harbor Laboratory). https://pubmed.ncbi.nlm.nih.gov/38585884/.

9 Mayo Clinic Staff. 2023. "Puberty Blockers for Transgender and Gender-Diverse Youth." *Mayo Clinic.* https://www.mayoclinic.org/diseases-conditions/gender-dysphoria/in-depth/pubertal-blockers/art-20459075.

10 Biggs, Michael. 2021. "Revisiting the Effect of GnRH Analogue Treatment on Bone Mineral Density in Young Adolescents with Gender Dysphoria." *Journal of Pediatric Endocrinology and Metabolism* 34 (7). https://doi.org/10.1515/jpem-2021-0180.

11 Baxendale, Sallie. 2024. "The Impact of Suppressing Puberty on Neuropsychological Function: A Review." *Acta Pædiatrica* 113 (6). https://doi.org/10.1111/apa.17150.

12 Boskey, Elizabeth. 2023. "Testosterone for Transgender Men and Trans-masculine People." *Verywell Health*. https://www.verywellhealth.com/testosterone-for-transgender-men-4688488.

13 Pak, Jae. 2023. "Trans Male Pattern Baldness: Everything You Need to Know." *Jae Pak MD*. https://jaepakmd.com/resources/trans-male-pattern-baldness/.

14 Krakowsky, Yonah, Emery Potter, Jason Hallarn, Bern Monari, Hannah Wilcox, Greta R. Bauer, Jacques Ravel, and Jessica L. Prodger. 2022. "The Effect of Gender-Affirming Medical Care on the Vaginal and Neovaginal Microbiomes of Transgender and Gender-Diverse People." *Frontiers in Cellular and Infection Microbiology* 11. https://doi.org/10.3389/fcimb.2021.769950.

15 Moravek, Molly B., Hadrian M Kinnear, Jenny S. George, Jourdin Batchelor, Ariella Shikanov, Vasantha Padmanabhan, and John F. Randolph. 2020. "Impact of Exogenous Testosterone on Reproduction in Transgender Men." *Endocrinology* 161 (3). https://doi.org/10.1210/endocr/bqaa014.

16 Obedin-Maliver, Juno. 2016. "Pelvic Pain and Persistent Menses in Transgender Men | Gender Affirming Health Program." https://transcare.ucsf.edu/guidelines/pain-transmen.

17 Cruz, Aa, Josefa Cruz, Sadikah Behbehani, Samar Nahas, Stephanie Handler, and Mallory Stuparich. 2024. "Hysterectomy and Oophorectomy for Transgender Patients: Preoperative and Intraoperative Considerations." *Journal of Minimally Invasive Gynecology* 31 (4). https://doi.org/10.1016/j.jmig.2023.12.009.

18 Haghighi, Anna Smith. 2023. "What to Know About Estrogen in Men." *Medical News Today*. https://www.medicalnewstoday.com/articles/estrogen-in-men#symptoms-of-high-estrogen.

19 Kassel, Gabrielle. 2023. "How Does Estrogen Affect People Assigned Male at Birth?" *Healthline*. https://www.healthline.com/health/effects-of-estrogen-on-male-body#typical-levels.

20 Jackson, Mary. 2020. "Study: Effects of Puberty-Blockers Can Last a Lifetime." *World News Group*. https://wng.org/roundups/study-effects-of-puberty-blockers-can-last-a-lifetime-1617220389.

21 Martin, Daniel. 2024. "Doctors Admit Link Between Transgender Hormone Therapy and Cancer in Leaked Emails." *The Telegraph*. https://www.telegraph.co.uk/news/2024/03/05/wpath-transgender-hormone-therapy-cancer-links-leaked-emails/.

22 Tang, Annie, J. Carlo Hojilla, Jordan E. Jackson, Kara A. Rothenberg, Rebecca Gologorsky, Douglas Stram, Colin M Mooney, Stephanie L Hernandez, and Karen M. Yokoo. 2022. "Gender-Affirming Mastectomy Trends and Surgical Outcomes in Adolescents." *Annals of Plastic Surgery* 88 (4). https://doi.org/10.1097/sap.0000000000003135.

23 Osborn, Corinne O'Keefe. 2018. "Vaginoplasty: Gender Confirmation Surgery." *Healthline*. September 29, 2018. https://www.healthline.com/health/transgender/vaginoplasty#technique.

24 Boskey, Elizabeth. 2023. "Neovagina Surgery: Types of Vaginoplasty." *Verywell Health*. https://www.verywellhealth.com/different-types-of-vaginoplasty-4171503.

25 Respaut, Robin, and Chad Terhune. 2022. "Putting Numbers on the Rise in Children Seeking Gender Care." *Reuters*. https://www.reuters.com/investigates/special-report/usa-transyouth-data/.

26 Sun, Ching-Fang, Hui Xie, Vemmy Metsutnan, John H. Draeger, Yezhe Lin, Maria Stack Hankey, and Anita S. Kablinger. 2023. "The Mean Age of Gender Dysphoria Diagnosis Is Decreasing." *General Psychiatry* 36 (3). https://www.ncbi.nlm.nih.gov/pmc/articles/PMC10314610/#:~:text=The%20mean%20(standard%20error%20(SE,age%2023%20(figure%201B).

27 Zucker, Kenneth J., Anne A. Lawrence, and Baudewijntje P.C. Kreukels. 2016. "Gender Dysphoria in Adults." *Annual Review of Clinical Psychology* 12 (1). https://doi.org/10.1146/annurev-clinpsy-021815-093034.

28 Hughes, Mia. 2023. "The WPATH Files: Pseudoscientific Surgical AND Hormonal Experiments on Children, Adolescents, and Vulnerable Adults." *Environmental Progress*. https://static1.squarespace.com/static/56a45d683b0be33df885def6/t/65e6d9bea9969715f-ba29e6f/1709627904275/U_WPATH+Report+and+Files.pdf.

29 Wyckoff, Alyson Sulaski. 2023. "AAP Reaffirms Gender-affirming Care Policy, Authorizes Systematic Review of Evidence to Guide Update." *American Academy of Pediatrics*. https://publications.aap.org/aapnews/news/25340/AAP-reaffirms-gender-affirming-care-policy?

30 "Government Bill (House of Commons) C-4 (44-1) - First Reading - an Act to Amend the Criminal Code (Conversion Therapy) - Parliament of Canada." *Government Bill (House of Commons) C-4 (44-1) - First Reading - An Act to Amend the Criminal Code (Conversion Therapy) - Parliament of Canada*, www.parl.ca/DocumentViewer/en/44-1/bill/C-4/first-reading.

31 Sam Killermann. 2015. "The Genderbread Person version 3." *It's Pronounced Metrosexual*. https://www.itspronouncedmetrosexual.com/2015/03/the-genderbread-person-v3/.

32 Christenson, Josh. 2023. "Nearly 6,000 US Public Schools Hide Child's Gender Status from Parents." *New York Post*. https://nypost.com/2023/03/08/us-public-schools-conceal-childs-gender-status-from-parents/.

33 Though research is scarce when it comes to children, there are more comprehensive studies on suicide rates with the adult population. The most comprehensive study ever conducted was in Sweden, and it showed that posttransition adult clients were 4.9 times more likely to have made a suicide attempt. They were 19.1 times more likely to have died from suicide, after adjusting for prior psychiatric comorbidity. See Dhejne, Cecilia, Paul Lichtenstein, Magnus Boman, Anna L.V. Johansson, Niklas Långström, and Mikael Landén. 2011. "Long-Term Follow-Up of Transsexual Persons Undergoing Sex Reassignment

Surgery: Cohort Study in Sweden." *PloS One* 6 (2). https://doi.org/10.1371/journal.pone.0016885.

34 Ruuska, Sami-Matti, Katinka Tuisku, Timo Holttinen, and Riittakerttu Kaltiala. 2024. "All-Cause and Suicide Mortalities Among Adolescents and Young Adults Who Contacted Specialised Gender Identity Services in Finland in 1996–2019: A Register Study." *BMJ Mental Health* 27 (1). https://doi.org/10.1136/bmjment-2023-300940.

35 Cohen-Kettenis, PT, HA Delemarre-van de Waal, and LJ Gooren. 2008. "The Treatment of Adolescent Transsexuals: Changing Insights." *Journal of Sexual Medicine* 5 (8). https://pubmed.ncbi.nlm.nih.gov/18564158/.

36 Paul, Pamela. 2024. "As Kids, They Thought They Were Trans. They No Longer Do." *New York Times.* https://www.nytimes.com/2024/02/02/opinion/transgender-children-gender-dysphoria.html.

37 Lindquist, Spencer. 2022. "Detransitioner Gives Heartbreaking Testimony: 'There's No Fixing It.'" *Breitbart.* https://www.breitbart.com/social-justice/2022/09/01/detransitioner-gives-heartbreaking-testimony-theres-no-fixing-it/.

38 McHugh, Paul. 2015. "Transgenderism: A Pathogenic Meme." *Public Discourse.* https://www.thepublicdiscourse.com/2015/06/15145/.

39 "Puberty Suppression Treatment for Patients With Gender Dysphoria." https://flboardofmedicine.gov/forms/Puberty-Suppression-Treatment-for-Patients-with-Gender-Dysphoria-Patient-Information-and-Parental-Consent-and-Assent-for-Minors.pdf.

40 "Lupron Depot Injection: Uses, Dosage, Side Effects, Warnings." https://www.drugs.com/lupron.html.

41 Nanos, Janelle. 2016. "Taming the Beast Within." *Boston Magazine.* https://www.bostonmagazine.com/news/2014/02/25/chemical-castration/.

42 Boghani, Priyanka. 2015. "When Transgender Kids Transition, Medical Risks Are Both Known and Unknown." *Frontline.* https://www.pbs.org/wgbh/frontline/article/when-transgender-kids-transition-medical-risks-are-both-known-and-unknown/.

43 Hughes, Mia. 2023. "The WPATH Files: Pseudoscientific Surgical and Hormonal Experiments on Children, Adolescents, And Vulnerable Adults." *Environmental Progress.* https://static1.squarespace.com/static/56a45d683b0be33df885def6/t/65e6d9bea9969715f-ba29e6f/1709627904275/U_WPATH+Report+and+Files.pdf.

44 2022. "Agency for Health Care Administration Hearing on General Medicaid Policy Rule." *The Florida Channel.* https://thefloridachannel.org/videos/7-8-22-agency-for-health-care-administration-hearing-on-general-medicaid-policy-rule/.

45 Davis, Elliott. 2024. "States That Have Restricted Gender-Affirming Care for Trans Youth." *U.S. News.* https://www.usnews.com

com/news/best-states/articles/2023-03-30/
what-is-gender-affirming-care-and-which-states-have-restricted-it-in-2023.

[46] Campbell, Denis. 2024. "Children to Stop Getting Puberty Blockers at Gender Identity Clinics, Says NHS England." *The Guardian.* https://www.theguardian. com/society/2024/mar/12/children-to-stop-getting-puberty-blockers-at-gender-identity-clinics-says-nhs-england.

[47] Ghorayshi, Azeen. 2023. "England Limits Use of Puberty-Blocking Drugs to Research Only." *New York Times.* https://www.nytimes.com/2023/06/09/health/puberty-blockers-transgender-children-britain-nhs.html#:~:-text=The%20change%20is%20part%20of%20a%20broader%20push.

[48] 2023. "Denmark Joins the List of Countries That Have Sharply Restricted Youth Gender Transitions." *Society for Evidence Based Gender Medicine.* https:// segm.org/Denmark-sharply-restricts-youth-gender-transitions.

[49] Kelleher, Rose. 2023. "Norway Takes a Step Forward in Ending 'Experiment' in Youth Gender Medicine." *Genspect.* https://genspect.org/norway-takes-a-step-forward-in-ending-experiment-in-youth-gender-medicine/.

[50] "Empowering Detransitioners: Advocacy and Justice." *Campbell Miller Payne, PLLC.* https://www.cmppllc.com/.

[51] Hains, Tim "Argentine President-Elect Milei: 'I Didn't Come Here to Guide Lambs, but to Awaken Lions,'" November 24, 2023 https://www.realclear-politics.com/video/2023/11/24/argentine_president-elect_milei_i_didnt_come_here_to_guide_lambs_but_to_awaken_lions.html.

PORNOGRAPHY

[1] Connor is a real person and a good man. I appreciate his honesty in these tough conversations. He writes a Substack about politics and culture called *Forge and Anvil.* You can find it here: https://forgeandanvil.substack.com/.

[2] Robb, Michael B., and Supreet Mann. "New Report Reveals Truths About How Teens Engage with Pornography." *Common Sense Media.* https:// www.commonsensemedia.org/press-releases/new-report-reveals-truths-about-how-teens-engage-with-pornography.

[3] From the majority opinion in *Reno:* "We are persuaded that the CDA lacks the precision that the First Amendment requires when a statute regulates the content of speech. In order to deny minors access to potentially harmful speech, the CDA effectively suppresses a large amount of speech that adults have a constitutional right to receive and to address to one another. That burden on adult speech is unacceptable if less restrictive alternatives would be at least as effective in achieving the legitimate purpose that the statute was enacted to

serve... It is true that we have repeatedly recognized the governmental interest in protecting children from harmful materials... But that interest does not justify an unnecessarily broad suppression of speech addressed to adults." https://supreme.justia.com/cases/federal/us/521/844/.

4   1999. Omnibus Consolidated and Emergency Supplemental Appropriations Act, 1999. Sec. 1402. https://www.govinfo.gov/content/pkg/PLAW-105publ277/html/PLAW-105publ277.htm.

5   2004. *Ashcroft v. ACLU*, 542 U.S. 656.

6   Breyer, S. 2004. *Ashcroft v. ACLU*, 542 U.S. 656. Dissenting opinion.

7   Robb, Michael B., and Supreet Mann. "New Report Reveals Truths About How Teens Engage with Pornography." *Common Sense Media.* https://www.commonsensemedia.org/press-releases/new-report-reveals-truths-about-how-teens-engage-with-pornography.

8   Reuters. 2021. "Billie Eilish Says Watching Porn as a Child 'Destroyed My Brain.'" *The Guardian.* https://www.theguardian.com/music/2021/dec/15/billie-eilish-says-watching-porn-gave-her-nightmares-and-destroyed-my-brain.

9   Michele L. Ybarra et al. 2011. "X-Rated Material and Perpetration of Sexually Aggressive Behavior Among Children and Adolescents: Is There a Link?" *Aggressive Behavior* 37 (1). https://pubmed.ncbi.nlm.nih.gov/21046607/.

10 Elena Martellozzo et. al. 2017. "... I Wasn't Sure It Was Normal to Watch It..." *Middlesex University.* https://learning.nspcc.org.uk/media/1187/mdx-nspcc-occ-pornography-report.pdf.

11 Myers, Evan. 2023. "Parents vs. Porn." *National Review.* https://www.national-review.com/magazine/2023/04/17/parents-vs-porn/.

12 2022. "Global Average Internet Speed, 1990-2050." *FutureTimeline.* https://futuretimeline.net/data-trends/2050-future-internet-speed-predictions.htm#:~:text=Figure%202%3A%20Average%20internet%20access,%2C%20 2005%20(1%2C116%20kbps).&text=%22In%202000%2C%20the%20 average%20global,per%20second%20(Kbps).%22&text=2006%20(1.55%20 Mbit%2Fs).

13 Bennett, Morgan. 2013. "The New Narcotic." *Public Discourse.* https://www.thepublicdiscourse.com/2013/10/10846/.

14 2024. "Age Verification Bill Tracker." *Free Speech Coalition.* https://action.freespeechcoalition.com/age-verification-bills/.

15 Brown, Elizabeth Nolan. 2024. "Pornhub Pulls Out of Seventh State." *Reason.* https://reason.com/2024/03/18/pornhub-pulls-out-of-seventh-state/.

16 2023. "American Principles Project National Survey," *RGM Research Inc.* https://americanprinciplesproject.org/wp-content/uploads/2023/08/RMG-Poll-Toplines-8-16-23.pdf.

THE ECONOMY

1   2011. "Coal-Fired Power Plants Targeted by Sierra Club in Washington, D.C." *HuffPost*. https://www.huffpost.com/entry/coal-fired-power-plant-sierra-club-dc_n_899509.

2   Ilnyckyj, Milan. 2011. "Sierra Club 'New Filter' Ads." *Bury Coal*. https://bury-coal.com/blog/2011/09/27/sierra-club-new-filter-ads/.

3   Kelley, Alexandra. 2019. "Biden Tells Coal Miners to 'Learn to Code.'" *The Hill*. https://thehill.com/changing-america/enrichment/education/476391-biden-tells-coal-miners-to-learn-to-code/.

4   "Current Campaigns." Sierra Club. https://www.sierraclub.org/wisconsin/current-campaigns.

5   Jenkins, Jeff. 2015. "Boone County Looks to Close One-Third of Its Elementary Schools." *WV MetroNews*. https://wvmetronews.com/2015/11/02/boone-county-looks-to-close-one-third-of-its-elementary-schools/.

6   2024. "Nellis Elementary School (Closed 2021)." *Public School Review*. https://www.publicschoolreview.com/nellis-elementary-school-profile.

7   2024. "Jeffrey-Spencer Elementary School (Closed 2021)." *Public School Review*. https://www.publicschoolreview.com/jeffrey-spencer-elementary-school-profile.

8   2024. "Wharton Elementary School (Closed 2021)." *Public School Review*. https://www.publicschoolreview.com/wharton-elementary-school-profile/25208.

9   Jasso, Caleb. 2019. "The Life of Julia: A Failed Progressive Political Campaign." *Pepperdine Policy Review* 11 (1). https://digitalcommons.pepperdine.edu/ppr/vol11/iss1/1. https://digitalcommons.pepperdine.edu/ppr/vol11/iss1/1/.

10 James, Frank. 2011. "Romney's 'Corporations Are People' a Gift to Political Foes." *NPR*. https://www.npr.org/sections/itsallpolitics/2011/08/11/139551684/romneys-corporations-are-people-getting-lots-of-mileage.

11 2015. "Obama to Business Owners: 'You Didn't Build That.'" *Fox News*. https://www.foxnews.com/politics/obama-to-business-owners-you-didnt-build-that.

12 Horn, Wade F. 2001. "Wedding Bell Blues: Marriage and Welfare Reform." *Brookings*. https://www.brookings.edu/articles/wedding-bell-blues-marriage-and-welfare-reform/.

13 Dubay, Curtis. 2010. "The Economic Case against the Death Tax." *The Heritage Foundation*. https://www.heritage.org/taxes/report/the-economic-case-against-the-death-tax.

14 Sohrab Ahmari. 2023. Tyranny, Inc. Forum Books. Pgs. 19-22.

15 Schneider, Daniel, and Kristen Harknett. 2019. "Parental Exposure to Routine Work Schedule Uncertainty and Child Behavior." *Equitable Growth*. https://

equitablegrowth.org/working-papers/parental-exposure-to-routine-work-schedule-uncertainty-and-child-behavior/.

16 Miller, Claire Cain. 2019. "How Unpredictable Work Hours Turn Families Upside Down." *New York Times.* https://www.nytimes.com/2019/10/16/upshot/unpredictable-job-hours.html.

17 2024. "USDA Finalizes Voluntary 'Product of USA' Label Claim to Enhance Consumer Protection." *USDA.* https://www.usda.gov/media/press-releases/2024/03/11/usda-finalizes-voluntary-product-usa-label-claim-enhance-consumer.

18 Savransky, Rebecca. 2016. "Obama to Trump: 'What Magic Wand Do You Have?'" *The Hill.* https://thehill.com/blogs/blog-briefing-room/news/281936-obama-to-trump-what-magic-wand-do-you-have/.

19 Ahmari, Sohlrab. 2023. *Tyranny, Inc. Forum Books.*

20 Ahmari, Sohlrab. 2023. *Tyranny, Inc. Forum Books.*

21 Rector, Robert. 2014. "How Welfare Undermines Marriage and What to Do About It." *The Heritage Foundation.* https://www.heritage.org/welfare/report/how-welfare-undermines-marriage-and-what-do-about-it.

22 Rector, Robert. 2014. "How Welfare Undermines Marriage and What to Do About It." *The Heritage Foundation.* https://www.heritage.org/welfare/report/how-welfare-undermines-marriage-and-what-do-about-it.

23 Brown, Anna. 2021. "Growing Share of Childless Adults in U.S. Don't Expect to Ever Have Children." *Pew Research Center.* https://www.pewresearch.org/short-reads/2021/11/19/growing-share-of-childless-adults-in-u-s-dont-expect-to-ever-have-children/.

24 Appelbaum, Yoni. 2018. "Yoni Appelbaum: Americans Aren't Practicing Democracy." *The Atlantic.* https://www.theatlantic.com/magazine/archive/2018/10/losing-the-democratic-habit/568336/.

25 Jones, J. M. 2024. "Church Attendance Has Declined in Most U.S. Religious Groups." *Gallup, Inc.* https://news.gallup.com/poll/642548/church-attendance-declined-religious-groups.aspx.

26 Kraft, Dina. 2018. "Israel Booms with Babies as Developed World's Birth Rates Plummet. Here's Why." *Christian Science Monitor.* https://www.csmonitor.com/World/Middle-East/2018/1214/Israel-booms-with-babies-as-developed-world-s-birth-rates-plummet.-Here-s-why.

27 2019. "All You Need to Know about the Latest in Hungary's Pro-Family Policy." *Fidesz - Magyar Polgári Szövetség.* https://fidesz-eu.hu/en/all-you-need-to-know-about-the-latest-in-hungarys-pro-family-policy/.

28 Martin, David. 2018. "Are Family Policy Reforms to Thank for Germany's Rising Birth Rates?" *Deutsche Welle.* https://www.dw.com/en/are-family-policy-reforms-to-thank-for-germanys-rising-birth-rates/a-43188961.

29 "2019. "All You Need to Know about the Latest in Hungary's Pro-Family Policy." *Fidesz - Magyar Polgári Szövetség.* https://fidesz-eu.hu/en/all-you-need-to-know-about-the-latest-in-hungarys-pro-family-policy/.

30 "2019. "All You Need to Know about the Latest in Hungary's Pro-Family Policy." *Fidesz - Magyar Polgári Szövetség*. https://fidesz-eu.hu/en/all-you-need-to-know-about-the-latest-in-hungarys-pro-family-policy/.

31 Pascale, Federica. 2023. "Italy Looks to Hungary to Solve Birth Rate Crisis." *EURACTIV*. https://www.euractiv.com/section/politics/news/italy-looks-to-hungary-to-solve-birth-rate-crisis/.

32 Pascale, Federica. 2023. "Italy Looks to Hungary to Solve Birth Rate Crisis." *EURACTIV*. https://www.euractiv.com/section/politics/news/italy-looks-to-hungary-to-solve-birth-rate-crisis/.

TAXES

1 Loughead, Katherine. 2024. "State Corporate Income Tax Rates and Brackets for 2024." *Tax Foundation*. https://taxfoundation.org/data/all/state/state-corporate-income-tax-rates-brackets-2024/.

2 "Overview of PRC Taxation System." *PwC*. https://www.pwccn.com/en/services/tax/accounting-and-payroll/overview-of-prc-taxation-system.html.

3 Yushkov, Andrey. 2024. "2024 State Individual Income Tax Rates and Brackets." *Tax Foundation*. https://taxfoundation.org/data/all/state/state-income-tax-rates-2024/.

4 Walczak, Jared. 2024. "State and Local Sales Tax Rates, 2024." *Tax Foundation*. https://taxfoundation.org/data/all/state/2024-sales-taxes/.

5 Hoffer, Adam, and Jessica Dobrinsky-Harris. 2023. "How High Are Gas Taxes in Your State?" *Tax Foundation*. https://taxfoundation.org/data/all/state/state-gas-tax-rates-2023/.

6 "Assembly's Proposed $245.8 Billion SFY 2024-25 Budget Invests in Making New York State a More Affordable Place to Live." *Speaker's Press Releases: New York State Assembly*. https://nyassembly.gov/Press/?sec=story&story=109523.

7 FPI Staff. 2024. "Florida Budget Proposals in Brief (FY 2024-25)." *Florida Policy Institute*. https://www.floridapolicy.org/posts/florida-budget-proposals-in-brief-fy-2024-25.

8 Tikkanen, Amy. "List of U.S. States by Population." *Encyclopædia Britannica*. https://www.britannica.com/topic/largest-U-S-state-by-population.

9 1992. "Presidential Debate in East Lansing, Michigan." *The American Presidency Project*. https://www.presidency.ucsb.edu/documents/presidential-debate-east-lansing-michigan.

10 Kartch, John. 2021. "A Timeline of Obama's $250,000 Tax Pledge." Americans for Tax Reform. https://www.atr.org/timeline-obamas-tax-pledge-a4529/.

11 Kartch, John. 2023. "Documentation of Biden's $400,000 Tax Pledge." *Americans for Tax Reform*. https://www.atr.org/bidenpledge/.

12 "Decennial Census of Population and Housing Data Tables." *United States Census Bureau.* https://www2.census.gov/programs-surveys/decennial/tables/time-series/coh-phone/phone-tab.txt.

13 2024. "What Is the Alternative Minimum Tax (AMT)?" *Tax Foundation.* https://taxfoundation.org/taxedu/glossary/alternative-minimum-tax-amt/.

14 Fleenor, Patrick, and Andrew Chamberlain. 2005. "Backgrounder on the Individual Alternative Minimum Tax (AMT)." *Tax Foundation.* https://taxfoundation.org/research/all/federal/backgrounder-individual-alternative-minimum-tax-amt/.

15 2024. "Who Pays the AMT?" *Tax Policy Center.* https://www.taxpolicycenter.org/briefing-book/who-pays-amt.

16 2017. "104 Years of the Income Tax: Then and Now." *Americans for Tax Reform.* https://www.atr.org/104-years-income-tax-then-and-now/.

17 Luscombe, Mark. 2022. "Historical Income Tax Rates." *Wolters Kluwer.* https://www.wolterskluwer.com/en/expert-insights/whole-ball-of-tax-historical-income-tax-rates.

18 Durante, Alex. 2024. "2024 Tax Brackets." *Tax Foundation.* https://taxfoundation.org/data/all/federal/2024-tax-brackets/.

19 2023. "IRS Provides Tax Inflation Adjustments for Tax Year 2024." *Internal Revenue Service.* https://www.irs.gov/newsroom/irs-provides-tax-inflation-adjustments-for-tax-year-2024.

20 2023. "IRS Provides Tax Inflation Adjustments for Tax Year 2024." *Internal Revenue Service.* https://www.irs.gov/newsroom/irs-provides-tax-inflation-adjustments-for-tax-year-2024.

21 2024. "Historical Federal Individual Income Tax Rates & Brackets, 1862-2021." *Tax Foundation.* https://taxfoundation.org/data/all/federal/historical-income-tax-rates-brackets/.

22 Carlson, Drew. 2021. "Poll: Raising Taxes on Businesses Will Increase Cost of Goods and Services, Harm Americans Making Less than $400K." *Americans for Tax Reform.* https://www.atr.org/poll-raising-taxes-on-businesses-will-increase-cost-of-goods-and-services-harm-americans-making-less-than-400k/.

23 Walczak, Jared. 2024. "State and Local Sales Tax Rates, 2024." *Tax Foundation.* https://taxfoundation.org/data/all/state/2024-sales-taxes/.

24 Yushkov, Andrey. 2024. "2024 State Individual Income Tax Rates and Brackets." *Tax Foundation.* https://taxfoundation.org/data/all/state/state-income-tax-rates-2024/.

25 2023. "Historical Highest Marginal Income Tax Rates." *Tax Policy Center.* https://www.taxpolicycenter.org/statistics/historical-highest-marginal-income-tax-rates.

26 2021. "Historical Federal Individual Income Tax Rates & Brackets, 1862-2021." *Tax Foundation.* https://taxfoundation.org/data/all/federal/historical-income-tax-rates-brackets/.

27 1996. "The Reagan Tax Cuts: Lessons for Tax Reform." *United States Congress Joint Economic Committee.* https://crab.rutgers.edu/users/mchugh/taxes/The%20Reagan%20Tax%20Cuts%20Lessons%20for%20Tax%20Reform.htm.

28 2021. "Historical Federal Individual Income Tax Rates & Brackets, 1862-2021." *Tax Foundation.* https://taxfoundation.org/data/all/federal/historical-income-tax-rates-brackets/.

29 1996. "The Reagan Tax Cuts: Lessons for Tax Reform." *United States Congress Joint Economic Committee.* https://crab.rutgers.edu/users/mchugh/taxes/The%20Reagan%20Tax%20Cuts%20Lessons%20for%20Tax%20Reform.htm.

30 1996. "The Reagan Tax Cuts: Lessons for Tax Reform." *United States Congress Joint Economic Committee.*

31 2022. "Monthly Budget Review: March 2022." *Congressional Budget Office.* https://www.cbo.gov/system/files/2022-04/57909-MBR.pdf.

32 2022. "Historical Budget Data." *Congressional Budget Office.* https://www.cbo.gov/system/files/2022-05/51134-2022-05-Historical-Budget-Data.xlsx.

33 2020. "Employment Expansion Continued in 2019, But Growth Slowed in Several Industries: Monthly Labor Review." *U.S. Bureau of Labor Statistics.* https://www.bls.gov/opub/mlr/2020/article/employment-expansion-continued-in-2019-but-growth-slowed-in-several-industries.htm.

34 Semega, Jessica, Melissa Kollar, Emily A. Shrider, and John Creamer. 2020. "Income and Poverty in the United States: 2019." *United States Census Bureau.* https://www.census.gov/library/publications/2020/demo/p60-270.html.

35 2024. Yushkov, Andrey. "2024 State Individual Income Tax Rates and Brackets." *Tax Foundation.* https://taxfoundation.org/data/all/state/state-income-tax-rates-2024/.

36 Kartch, John. 2019. "Kartch: Vice Gets History of the Death Tax Tragically Wrong." *The Daily Caller.* https://dailycaller.com/2019/01/05/kartch-vice-tax/.

DEBT

1 Heritage Foundation. 2024. "Public Debt for Every American." *Federal Budget in Pictures.* https://www.federalbudgetinpictures.com/public-debt-for-every-american/.

2 Heritage Foundation. 2024. "Public Debt for Every American." *Federal Budget in Pictures.* https://www.federalbudgetinpictures.com/public-debt-for-every-american/.

3 Ford, George S., Hyeongwoo Kim, and Lawrence J. Spiwak. 2017. "What Is the 'Cost per Regulator' on GDP and Private Sector Job Creation? An Update on Prior Research." *Phoenix Center for Advanced Legal & Economic Public Policy*

Studies. https://www.phoenix-center.org/perspectives/Perspective17-01Final.
pdf.

4   Riedl, Brian. 2023. "The Limits of Taxing the Rich." *Manhattan Institute.*
    https://manhattan.institute/article/the-limits-of-taxing-the-rich.

5   Source: 2024. "The Long-Term Budget Outlook: 2024 to 2054." *Congressional
    Budget Office.* https://www.cbo.gov/publication/60127.

6   2023. "The 2023 Annual Report of the Board of Trustees of the Federal Old-
    Age and Survivors Insurance and Federal Disability Insurance Trust Funds."
    Social Security Administration. https://www.ssa.gov/OACT/TR/2023/.

7   Higgs, Robert. 1987. *Crisis and Leviathan: Critical Episodes in the Growth of
    American Government.* Oxford University Press.

8   Source: Perry, Mark J. @Mark_J_Perry. 2024. X post. https://x.com/
    Mark_J_Perry/status/1747995005518516419.

9   Perry, Mark J. @Mark_J_Perry. 2024. X post. https://x.com/Mark_J_Perry/
    status/1747995005518516419.

10 Reinhart, Carmen M., and Kenneth S. Rogoff. 2010. "Growth in a Time
    of Debt." *National Bureau of Economic Research.* https://doi.org/10.3386/
    w15639.

11 2024. "The Long-Term Budget Outlook: 2024 to 2054." *Congressional Budget
    Office.* https://www.cbo.gov/publication/60127.

12 Source: 2024. "The Long-Term Budget Outlook: 2024 to 2054." *Congressional
    Budget Office.* https://www.cbo.gov/publication/60127.

13 Stein, Herbert. 1998. *What I Think: Essays on Economics, Politics, and Life.*
    American Enterprise Institute.

14 Mitchell, Daniel J. 2014. "The Golden Rule of Spending Restraint." *Inter-
    national Liberty.* https://danieljmitchell.wordpress.com/2014/04/07/the-
    golden-
    rule-of-spending-restraint/.

15 Source: Mitchell, Daniel J. 2023. "The Simple (But Definitely Not Easy) Way
    to Avert America's Fiscal Crisis." *International Liberty.* https://danieljmitchell.
    wordpress.com/2023/02/16/the-simple-but-definitely-not-easy-
    way-to-avert-americas-fiscal-crisis/.

16 Mitchell, Daniel J. 2023. "More Evidence for Switzerland's Spending Cap."
    International Liberty. https://danieljmitchell.wordpress.com/2023/03/18/
    more-evidence-for-switzerlands-spending-cap/.

17 Source: Mitchell, Daniel J. 2023. "More Evidence for Switzerland's Spending
    Cap." *International Liberty.* https://danieljmitchell.wordpress.com/
    2023/03/18/more-evidence-for-switzerlands-spending-cap/.

ENERGY

[1] "Climate Change." *UNICEF.* https://www.unicefusa.org/what-unicef-does/
     emergency-response/climate-change#:~:text=Yet%20nearly%20half%20
     the%20world's,environmental%20hazards%2C%20shocks%20and%20stresses.
[2] 2024. "Biden-Harris Administration Announces Temporary Pause on Pending
     Approvals of Liquefied Natural Gas Exports." *The White House.* https://
     www.whitehouse.gov/briefing-room/statements-releases/2024/01/26/
     fact-sheet-biden-harris-administration-announces-temporary-pause-on-pend-
     ing-approvals-of-liquefied-natural-gas-exports/#:~:text=Today%2C%20
     the%20Biden%2DHarris%20Administration,the%20underlying%20
     analyses%20for%20authorizations.
[3] Daly, Matthew. 2024. "Liquefied Natural Gas: What to Know About LNG and
     Biden's Decision to Delay Gas Export Proposals." *Associated Press.* https://
     apnews.com/article/lng-exports-biden-europe-climate-russia-24a7730a3b-
     8449273fec73824ce26001.
[4] "Fifth Amendment." *United States Constitution.* https://www.law.cornell.
     edu/wex/fifth_amendment#:~:text=A%20right%20against%20forced%20
     self,market%20value%20of%20the%20property.

ESG AND DEI

[1] ARTE.tv Documentary. 2023. "Sri Lanka: Food Crisis." YouTube video.
     https://www.youtube.com/watch?v=v1OvVzFuNOI.
[2] Stiglitz, Joseph E. 2016. "What's Next for Sri Lanka?" *World Economic Forum.*
     https://www.weforum.org/agenda/2016/02/what-next-for-sri-lanka/.
[3] 2021. "Speech by President Gotabaya Rajapaksa at the 'Rediscovering Nitro-
     gen: Solutions and Synergies for Climate Change, Health, Biodiversity and
     Circular Economy.'" https://web.archive.org/web/20230619183900/https:/
     slembassyusa.org/new/media-center/news/2409-speech-by-president-gota-
     baya-rajapaksa-at-the-rediscovering-nitrogen-solutions-and-synergies-for-cli-
     mate-change-health-biodiversity-and-circular-economy-cop26-side-event-scot-
     land-uk-on-31-october-2021.html.
[4] Mashal, Mujib, and Skandha Gunasekara. 2023. "Sri Lanka is Calm Again. That
     Doesn't Mean Things are Any Better." *New York Times.* https://www.nytimes.
     com/2023/01/31/business/sri-lanka-economy.html.
[5] Shukla, Archana. 2022. "Sri Lanka's Children Go Hungry as Food Prices Soar."
     BBC. https://www.bbc.com/news/business-63868497.
[6] Blackmon, David. 2022. "Rising Social Unrest Over Energy,
     Food Shortages Threatens Global Stability," *Forbes.* https://
     www.forbes.com/sites/davidblackmon/2022/07/10/

rising-social-unrest-over-energy-food-shortages-threatens-global-stability/?sh=1861ae40568b.

7   Ashing, Inger. 2021. "Children Face Life with More Heatwaves, Floods, Droughts and Wildfires than Their Grandparents." *World Economic Forum.* https://www.weforum.org/agenda/2021/10/climate-change-crisis-child-rights-crisis-save-the-children-cop26/.

8   Peries, Marilu Gresens. 2021. "Tool for Investors on Integrating Children's Rights into ESG Assessment," *UNICEF.* https://www.unicef.ca/sites/default/files/2021-04/Tool-for-Investors-on-Integrating-Childrens-Rights-Into-ESG-Assessment.pdf.

9   2021. "Speech by President Gotabaya Rajapaksa at the 'Rediscovering Nitrogen: Solutions and Synergies for Climate Change, Health, Biodiversity and Circular Economy.'" https://web.archive.org/web/20230619183900/https:/slembassyusa.org/new/media-center/news/2409-speech-by-president-gotabaya-rajapaksa-at-the-rediscovering-nitrogen-solutions-and-synergies-for-climate-change-health-biodiversity-and-circular-economy-cop26-side-event-scotland-uk-on-31-october-2021.html.

10   Phillips, Matt. 2021. "Exxon Board Defeat Signals Rise of Social-Good Activists." *New York Times.* https://www.nytimes.com/2021/06/09/business/exxon-mobil-engine-no1-activist.html.

11   Ramaswamy, Vivek. 2022. "Shareholder Stand Up for Profit and Against ESG at Chevron." *Wall Street Journal.* https://www.wsj.com/articles/shareholders-stand-up-for-profit-at-chevron-esg-big-three-blackrock-vanguard-state-street-paris-agreement-scope-3-emissions-strive-11662558395.

12   Blunt, Katherine. 2020. "California Blackouts a Warning for States Ramping Up Green Power." *Wall Street Journal.* https://www.wsj.com/articles/california-blackouts-a-warning-for-states-ramping-up-green-power-11597706934.

13   Upham, Becky. 2022. "Severe Weather and Power Outages Create a Perfect Storm for Carbon Monoxide Poisoning." *Everyday Health.* https://www.everydayhealth.com/public-health/severe-weather-and-power-outages-create-a-perfect-storm-for-carbon-monoxide-poisoning/.

14   Northrop, Alexander J., Nina M. Flores, Vivian Do, Perry E. Sheffield, and Joan A. Casey. 2024. "Power Outages and Pediatric Unintentional Injury Hospitalizations in New York State." *Environmental Epidemiology* 8 (1). https://www.ncbi.nlm.nih.gov/pmc/articles/PMC10852386/.

15   Shellenberger, Michael. 2019. "Why Climate Alarmism Hurts Us All." *Forbes.* https://www.forbes.com/sites/michaelshellenberger/2019/12/04/why-climate-alarmism-hurts-us-all/?sh=9cdcf8736d89.

16   Shellenberger, Michael. 2019. "Why Climate Alarmism Hurts Us All." *Forbes.* https://www.forbes.com/sites/michaelshellenberger/2019/12/04/why-climate-alarmism-hurts-us-all/?sh=9cdcf8736d89.

[17] Shead, Sam. 2021. "Climate Change is Making People Think Twice About Having Children." *CNBC*. https://www.cnbc.com/2021/08/12/climate-change-is-making-people-think-twice-about-having-children.html.

[18] Tolhurst, Ben. 2023. "Over 300 Business Leaders are Joining XR's Climate Protest—Here's Why." *Business Green*. https://www.businessgreen.com/opinion/4112583/300-business-leaders-joining-xrs-climate-protest-heres.

[19] Kenway, Natalie. 2021. "BlackRock to Vote Against Corporates with Limited Net-Zero Planning." *PA Future*. https://future.portfolio-adviser.com/blackrock-to-vote-against-corporates-with-limited-net-zero-planning/.

[20] "Diversity Equity and Inclusion: Our Differences Makes Us Stronger." *Vanguard*. https://corporate.vanguard.com/content/corporatesite/us/en/corp/who-we-are/we-care-about/diversity-equity-inclusion.html.

[21] 2022. "BlackRock Impact Opportunities Fund: Annual Impact Report—Inaugural Edition." *BlackRock*. https://www.blackrock.com/us/individual/literature/presentation/bio-annual-impact-report-2022.pdf.

[22] Hirst, Scott, and Lucian Bebchuk. 2022. "Big Three Power, and Why it Matters." *Boston University Law Review* 102. https://scholarship.law.bu.edu/cgi/viewcontent.cgi?article=4318&context=faculty_scholarship.

[23] Hronich, Maggie. 2022. "Leaked Videos Expose Disney's 'Not-At-All-Secret Gay Agenda.'" *Daily Signal*. https://www.dailysignal.com/2022/03/30/leaked-videos-expose-disneys-not-at-all-secret-gay-agenda/.

[24] Lencki, Maria. 2023. "Disney Is 'Digging Its Own Grave' with Woke Nonsense: Karol Markowicz," Fox News. https://www.foxnews.com/media/disney-digging-grave-woke-nonsense-karol-markowicz.

[25] "2022-2023 ESG Report." *Paramount*. https://www.paramount.com/sites/g/files/dxjhpe226/files/2023-10/2023_Paramount_ESG_Report_v3.pdf.

[26] Clark, Kelby. 2020. "How MTV News and Logo Give Voice to Marginalized Audiences." *Paramount*. https://www.paramount.com/news/how-mtv-news-and-logo-give-voice-to-marginalized-audiences.

[27] "Trans Lifeline: Finalists in LGBTQ+." *5th Annual Shorty Social Good Awards*. https://shortyawards.com/5th-socialgood/trans-lifeline.

[28] Artavia, David. 2021. "'Blues Clues' Rings in Pride Month in New Sing-Sing, Starring Drag Queen Nina West, Celebrating LGBTQ Families." *Yahoo*. https://www.yahoo.com/entertainment/blues-clues-rings-pride-month-drag-queen-nina-west-lgbtq-families-174301686.html.

[29] Anderson, Ryan T. 2018. "Transgender Ideology Hurts Kids." *Heritage Foundation*. https://www.heritage.org/gender/commentary/transgender-ideology-hurts-kids.

[30] Kennedy, Dana. 2023. "Inside the CEI System Pushing Brands to Endorse Celebs Like Dylan Mulvaney." *New York Post*. https://nypost.com/2023/04/07/inside-the-woke-scoring-system-guiding-american-companies/.

[31] 2024. "Corporate Sponsors," Human Rights Campaign. https://www.hrc.org/about/corporate-partners.

32 Dickson, EJ. 2024. "The Right Is Trying to Make Bud Light Happen All Over Again with a Doritos Boycott." *Rolling Stone.* https://www.rollingstone.com/culture/culture-news/boycottdoritos-spanish-trans-influencer-samantha-hudson-1234981041/.

33 Grossman, Hannah. 2024. "North Face Offers Discount for Customers Taking Equity Course that Says Black People Can't Enjoy the Outdoors." *Fox Business.* https://www.foxbusiness.com/media/north-face-offers-discount-customers-taking-equity-course-says-black-people-cant-enjoy-outdoors.

34 Zilber, Ariel. 2023. "Target's 'Tuck-Friendly' Swimwear for Kids Sparks Outcry: 'Bud Light 2.0.'" *New York Post.* https://nypost.com/2023/05/19/targets-tuck-friendly-swimwear-for-kids-sparks-controversy/.

35 Flood, Brian, and Suzanne O'Halloran. 2023. "Target Market Cap Losses Hit $15.7 Billion, Shares Approach 52-Week Low Amid Woke Backlash." *Fox Business.* https://www.foxbusiness.com/media/target-market-cap-losses-hit-15-7-billion-share-near-52-week-low-amid-woke-backlash.

36 Aratani, Lauren. "Target Sees Drop in Sales After Rightwing Backlash to Pride Merchandise." *The Guardian.* https://www.theguardian.com/us-news/2023/aug/16/target-sales-drop-second-quarter-lgbt-pride-merchandise-conservative.

RELIGIOUS LIBERTY

1 2018. "Brief of Amici Curiae Former Foster Children and Foster/Adoptive Parents and Catholic Association Foundation in Support of Petitioners." *United States District Court for the Eastern District of Pennsylvania.* https://becketnews-ite.s3.amazonaws.com/Declaration-of-Doe-Foster-Mother-1-in-Sharonell-Fulton-v.-City-of-Philadelphia.pdf.

2 "Catholic Charity Statistics: Market Report & Data." https://gitnux.org/catholic-charity-statistics/.

3 Zinsmeister, Karl. 2019. "Less God, Less Giving?" *Philanthropy Magazine.* https://www.philanthropyroundtable.org/magazine/less-god-less-giving/.

4 King, David P. 2018. "Religion, Charity, and Philanthropy in America." *Oxford Research Encyclopedia of Religion.* https://oxfordre.com/religion/display/10.1093/acrefore/9780199340378.001.0001/acrefore-9780199340378-e-435?p=emailAaKvgKXVHeQ8o&d=/10.1093/acrefore/9780199340378.001.0001/acrefore-9780199340378-e-435.

5 2009. "Mental Health Effects of Poverty, Hunger, and Homelessness on Children and Teens." *American Psychological Association.* https://www.apa.org/topics/socioeconomic-status/poverty-hunger-homelessness-children.

6 Rothman, Lily. 2015. "When Fidel Castro Canceled Santa Claus." *TIME.* https://time.com/3652532/cuba-epiphany-feast-christmas/.

[7]   2023. "Maryland Parents Sue for Right to Opt Kids Out of 'Pride' Storybooks." *Becket Law.* https://www.becketlaw.org/media/maryland-parents-sue-for-right-to-opt-kids-out-of-pride-storybooks/.

[8]   2023. "School Board and County Officials Hide While Students are Doxed." *Clean Slate MoCo.* https://www.cleanslatemoco.com/school-board-and-county-officials-hide-while-students-are-doxed/1285.

[9]   Haidt, Jonathan. "Why the Mental Health of Liberal Girls Sank First and Fastest." *The Free Press.* https://www.thefp.com/p/why-the-mental-health-of-liberal.

[10]   Fernández, Víctor Manuel, and Armando Matteo. 2024. "Declaration of the Dicastery for the Doctrine of the Faith 'Dignitas Infinita' on Human Dignity." *Holy See Press Office.* https://press.vatican.va/content/salastampa/en/bollettino/pubblico/2024/04/08/240408c.html.

[11]   2019. Barr, William. "Attorney General William P. Barr Delivers Remarks to the Law School and the de Nicola Center for Ethics and Culture at the University of Notre Dame." *Office of Public Affairs, U.S. Department of Justice.* https://www.justice.gov/opa/speech/attorney-general-william-p-barr-delivers-remarks-law-school-and-de-nicola-center-ethics.

[12]   Zinsmeister, Karl. 2019. "Less God, Less Giving?" *Philanthropy Magazine.* https://www.philanthropyroundtable.org/magazine/less-god-less-giving/.

[13]   Foley, Ryan. 2022. "Christiam Millennials Give 3 Times More Money to Charity Than Non-Religious Counterparts: Study." *Christian Post.* https://www.christianpost.com/news/christian-young-adults-give-more-to-charity-than-non-christians.html.

[14]   Zinsmeister, Karl. 2019. "Less God, Less Giving?" *Philanthropy Magazine.* https://www.philanthropyroundtable.org/magazine/less-god-less-giving/.

[15]   *Fulton et al. v. City of Philadelphia, Pennsylvania, et al.* https://becketnewsite.s3.amazonaws.com/Former-Foster-Children-and-Parents-and-TCA-Fulton-Amicus-Brief.pdf.

[16]   *Fulton et al. v. City of Philadelphia, Pennsylvania, et al.* https://becketnewsite.s3.amazonaws.com/Former-Foster-Children-and-Parents-and-TCA-Fulton-Amicus-Brief.pdf.

EDUCATION

[1]   Allen, Virginia. 2022. "This Mom Says Transgender Movement Took Her Daughter's Life." *Daily Signal.* https://www.dailysignal.com/2022/03/21/this-mom-says-transgender-movement-took-her-daughters-life/.

[2]   Mordock, Jeff. 2022. "Biden Tells Teachers That Kids Are 'Like Yours When They Are in the Classroom.'" *Washington Times.* https://www.washingtontimes.com/news/2022/apr/28/biden-tells-teachers-kids-are-yours-when-they-are-/.

3   Stewart, Steve. 2021. "Tallahassee Mom: 'Gender Ideology Almost Destroyed My Family.'" *Tallahassee Reports*. https://tallahasseereports.com/2021/12/02/tallahassee-mom-gender-ideology-almost-destroyed-my-family/.

4   "Whole School, Whole Community, Whole Child (WSCC)." *CDC Healthy Schools*. https://www.cdc.gov/healthyschools/wscc/index.htm.

5   "The Nation's Report Card | NAEP." https://nces.ed.gov/nationsreportcard/. *National Center for Education Statistics*.

6   Jemal, Alexis. 2017. "Critical Consciousness: A Critique and Critical Analysis of the Literature." *The Urban Review* 49 (4). https://doi.org/10.1007/s11256-017-0411-3; El-Amin, Aaliyah, Daren Graves, Jamie Johannsen, Jalene Tamerat, Madora Soutter, Shelby Clark, Saira Malhotra, and Scott Seider. 2024. "Critical Consciousness: A Key to Student Achievement." *Kappan*. https://kappanonline.org/critical-consciousness-key-student-achievement/.

7   Gewertz, Catherine. 2023. "Teaching Math Through a Social Justice Lens." *Education Week*. https://www.edweek.org/teaching-learning/teaching-math-through-a-social-justice-lens/2020/12.

8   Quayson, Ato, and Ankhi Mukherjee, eds. 2024. *Decolonizing the English Literary Curriculum*. Cambridge University. https://assets.cambridge.org/97810092/99954/frontmatter/9781009299954_frontmatter.pdf.

9   Donlevy, Katherine, and Steven Vago. 2023. "Cooper Union Barricades Jewish Students Inside Library." *New York Post*. https://nypost.com/2023/10/25/news/cooper-union-barricades-jewish-students-inside-library/.

10   Eden, Max. 2019. "Graduation Inflation Is Harming Students." *RealClear Education*. https://www.realcleareducation.com/articles/2019/02/13/graduation_inflation_is_harming_students_110315.html.

11   Van Fleet, Xi. 2023. *Mao's America*. Center Street.

12   Turner, Cory. 2020. "When Should Schools Close for Coronavirus?" *NPR*. https://www.npr.org/2020/03/11/814438424/when-should-schools-close-for-coronavirus.

13   Mervosh, Sarah, Claire Cain Miller, and Francesca Paris. 2024. "What the Data Says about Pandemic School Closures, Four Years Later." *New York Times*. https://www.nytimes.com/2024/03/18/upshot/pandemic-school-closures-data.html.

14   American Academy of Pediatrics. (@AmerAcadPeds). 2021. X post. https://x.com/AmerAcadPeds/status/1425857041457942542.

15   Wyckoff, Alyson Sulaski. 2023. "AAP Reaffirms Gender-Affirming Care Policy, Authorizes Systematic Review of Evidence to Guide Update." *American Academy of Pediatrics*. https://publications.aap.org/aapnews/news/25340/AAP-reaffirms-gender-affirming-care-policy?

16 Antonucci, Mike. 2021. "New Numbers: The National Education Association and the American Federation of Teachers Now Represent 1 in 4 U.S. Union Members." *The 74*. https://www.the74million.org/article/aft-nea-1-in-4-us-union-members/.

17 jduffus. 2022. "New GAI Report Shows Where the Money Goes." *Government Accountability Institute*. https://g-a-i.org/2022/10/31/from-academics-to-activists-teachers-unions-reimagine-spending-priorities/.

18 jduffus. 2022. "New Report from GAI Exposes Teachers Union Misuse of Power." *Government Accountability Office*. https://g-a-i.org/2022/02/27/teachers-unions-from-academics-to-activists/.

19 Post Editorial Board. 2022. "New York Keeps Spending More on Schools and Getting Less Results." *New York Post*. https://nypost.com/2022/01/30/new-york-keeps-spending-more-on-schools-and-getting-less-results/.

20 Zimmer, Amy, and Alex Zimmerman. 2023. "Participation in Parent Conferences Has Plunged 40% since COVID Remote Meetings Began." *The City*. https://www.thecity.nyc/2023/11/13/parent-teacher-conferences-remote-covid-teachers-union/.

21 2014. "Mission." American Federation of Teachers. https://www.aft.org/about/mission.

22 Chasmar, Jessica. 2023. "Randi Weingarten Says 'Biden Transition Team' Was First to Solicit Union's Advice on Schools Reopening." *Fox News*. https://www.foxnews.com/politics/randi-weingarten-covid-19-school-lockdowns.

23 2020. "As K12 Education Funding Jumps Dramatically, Still Just 54% of Funding Spent on Instruction." *MacIver Institute*. https://www.maciverinstitute.com/2020/03/as-school-spending-rises-just-54-of-funding-spent-on-instruction/.

24 Milyutin, Evgeny. 2022. "Why Don't We Spend More Time Teaching Math?" *District Administration*. https://districtadministration.com/da-op-ed-why-dont-we-spend-more-time-teaching-math/; Eden, Max. 2022. "The Trouble with Social Emotional Learning." *American Enterprise Institute*. https://www.aei.org/research-products/testimony/the-trouble-with-social-emotional-learning/.

25 Bernstein, Brittany. 2021. "Speaker Kicked Out of Florida School Board Meeting for Reading from Sexually Explicit School Library Book." *National Review*. https://www.nationalreview.com/news/speaker-kicked-out-of-florida-school-board-meeting-for-reading-from-sexually-explicit-school-library-book/.

26 Poff, Jeremiah. 2022. "Florida Parents Sue School District over Daughter's Secret Gender Transition." *Washington Examiner*. https://www.washingtonexaminer.com/news/2872212/florida-parents-sue-school-district-over-daughters-secret-gender-transition/.

27 Lyell, Kelly. 2023. "PSD Faces Lawsuit after 2021 Gender and Sexualities Alliance Meeting in Wellington." *Fort Collins Coloradoan*. https://www.coloradoan.

com/story/news/2023/05/04/poudre-school-district-being-sued-over-transgender-policies/70183728007/.

[28] Sacca, Paul. 2023. "Twitter Begins Suspending Users for Using the Term 'Groomer' After Pressure from the Left; Cultural Critic James Lindsay Locked out of His Account." *Blaze Media.* https://www.theblaze.com/news/twitter-groomer-bans-james-lindsay.

[29] Five years ago, neither Tina nor I had any idea we would be spearheading the largest parental rights movement in the country. We were just selling T-shirts that read, "We do not coparent with the government." The $150,000 of sales tipped us off that it was time for moms to unite.

[30] Details in the family chapter of this book.

[31] *Meyer v. Nebraska* (1923). This case dealt with a Nebraska law that prohibited the teaching of any modern language other than English in both public and private schools until the ninth grade. The Supreme Court held that the law violated the Due Process Clause of the Fourteenth Amendment because it infringed upon the rights of parents to control the education of their children.

Pierce v. Society of Sisters (1925). The Court ruled in this case that an Oregon law requiring children to attend public schools was unconstitutional. The decision affirmed the rights of parents to choose alternative forms of education, such as private or religious schools, for their children.

Wisconsin v. Yoder (1972). This case involved Amish parents who objected to a Wisconsin law requiring their children to attend school until age sixteen. The Supreme Court held that the state's interest in compulsory education did not outweigh the parents' First Amendment right to freedom of religion, affirming the parents' authority to direct the upbringing and education of their children.

Troxel v. Granville (2000). In this case, the Court addressed the issue of grandparent visitation rights. The Court ruled that a Washington state law allowing any person to petition for visitation rights over a parent's objections was unconstitutional. The decision upheld the fundamental right of parents to make decisions concerning the care, custody, and control of their children.

[32] "About Moms for Liberty." *Moms for Liberty.* https://www.momsforliberty.org/.

[33] Seville, Michael. 2005. "Getting Parents Involved Is the Foundation of Student Success." *Edutopia.* https://www.edutopia.org/parent-involvement-mcauliffe-step.

[34] Dunleavy, Jerry. 2021. "Garland Defends DOJ Memo Despite NSBA Letter Being Withdrawn." *Washington Examiner.* https://www.washingtonexaminer.com/news/1077243/garland-defends-doj-memo-despite-nsba-letter-being-withdrawn/.

[35] Nelson, Joshua Q. 2023. "Moms for Liberty Founder's Testimony Torches DOJ for Targeting Parents: 'There Must Be Accountability.'" *Fox News.* https://

www.foxnews.com/media/moms-liberty-founders-testimony-torches-doj-targeting-parents-accountability.

36 Brooks, Emily. 2023. "Tensions Flare in 'Weaponization' Panel Hearing with Sidelined FBI Agents." *The Hill.* https://thehill.com/homenews/house/4011296-tensions-flare-in-weaponization-panel-hearing-with-sidelined-fbi-agents.

37 2025. *Mandate for Leadership: The Conservative Promise.* Heritage Foundation. https://shop.heritage.org/products/mandate-for-leadership-2025.

38 Poff, Jeremiah. 2023. "Every State That Passed or Expanded School Choice in 2023." *Washington Examiner.* https://www.washingtonexaminer.com/news/1629825/every-state-that-passed-or-expanded-school-choice-in-2023/.

39 DeAngelis, Corey A. 2021. "The COVID-19 Pandemic Has Shown Why We Should Fund Students, Not Systems." *Reason Foundation.* https://reason.org/commentary/the-covid-19-pandemic-has-shown-why-we-should-fund-students-not-systems/.

40 Staff. 2023. "Governor Ron DeSantis Signs Historic Legislation to Expand School Choice Options to All Florida Students." *Ron DeSantis.* https://www.flgov.com/2023/03/27/governor-ron-desantis-signs-historic-legislation-to-expand-school-choice-options-to-all-florida-students/; Staff. 2022; "Governor Ron DeSantis Announces $89 Million for Workforce Education Initiatives, Bringing Total Investment to Greater Than $3.5 Billion Since 2019." *Ron DeSantis.* https://www.flgov.com/2022/02/02/governor-ron-desantis-announces-89-million-for-workforce-education-initiatives-bringing-total-investment-to-greater-than-3-5-billion-since-2019/.

41 Staff. 2024. "Governor DeSantis Signs Legislation Further Enhancing Florida's Education Standards on the Evils of Communism." *Ron DeSantis.* https://www.flgov.com/2024/04/17/governor-desantis-signs-legislation-further-enhancing-floridas-education-standards-on-the-evils-of-communism/#:~:text=HIALEAH%20GARDENS%2C%20Fla.%E2%80%94Today,%2C%E2%80%9D%20said%20Governor%20Ron%20DeSantis.

42 Atterbury, Andrew. 2022. "Review of DeSantis Lays out "Blueprint" to Elect More Conservatives on School Boards." *Politico.* https://www.politico.com/news/2022/12/20/desantis-lays-out-blueprint-to-elect-more-conservatives-on-school-boards-00074806.

43 "Senate Bill 256 (2023)." *The Florida Senate.* https://www.flsenate.gov/Session/Bill/2023/256.

44 Burgess, Brian. 2022. "Inside the DeSantis Freedom Blueprint Education Conference." *The Capitolist.* https://thecapitolist.com/inside-the-desantis-freedom-blueprint-education-conference/.

45 "Protecting Parental Rights at the State Level." *Parental Rights Foundation.* https://parentalrights.org/states/.

46 Jacobson, Linda. 2023. "The Mystery of Ryan Walters: How a Beloved History Teacher Became Oklahoma's Culture-Warrior-in-Chief." *The 74.* https://www.

the74million.org/article/the-mystery-of-ryan-walters-how-a-beloved-history-teacher-became-oklahomas-culture-warrior-in-chief/

[47]   Graham Lee, "Governor Henry McMaster Signs 'Read to Succeed' Bill at Local Elementary School," March 27, 2024 https://www.wjbf.com/news/south-carolina-news/governor-henry-mcmaster-signs-read-to-succeed-bill-at-local-elementary-school/; "Arkansas." *LEARNS*, https://learns.ade.arkansas.gov/

[48]   Grajeda, Antoinette. 2023. "What Is the Arkansas LEARNS Act?" *Arkansas Advocate*. https://arkansasadvocate.com/2023/03/08/how-will-the-learns-act-impact-arkansas-families/.

[49]   2023. "2022 K-12 Louisiana Student Standards for Social Studies." *Louisiana Department of Education*. https://www.louisianabelieves.com/docs/default-source/academic-curriculum/k-12-louisiana-student-standards-for-social-studies.pdf?sfvrsn=df396518_34.

DIGITAL TECHNOLOGY

[1]   Steadman, Otillia. 2020. "Lost Year," Buzzfeed News. https://www.buzzfeednews.com/article/otilliasteadman/lost-year-coronavirus-little-boy-bronx.

[2]   2020. "City of Columbus Announces CARES Act Funding for Columbus City Schools," *Inside Columbus City Schools*. https://www.ccsoh.us/site/default.aspx?PageType=3&DomainID=1643&ModuleInstanceID=125&ViewID=6446EE88-D30C-497E-9316-3F8874B3E108&RenderLoc=0&FlexDataID=24507&PageID=2383.

[3]   Stokes, Kyle. 2020. "In LAUSD, 'Just About Every' Student Now Has a Laptop To Use During the Pandemic." *LAist*. https://laist.com/news/lausd-schools-laptop-chromebook-ipad-distribution-complete-beutner-update.

[4]   2022. "Reading and Mathematics Scores Decline During COVID-19 Pandemic." *The Nation's Report Card*, 2022. https://www.nationsreportcard.gov/highlights/ltt/2022/; Cineas, Fabiola. 2024. "Why So Many Kids Are Still Missing School." *Vox*. https://www.vox.com/2024/1/9/23904542/chronic-absenteeism-school-attendance.

[5]   Singer, Natasha. 2017. "Apple's Devices Lose Luster in American Classrooms." *New York Times*. https://www.nytimes.com/2017/03/02/technology/apple-products-schools-education.html.

[6]   Singer, Natasha. 2017/ "How Google Took Over the Classroom." *New York Times*. https://www.nytimes.com/2017/05/13/technology/google-education-chromebooks-schools.html.

7   Hirsh-Pasek, K., J.M. Zosh, R.M. Golinkoff, J.H. Gray, M.B. Robb, and J. Kaufman. 2015. "Putting Education in 'Educational' Apps: Lessons from the Science of Learning." *Psychological Science in the Public Interest* 16 (1). https://doi.org/10.1177/1529100615569721.

8   Lenhart, Amanda. 2015. "A Majority of American Teens Report Access to a Computer, Game Console, Smartphone and a Tablet." *Pew Research Center.* https://www.pewresearch.org/internet/2015/04/09/a-majority-of-american-teens-report-access-to-a-computer-game-console-smartphone-and-a-tablet/.

9   2018. "Screen Time vs. Lean Time." Centers for Disease Control and Prevention. https://archive.cdc.gov/#/details?url=https://www.cdc.gov/nccdphp/dnpao/multimedia/infographics/getmoving.html.

10   GilPress. 2023. "Average Screen Time Statistics (2024)." *What's the Big Data.* https://whatsthebigdata.com/average-screen-time-stats/#google_vignette.

11   Guilherme Borges et al. 2021. "Gaming Disorder in DSM-5 and ICD-11: A Case of the Glass Half Empty or Half Full." *Canadian Journal of Psychiatry* 66 (5). https://journals.sagepub.com/doi/10.1177/0706743720948431.

12   Kardaras, Nicholas. 2016. *Glow Kids: How Screen Addiction Is Hijacking Our Kids—and How to Break the Trance.* St. Martin's Press.

13   Brockmyer, JF. 2022. "Desensitization and Violent Video Games: Mechanisms and Evidence." *Child and Adolescent Psychiatric Clinics of North America* 31 (1). https://pubmed.ncbi.nlm.nih.gov/34801150/.

14   Kardaras, Nicholas. 2016. *Glow Kids: How Screen Addiction Is Hijacking Our Kids—and How to Break the Trance.* St. Martin's Press.

15   Haidt, Jon. 2024. "Marshall McLuhan on Why Content Moderation Is a Red Herring." *After Babel.* Substack. https://www.afterbabel.com/p/content-moderation-red-herring.

16   2014. "Reading Apps for Kids Are A 'Digital Wild West' with Few Guideposts." *Joan Ganz Cooney Center.* https://joanganzcooneycenter.org/press/reading-apps-for-kids-are-a-digital-wild-west-with-few-guideposts/.

17   DeLisa, Caden. 2023. "New Law Protects Student Data Privacy, Restricts Targeted Advertising on Education Apps." *The Capitolist.* https://thecapitolist.com/new-law-protects-student-data-privacy-restricts-targeted-advertising-on-education-apps/.

18   Stokes, Kyle. 2020. "In LAUSD, 'Just About Every' Student Now Has a Laptop to Use During the Pandemic." *LAist.* https://laist.com/news/lausd-schools-laptop-chromebook-ipad-distribution-complete-beutner-update.

19   Yeskel, Zach. 2014. "Previewing a New Classroom." *The Keyword.* https://laist.com/news/lausd-schools-laptop-chromebook-ipad-distribution-complete-beutner-update.

20 Ladd, Brian. 2008. "Roadkill: The New Machine Flattens Its Critics," from *Autophobia: Love and Hate in the Automotive Age.* University of Chicago Press. https://press.uchicago.edu/Misc/Chicago/467412.html.

21 Singer, Natasha. 2017. "How Google Took Over the Classroom." *New York Times.* https://www.nytimes.com/2017/05/13/technology/google-education-chromebooks-schools.html.

22 Lindsay, Jared. 2021. "Evolution of the Scientific Calculator." *BestReviews.* https://kdvr.com/reviews/br/electronics-br/calculators-br/evolution-of-the-scientific-calculator/#:~:text=The%20arithmometer%20and%20comptometer,arithmetic%20operations%20without%20human%20intervention.

23 Kosoff, Maya. 2019. "Big Calculator: How Texas Instruments Monopolized Math Class." *Medium.* https://gen.medium.com/big-calculator-how-texas-instruments-monopolized-math-class-67ee165045dc.

24 Pang, William. 2016. "The Common High-School Tool That's Banned in College." *The Atlantic.* https://www.theatlantic.com/education/archive/2016/12/the-conundrum-of-calculators-in-the-classroom/493961/.

25 Douglas, Ronald G., ed. 1986. *Toward a Lean and Lively Calculus. Mathematical Association of America.* https://maa.org/sites/default/files/pdf/pubs/books/members/NTE6_optimized.pdf.

26 Moran, Melanie. 2008. "Calculators Okay in Math Class, If Students Know the Facts First." *Vanderbilt University Research.* https://news.vanderbilt.edu/2008/08/19/calculators-okay-in-math-class-if-students-know-the-facts-first-62879/.

27 Schwartz, Charles I. 2023. "Screen Time and Children." *Medline Plus.* https://medlineplus.gov/ency/patientinstructions/000355.htm#:~:text=Most%20American%20children%20spend%20about,child%20to%20sleep%20at%20night.

28 Muppalla, SK, S Vuppalapati, A Reddy Pulliahgaru, and H Sreenivasulu. 2023. "Effects of Excessive Screen Time on Child Development: An Updated Review and Strategies for Management." *Cureus* 15 (6). https://www.ncbi.nlm.nih.gov/pmc/articles/PMC10353947/#:~:text=Studies%20have%20indicated%20that%20compared,poorer%20vocabulary%20acquisition%20%5B15%5D.

29 Hutton, John S. 2022. "Screen Usage Linked to Brain Differences in Brain Structure in Young Children." *Cincinnati Children's Hospital.* https://scienceblog.cincinnatichildrens.org/screen-usage-linked-to-differences-in-brain-structure-in-young-children/.

30 2015. "The Decrease of the Senses and the Evolution of the Fast Brain." *AWSNA Waldorf High School Research Project.* https://www.waldorflibrary.org/articles/617-the-decrease-of-the-senses-and-the-evolution-of-the-fast-brain.

31 Nelson, Carlota. 2024. "Babies Need Humans, Not Screens." *UNICEF.* https://www.unicef.org/parenting/child-development/babies-screen-time.

32 Bilton, Nick. 2024. "Steve Jobs Was a Low-Tech Parent." *New York Times*. https://www.nytimes.com/2014/09/11/fashion/steve-jobs-apple-was-a-low-tech-parent.html.

33 Leskin, Paige. 2018. "Google Ceo Sundar Pichai Says His Family TV Is 'Not Easily Accessible' and Requires 'Activation Energy' to Watch." *Business Insider*. https://www.businessinsider.com/google-ceo-sundar-pichai-limits-family-tech-tv-access-2018-11.

34 Hu, Charlotte. 2024. "Why Writing by Hand Is Better for Memory and Learning." *Scientific American*. https://www.scientificamerican.com/article/why-writing-by-hand-is-better-for-memory-and-learning/.

35 Creamer, Ella. 2023. "Reading Print Improves Comprehension Far More Than Looking at Digital Text, Say Researchers." https://www.theguardian.com/books/2023/dec/15/reading-print-improves-comprehension-far-more-than-looking-at-digital-text-say-researchers#:~:text=Reading%20print%20texts%20improves%20comprehension,which%20assessed%20nearly%20470%2C000%20participants.

36 Reber, Debbie. 2023. "Dr. Katie Davis on Digital Media's Role in the Lives of Differently Wired Kids." *Tilt Parenting* podcast, Episode 334. https://tiltparenting.com/2023/07/11/digital-media-kids/.

37 Oppenheimer, Todd. 2004. *The Flickering Mind: Saving Education from the False Promise of Technology*. Random House.

38 Justus J. Randolph et al. 2023. "Montessori Education's Impact on Academic and Nonacademic Outcomes: A Systematic Review." *Campbell Systematic Reviews* 19 (3). https://www.ncbi.nlm.nih.gov/pmc/articles/PMC10406168/.

39 Fliesler, Nancy. 2023. "Babies and Screen Time: New Research Calls for Caution." *Boston Children's Hospital*. https://answers.childrenshospital.org/screen-time-infants/.

40 Schuman, David. 2023. "Minnesota Middle School Bans Cellphone Use, Yielding Surprising Results." *CBS News*. https://www.cbsnews.com/minnesota/news/maple-grove-middle-school-cellphone-ban/.

THE ENVIRONMENT

1 Branson-Potts, H. 2020. "Kids Rejoiced When School Reopened. Then Fire Left Many Students Homeless." *Los Angeles Times*. https://www.latimes.com/california/story/2020-09-12/slater-fire-northern-california.

2 Papanek, M. 2020. "USFS: Slater, Devil Fires Finally Contained, Closures Remain in Place." *KRCR*. https://krcrtv.com/north-coast-news/

eureka-local-news/us-forest-service-slater-devil-fires-contained-after-burning-nearly-170000-acres.

3   Metz, J. & Masteron, L. 2023. "What to Know about Wildfire Insurance." *Forbes Advisor.* https://www.forbes.com/advisor/homeowners-insurance/wildfires/#:~:text=More%20than%204.5%20million%20U.S.,the%20National%20Interagency%20Fire%20Center; 2022. "Wildfires and Acres." *National Interagency Fire Center.* https://www.nifc.gov/fire-information/statistics/wildfires.

4   Holm, S. M., M.D. Miller, and J.R. Balmes. 2021. "Health Effects of Wildfire Smoke in Children and Public Health Tools: A Narrative Review." *Journal of Exposure Science & Environmental Epidemiology 31.* https://doi.org/10.1038/s41370-020-00267-4.

5   2024. "Atrocious Air." *First Street.* https://firststreet.org/research-library/atrocious-air.

6   Barnard, C. 2021. "From Trout to Polar Bears: How the Environmental Movement Lost America." *The American Conservative.* https://www.theamerican-conservative.com/from-trout-to-polar-bears-how-the-environmental-movement-lost-america/.

7   M.G. Burgess et al. 2024. "Climate Change Opinion and Recent Presidential Elections." *Zenodo.* https://zenodo.org/records/10494414.

8   2019. "Bernie Sanders in Climate Change 'Population Control' Uproar." *BBC News.* https://www.bbc.com/news/world-us-canada-49601678.

9   Nordhaus, T., and S. Shah. 2022. "In Sri Lanka, Organic Farming Went Catastrophically Wrong." *Foreign Policy.* https://foreignpolicy.com/2022/03/05/sri-lanka-organic-farming-crisis/.

10   Karembu, M. 2017. "How European-Based NGOs Block Crop Biotechnology Adoption in Africa." *ISAAA AfriCenter.* https://africenter.isaaa.org/european-based-ngos-block-crop-biotechnology-adoption-africa/.

11   2024. "What to Do About Deer." *The Humane Society of the United States.* https://www.humanesociety.org/resources/what-do-about-deer.

12   Newburger, E. 2022. "California Bans the Sale of New Gas-Powered Cars by 2035." *CNBC.* https://www.cnbc.com/2022/08/25/california-bans-the-sale-of-new-gas-powered-cars-by-2035.html; Albeck-Ripka, L. 2022. "Amid Heat Wave, California Asks Electric Vehicle Owners to Limit Charging." *New York Times.* https://www.nytimes.com/2022/09/01/us/california-heat-wave-flex-alert-ac-ev-charging.html.

13   Wells, K. 2023. "China's Monopoly Over Critical Minerals." *Georgetown Security Studies Review.* https://georgetownsecuritystudiesreview.org/2023/06/01/chinas-monopoly-over-critical-minerals/.

14   2020. "One in Five UK Children Report Nightmares About Climate Change." *Reuters.* https://www.reuters.com/article/idUSL1N2AV1FF/#:~:text=March%203%20.

15 C. Hickman et al. 2021. "Climate Anxiety in Children and Young People and Their Beliefs About Government Responses to Climate Change: A Global Survey." *The Lancet Planetary Health* 5 (12). https://doi.org/10.1016/s2542-5196(21)00278-3.

16 Jenkins, L.M. 2020. "1 in 4 Childless Adults Say Climate Change Has Factored Into Their Reproductive Decisions." *Morning Consult.* https://pro.morning-consult.com/articles/adults-children-climate-change-polling.

17 Burke, E. 1899. "Reflections on the Revolution in France." *The Works of the Right Honorable Edmund Burke* 3.

18 C3 Solutions. (2023). *Free Economies Are Clean Economies.* https://www.c3solutions.org/policy-paper/free-economies-are-clean-economies-2023/foreword/.

19 Regan, S. 2019. "Socialism Is Bad for the Environment." *PERC.* https://www.perc.org/2019/05/17/socialism-is-bad-for-the-environment/.

20 Bernstam, M.S. 1991. *The Wealth of Nations and the Environment.* Institute of Economic Affairs.

21 Ostrom, E. 1990. *Governing the Commons: The Evolution of Institutions for Collective Action.* Cambridge University Press.

22 Tyrrell, P., and M. Pontifis. 2019. "New Data Bucks Conventional Wisdom on Free Markets and the Environment." Heritage Foundation. https://www.heritage.org/international-economies/commentary/new-data-bucks-conventionalwisdom-free-markets-and-the.

23 Tupy, M.L., and G.L. Pooley. 2022. *Superabundance: The Story of Population Growth, Innovation, and Human Flourishing on an Infinitely Bountiful Planet.* Cato Institute.

24 Lopez, N. 2023. "Feds Allow Diablo Canyon to Stay Open While Seeking 20-Year Extension." *CalMatters.* https://calmatters.org/environment/2023/03/diablo-canyon-nuclear-power-plant/.

25 Mothers for Nuclear. https://www.mothersfornuclear.org/.

26 Gibbs, A. 2023. "Pregnant Woman Poses With 'Nuclear Waste' to Prove Point About Radiation." *Newsweek.* https://www.newsweek.com/pregnant-woman-poses-nuclear-waste-prove-point-about-radiation-idaho-1809500.

FOREIGN POLICY

1 Bowman, Tom. 2011. "A Marine's Death, and the Family He Left Behind," *National Public Radio.* https://www.npr.org/2011/11/03/141954997/a-marines-death-and-the-family-he-left-behind.

² Bowman, Tom. 2011. "A Marine's Death, and the Family He Left Behind," *National Public Radio.* https://www.npr.org/2011/11/03/141954997/a-marines-death-and-the-family-he-left-behind.

³ Benen, Steve. 2012. "The Importance of a Pride Flag in Afghanistan." *NBC News.* https://www.nbcnews.com/news/world/importance-pride-flag-afghanistan-flna637359.

⁴ "2022 National Veteran Suicide Prevention Report." *Department of Veterans Affairs.* https://www.mentalhealth.va.gov/docs/data-sheets/2022/2022-National-Veteran-Suicide-Prevention-Annual-Report-FINAL-508.pdf.

⁵ "Cost of War Project," *Brown University.* https://watson.brown.edu/costsofwar/.

⁶ Novak, Lisa M. 2010. "Decade of Navy Personnel Cuts Hinders Readiness." *Stars and Stripes.* https://www.stripes.com/migration/report-decade-of-navy-personnel-cuts-hinders-current-readiness-1.107245.

⁷ Britzky, Haley. 2022. "The Army Knows Its Op-Tempo Is Unsustainable." *Task and Purpose.* https://taskandpurpose.com/news/army-training-rotations-optempo-budget/; Barnhill, Jennifer. 2023. "Why Divorce Is Particularly Hard on Military Families." *Military.com.* https://www.military.com/daily-news/opinions/2023/06/22/why-divorce-particularly-hard-military-families.html.

⁸ "2023 Blue Star Family Military Lifestyle Survey," Blue Star Families Association. https://bluestarfam.org/research/mfls-survey-release-2024/.

⁹ Vergun, David. 2023. "DOD Addresses Recruiting Shortfall Challenges." *DOD News.* https://www.defense.gov/News/News-Stories/Article/Article/3616786/dod-addresses-recruiting-shortfall-challenges/#:~:text=Ashish%20Vazirani%20said%20that%20during,recruiting%20environment%2C%22%20he%20said.

¹⁰ "Washington's Farewell Address, 1796." *George Washington's Mount Vernon,* https://www.mountvernon.org/education/primary-source-collections/primary-source-collections/article/washington-s-farewell-address-1796/.

¹¹ "July 4, 1821: Speech to the U.S. House of Representatives on Foreign Policy," *National Archives,* https://millercenter.org/the-presidency/presidential-speeches/july-4-1821-speech-us-house-representatives-foreign-policy.

¹² Ravid, Barak. 2023. "Scoop: U.S. to Send Artillery Shells to Israel Originally Destined for Ukraine." *Axios.* https://www.axios.com/2023/10/19/us-israel-artillery-shells-ukraine-weapons-gaza.

¹³ Schmitt, Eric. 2023. "Pentagon Sends U.S. Arms Stored in Israel to Ukraine." *New York Times.* https://www.nytimes.com/2023/01/17/us/politics/ukraine-israel-weapons.html.

POLICING

1   Kaste, Martin. 2019. "New Study Says White Police Officers Are Not
    More Likely to Shoot Minority Suspects." *NPR.* https://www.npr.
    org/2019/07/26/745731839/new-study-says-white-police-officers-are-not-
    more-likely-to-shoot-minority-suspects; Force Science Institute. 2016. "New
    Washington State University Study: Even Tired Cops Are More Hesitant to
    Shoot Black Suspects." *Police1.* https://www.police1.com/use-of-force/arti-
    cles/new-washington-state-university-study-even-tired-cops-are-more-hesi-
    tant-to-shoot-black-suspects-VsQPXHtPEhHhCOjZ/.

2   Lott, John R. and Carlisle E. Moody. 2021. "Do White Police Officers Unfairly
    Target Black Suspects?" *Economics, Law and Policy* 4 (2). https://papers.ssrn.
    com/sol3/papers.cfm?abstract_id=2870189; Lott, John R. Jr. 2018. "Police
    Officers Are Not Disproportionately Killing Black Men—Here Are the Facts."
    Townhall. https://townhall.com/columnists/johnrlottjr/2018/08/27/police-
    shootings-n2513363.

3   Force Science Institute. 2016. "New Washington State University Study: Even
    Tired Cops Are More Hesitant to Shoot Black Suspects." *Police1.* https://
    www.police1.com/use-of-force/articles/new-washington-state-university-
    study-even-tired-cops-are-more-hesitant-to-shoot-black-suspects-VsQPXHt-
    PEhHhCOjZ/.

4   Hoffman, Ari. 2023. "Exclusive: Teen Files Claim Against Seattle Over City's
    'Indifference' to Deadly CHAZ Autonomous Zone." *Post Millennial.* https://
    thepostmillennial.com/exclusive-teen-files-claim-against-seattle-over-citys-
    indifference-to-deadly-chaz-autonomous-zone.

5   Colen, Aaron. 2020. "Seattle Police Chief Says Rapes and Robberies Are
    Occurring in Chaz Area and Officers Can't Respond to Them." *Blaze Media.*
    https://www.theblaze.com/news/seattle-police-chief-violence-chaz; Hoff-
    man, Ari. 2023. "Breaking: Seattle Forced to Pay $3.6 Million in 2020 CHAZ
    Damages to Business Owners." *Post Millennial.* https://thepostmillennial.
    com/breaking-seattle-forced-to-pay-3-6-million-in-2020-autonomous-zone-
    damages-to-business-owners.

6   Hoffman, Ari. 2022. "Seattle Council Members Who Defunded Police Blame
    Department for Lack of Detectives to Investigate Sexual Assaults." *Post Millen-
    nial.* https://thepostmillennial.com/seattle-council-members-who-defunded-
    police-blame-department-for-lack-of-detectives-to-investigate-sexual-assaults.

7   Daviscourt, Katie. 2022. "'We Won't Be Coming': Washington State Police
    Reform Goes into Effect, Law Enforcement Warns of Consequences." *Post Mil-
    lennial.* https://thepostmillennial.com/we-wont-be-coming-washington-state-
    police-reform-goes-into-effect-law-enforcement-warns-of-consequences/.

8   Ziegler, Suzie. 2022. "911 Audio: Suspect Tells Dispatcher to Call Off
    Seattle PD Pursuit, Citing New Law." *Police1.* https://www.police1.com/

suspect-pursuit/articles/911-audio-suspect-tells-dispatcher-to-call-off-seattle-pd-pursuit-citing-new-law-3xTnDZEnCK1hOkt3/.

[9] Goodell, Emily. 2023. "WSP Ended Pursuit of Speeding Driver Near Ellensburg. An Hour Later, 2 Kids Were Killed in a Wrong-Way Crash Near Sunnyside." *AppleValleyNewsNow.com*. https://www.applevalleynewsnow.com/news/crime/wsp-ended-pursuit-of-speeding-driver-near-ellensburg-an-hour-later-2-kids-were-killed/article_7dcf0228-b89a-11ed-8b9d-337cb5340a3d.html.

[10] Meyers, Donald W. 2024. "Affidavit: Troopers Tried Four Times to Stop Driver Accused of Killing Two Children in I-82 Crash." *Yakima Herald-Republic*. https://www.yakimaherald.com/news/local/crime_and_courts/affidavit-troopers-tried-four-times-to-stop-driver-accused-of-killing-two-children-in-i/article_a4c3021e-bd52-11ed-8115-dfe44d5c6c2b.html.

[11] Davis, Brett. 2023. "Republican Lawmakers Pressure Sen. Dhingra on Police Pursuit Reform Bill." The Center Square. https://www.thecentersquare.com/washington/article_76ff02a0-9d05-11ed-aa2d-ab844e5ada31.html.

[12] Hoffman, Ari. 2023. "Seattle Police Ordered Not to Pursue Suspects as Part of 'Reform' Plans." *Post Millennial*. https://thepostmillennial.com/seattle-police-ordered-not-to-pursue-suspects-as-part-of-reform-plans.

[13] Hoffman, Ari. 2023. "Seattle to Pay out $1.9 Million to Family after Delayed Police Response Resulted in Fatal Cardiac Arrest." *Post Millennial*. https://thepostmillennial.com/seattle-to-pay-out-1-9-million-to-family-after-delayed-police-response-resulted-in-fatal-cardiac-arrest.

[14] Beekman, Daniel. 2022. "Former Seattle 911 Manager Says He Warned City about Deadly Dispatch Problem." *Seattle Times*. http://www.seattletimes.com/seattle-news/law-justice/former-seattle-911-manager-says-he-warned-city-about-deadly-dispatch-problem/.

[15] Hoffman, Ari. 2022. "Seattle Social Worker Slain by Client as City Council Further Defunds Police." *Post Millennial*. https://thepostmillennial.com/seattle-social-worker-slain-by-client-as-city-council-further-defunds-police.

[16] Hoffman, Ari. 2022. "Seattle Slashes Police Budget, Eliminates Homeless Program." *Post Millennial*. https://thepostmillennial.com/seattle-slashes-police-budget-eliminates-homeless-program.

[17] 2024. "Crime in Washington: 2024." *Washington State House Republicans*. https://houserepublicans.wa.gov/crime-in-wa/.

[18] Hoffman. 2022. "Seattle Teacher Politicizes School Shooting: 'If You Don't Vote Blue Today, F*ck You.'" *Post Millennial*. https://thepostmillennial.com/seattle-teacher-politicizes-school-shooting-if-you-dont-vote-blue-today-fck-you.

[19] Hoffman, Ari. 2022. "Teens Threatened by Gunman at Seattle Public School After Police Banned from Campus: Report." *Post Millennial*. https://thepostmillennial.com/teens-gunman-seattle-public-school#:~:text=Several%20

students%20at%20a%20public%20high%20school%20in,the%20
school%27s%20parking%20lots.%20%22You%20should%20flip%20out.

[20] Hilsenrath, Jon. 2020. "Homicide Spike Hits Most Large U.S. Cities." *Wall Street Journal.* https://www.wsj.com/articles/homicide-spike-cit-ies-chicago-newyork-detroit-us-crime-police-lockdown-coronavirus-pro-tests-11596395181.

[21] Peter Nickeas et al. 2021. "Defund the Police Encounters Resistance as Violent Crime Spikes." *CNN.* https://www.cnn.com/2021/05/25/us/defund-police-crime-spike/index.html.

[22] Elinson, Zusha et al. 2021. "Cities Reverse Defunding the Police amid Rising Crime," *WSJ.* www.wsj.com/articles/cities-reverse-defunding-the-police-amid-rising-crime-11622066307.

[23] Hoffman, Ari. 2023. "Exclusive: WA School District Forced to Hire off-Duty Cops After Removing Police and Getting Increased Threats of Violence." *Post Millennial.* https://thepostmillennial.com/exclusive-wa-school-district-forced-to-hire-off-duty-cops-after-removing-police-and-getting-increased-threats-of-violence.

[24] Hoffman, Ari. 2024. "Washington State Legislature Restores Police Pursuits, Parental Rights After Citizen-Backed Initiatives." *Post Millennial.* https://the-postmillennial.com/washington-state-legislature-restores-police-pursuits-par-ental-rights-after-citizen-backed-initiatives#google_vignette.

BORDER SECURITY AND IMMIGRATION

[1] Congressman French Hill. "Bill Clinton on Illegal Immigration at 1995 State of the Union." YouTube video. https://www.youtube.com/watch?v=1IrDrBs13oA.

[2] Brad Warthen. 2006. "Joe Biden at Rotary." YouTube video. https://www.youtube.com/watch?v=15djRzWG3_0.

[3] Barack Obama. 2006. "Obama Sobre 'Secure Fence Act." C-SPAN video. https://www.c-span.org/video/?c4589456/user-clip-obama-sobre-secure-fence-act-2006.

[4] 2024. "Immigration Benefits All Americans and Strengthens the Economy." *fwd.us.* https://www.fwd.us/news/americans-and-immigration/.

[5] Watson, Tara. 2024. "How Immigration Reforms Could Bolster Social Security and Medicare Solvency and Address Direct Care Workforce Issues." *Brookings.* https://www.brookings.edu/articles/how-immigration-reforms-could-bolster-social-security-and-medicare-solvency-and-address-direct-care-workforce-issues/.

6   Editorial Board. 2022."The U.S. Needs More Immigrants and More Babies."
    Washington Post. https://www.washingtonpost.com/opinions/2022/02/07/
    us-needs-more-immigrants-more-babies/.

7   Following the government's COVID-19 response of shutting down busi-
    nesses, the Left has also argued that increased immigration is essential to fill
    the labor demand generated by businesses reopening. Yurkevich, Vanessa.
    2022. "America Needs Immigrants to Solve its Labor Shortage." *CNN.* https://
    www.cnn.com/2022/12/22/economy/immigration-jobs/index.html. How-
    ever, employment for native-born workers is millions below its prepandemic
    trend. Meanwhile, foreign-born employment is 3.3 million above its prepan-
    demic level. Antoni, E.J. 2024. "Biden's Swiss Cheese Labor Market." *Heritage
    Foundation.* https://www.heritage.org/jobs-and-labor/commentary/bidens-
    swiss-cheese-labor-market.

8   Omar, Erik. 2020. "Racism and the U.S. Immigration Sys-
    tem." *Immigrant Legal Center.* https://www.immigrantlc.org/
    racism-and-the-us-immigration-system/.

9   Bryant, Erica. 2023. "The Immigration System Is Racist; Solutions Exist." *Vera.*
    https://www.vera.org/news/the-immigration-system-is-racist-solutions-exist.

10 2024. "Rules for Radicals." *The Citizen's Handbook.* https://www.citizenshand-
    book.org/rules.html.

11 Dierker, Benjamin R. 2018. "How The Left's War on Words Manipulates
    Your Mind." *The Federalist.* https://thefederalist.com/2018/05/01/lefts-war-
    words-
    manipulates-mind/.

12 Rose, Joel. 2021. "Immigration Agencies Ordered Not to Use Term 'Illegal
    Alien' Under New Biden Policy." *NPR.* https://www.npr.org/2021/04/
    19/988789487/immigration-agencies-ordered-not-to-use-term-illegal-
    alien-under-new-biden-polic#:~:text=Evan%20Vucci%2FAP-,President%20
    Biden%20signs%20an%20executive%20order%20on,February%20in%20
    the%20Oval%20Office.&text=Evan%20Vucci%2FAP-,The%20Biden%20
    administration%20is%20ordering%20U.S.%20immigration%20enforce-
    ment%20agencies%20to,noncitizen%22%20and%20%22integration.%22;
    Trinko, Katrina. 2024. "The Left's Long War on Using 'Illegal Aliens.'" *The
    Daily Signal.* The Left's Long War on Using 'Illegal Aliens' (dailysignal.com).

13 Sacchetti, Maria. 2021. "ICE, CBP to Stop Using 'Illegal Alien' and 'Assimila-
    tion' Under New Biden Administration Order." *Washington Post.* https://
    www.washingtonpost.com/immigration/illegal-alien-assimilation/2021/
    04/19/9a2f878e-9ebc-11eb-b7a8-014b14aeb9e4_story.html.

14 Never stopping their word games, the Left quickly replaced "noncitizen" with
    "asylum seeker" to paint all illegal aliens coming to the U.S. as more sympa-
    thetic. More recently, the White House and its parrot media have started using
    the word "newcomers" to refer to aliens. 2024. "Biden-Harris Administration

Calls on Congress to Immediately Pass the Bipartisan National Security Agreement." *The White House.* https://www.whitehouse.gov/briefing-room/statements-releases/2024/02/04/fact-sheet-biden-harris-administration-calls-on-congress-to-immediately-pass-the-bipartisan-national-security-agreement/.

15 Typical scenarios for receiving immigration parole into the U.S. include emergency surgery and testifying in a criminal trial.

16 The most egregious "pathway" that the Biden administration has created allows aliens outside the U.S. to avoid the visa process by using a Customs and Border Protection (CBP) Mobile One application to schedule their parole appointment at a port of entry inside the U.S. "CBP One Mobile Application." *U.S. Customs and Border Protection.* https://www.cbp.gov/about/mobile-apps-directory/cbpone. Then, inadmissible aliens fly into the U.S. at designated airports and CBP paroles them into the U.S. "Processes for Cubans, Haitians, Nicaraguans, and Venezuelans." *U.S. Citizenship and Immigration Services.* https://www.uscis.gov/CHNV.

17 2023. "Secretary Antony J. Blinken and Secretary of Homeland Security Alejandro Mayorkas at a Joint Press Availability." *U.S. Department of State.* https://www.state.gov/secretary-antony-j-blinken-and-secretary-of-homeland-security-alejandro-mayorkas-at-a-joint-press-availability/.

18 Unaccompanied Alien Child Protection Act of 2000, S. 3117, 106th Congress (2000).

19 William Wilberforce Trafficking Victims Protection Reauthorization Act of 2008 (TVPRA), Public Law 110–457, 122 Stat. 5044 (2008).

20 TVPRA sec. 235(a)(1).

21 Children from Canada and Mexico are returned to their home country.

22 Stimson, Charles, Hans von Spakovsky and Lora Ries. 2020 "Assessing the Trump Administration's Immigration Policies." *Heritage Foundation.* https://www.heritage.org/sites/default/files/2020-06/SR233_0.pdf.

23 TVPRA sec. 235.

24 "Total Unaccompanied Alien Children Apprehensions by Month - FY 2010-FY 2019." *U.S. Border Patrol.* https://www.cbp.gov/sites/default/files/assets/documents/2020-Jan/U.S.%20Border%20Patrol%20Total%20Monthly%20UAC%20Apprehensions%20by%20Sector%20%28FY%202010%20-%20FY%202019%29_0.pdf.

25 "Total Unaccompanied Alien Children Apprehensions by Month - FY 2010-FY 2019." *U.S. Border Patrol.* https://www.cbp.gov/sites/default/files/assets/documents/2020-Jan/U.S.%20Border%20Patrol%20Total%20Monthly%20UAC%20Apprehensions%20by%20Sector%20%28FY%202010%20-%20FY%202019%29_0.pdf.

26 "Total Unaccompanied Alien Children Apprehensions by Month - FY 2010-FY 2019." *U.S. Border Patrol.* https://www.cbp.gov/sites/default/files/assets/

documents/2020-Jan/U.S.%20Border%20Patrol%20Total%20Monthly%20
UAC%20Apprehensions%20by%20Sector%20%28FY%202010%20-%20
FY%202019%29_0.pdf.

27 "Total Unaccompanied Alien Children Apprehensions by Month - FY 2010-
    FY 2019." *U.S. Border Patrol.* https://www.cbp.gov/sites/default/files/assets/
    documents/2020-Jan/U.S.%20Border%20Patrol%20Total%20Monthly%20
    UAC%20Apprehensions%20by%20Sector%20%28FY%202010%20-%20
    FY%202019%29_0.pdf.
28 "Nationwide Encounters." *U.S. Customs and Border Protection.* https://www.
    cbp.gov/newsroom/stats/nationwide-encounters.
29 "Nationwide Encounters." *U.S. Customs and Border Protection.* https://www.
    cbp.gov/newsroom/stats/nationwide-encounters.
30 Singman, Brooke. 2021. "Biden DHS Secretary Promises US Will Not Expel
    Unaccompanied Minors." *Fox News.* https://www.foxnews.com/politics/
    biden-dhs-secretary-promises-us-will-not-expel-unaccompanied-minors.
31 "Statement by Secretary Mayorkas on U.S. Strategy for Immigration." *U.S.
    Department of Homeland Security.* https://www.dhs.gov/news/2021/07/29/
    statement-secretary-mayorkas-us-strategy-immigration.
32 Helsel, Phil. 2021. "Two Toddlers Dropped from 14-Foot Border Barrier into
    U.S., Officials Say." *NBC News.* https://www.nbcnews.com/news/us-news/
    two-toddlers-dropped-14-foot-border-barrier-u-s-officials-n1262701.
33 Ortiz, Fernie. 2023. *Border Report.* https://www.borderreport.com/immigra-
    tion/video-smuggler-abandons-1-year-old-guatemalan-boy-on-riverbank-on-
    border/.
34 "Ernst Pushes for Fingerprinting of Migrant Minors
    to Combat Child Recycling." *Joni Ernst, U.S. Sena-
    tor.* https://www.ernst.senate.gov/news/press-releases/
    ernst-pushes-for-fingerprinting-of-migrant-minors-to-combat-child-recycling.
35 Real America's Voice (@RealAmVoice). 2023. X post. https://x.com/
    RealAmVoice/status/1689050216945668096.
36 In 2002, the House Democrats successfully sought to transfer responsibility
    for unaccompanied alien children from the Justice Department's Immigra-
    tion and Naturalization Service (INS) to the Office of Refugee Resettlement
    (ORR) in the Department of Health and Human Services (HHS). Homeland
    Security Act of 2002, Pub. Law 107-296, 116 Stat. 2135, sec. 462(b) (2002).
    The Left argued that unaccompanied children would receive safer treatment
    from HHS. This transfer of immigration functions, however, further frag-
    mented the immigration bureaucracy across several federal agencies, including
    the Departments of Homeland Security, Justice, State, and Labor. This
    scattered model has resulted in dysfunction among the departments, blame
    shifting, and children falling through the bureaucratic cracks.

37   Becerra told staff regarding discharging unaccompanied children, "If Henry
      Ford had seen this in his plants, he would have never become famous and rich.
      This is not the way you do an assembly line." Dreier, Hannah. 2023. "Alone
      and Exploited, Migrant Children Work Brutal Jobs Across the U.S." *New York
      Times.* https://www.nytimes.com/2023/02/25/us/unaccompanied-mi-
      grant-child-workers-exploitation.html.
38   2022. "Governor Ron DeSantis Takes Additional Actions to Protect Floridians
      From Biden's Border Crisis." https://www.flgov.com/2022/06/17/gover-
      nor-ron-desantis-takes-additional-actions-to-protect-floridians-
      from-bidens-border-crisis/.
39   2023. "21st SW Grand Jury Releases Shocking Report." *Office of Attorney
      General, State of Florida.* https://www.myfloridalegal.com/newsrelease/
      21st-sw-grand-jury-releases-shocking-report.
40   2023. "Third Presentment of the Twenty-First Statewide Grand Jury
      Regarding Unaccompanied Alien Children (UAC)." *Supreme Court of
      Florida,* Case No.: SC22-796, March 29, 2023. https://acis-api.flcourts.gov/
      courts/68f021c4-6a44-4735-9a76-5360b2e8af13/cms/case/651d8f68-f322-
      4cd0-831f-74dc9b0d77a8/docketentrydocuments/8437d6e2-1c46-4575-bd2
      1-47de83302c61.
41   Dreier, Hannah. 2023. "Alone and Exploited, Migrant Children Work
      Brutal Jobs Across the U.S." *New York Times.* https://www.nytimes.
      com/2023/02/25/us/unaccompanied-migrant-child-workers-exploitation.
      html.
42   Foreign gang members regularly exploit these foolish TVPRA policies and
      procedures as well. Sometimes teenagers themselves, members of danger-
      ous groups easily enter the U.S. as unaccompanied minors and go on to
      inflict crimes—and even death—on too many Americans and migrants. To
      highlight one example of many, a seventeen-year-old MS-13 gang member
      sexually assaulted and strangled a twenty-year-old autistic woman to death
      in Aberdeen, Maryland, in July 2022, three months after entering the U.S.
      illegally as a UAC. 2023. "House Judiciary Report Faults Biden Admin for
      Release of Alleged MS-13 Member Now Charged with Murder." *U.S. House of
      Representatives Committee on the Judiciary.* https://judiciary.house.gov/media/
      in-thenews/house-judiciary-report-faults-biden-admin-release-alleged-ms-13-
      member-now.
43   In addition to claiming to protect children, the Left also wields "family
      reunification" as an all-purpose rationale to have unaccompanied children
      join family already in the U.S., or have family come to the U.S. to join their
      unaccompanied child they sent ahead of them. "Family Reunification Parole
      Processes." *U.S. Citizenship and Immigration Services.* https://www.uscis.gov/
      FRP. Regardless, for the Left, reunification only can occur here in the U.S.
      They do not advocate for reuniting unaccompanied children with their family

back in their home country. This is the giveaway—section 235 of the TVPRA is not about protecting unaccompanied children. Rather, it is another pathway to have more people immigrate into the U.S., using children as bait.

The Left also regularly advocates to legalize, or provide amnesty to, millions of illegal aliens living in the U.S., always starting with children. For over two decades, the Left has pushed to legalize illegal aliens who entered the U.S. as minors. Fitz, Marshall. 2010. "Myth vs. Fact: The DREAM Act." *Center for American Progress.* https://www.americanprogress.org/article/myth-vs-fact-the-dream-act/. The advocates' argument has been that such aliens came into the U.S. through no fault of their own; their parents brought them. Soon, however, the Left will expand their amnesty demands to include unaccompanied children. Advocates will argue that these illegal aliens deserve green cards because they entered the U.S. unaccompanied. This shows that the Left uses kids—both accompanied and unaccompanied—to achieve more immigration outside of the Immigration and Nationality Act's numerous and generous legal immigration avenues. Furthermore, this advocacy to legalize unaccompanied alien children would complete the Left's planned life cycle, as designed by section 235 to entice unaccompanied child border crossings. This is a perverse system.

44   Rector, Robert. 2007. "Look to Milton: Open Borders and the Welfare State." *Heritage Foundation.* https://www.heritage.org/immigration/commentary/look-milton-open-borders-and-the-welfare-state.

45   2024. "Department of Homeland Security Announces $300 Million in Direct Funding to Communities Receiving Migrants and $340 Million for a New Competitive Awards Process." *U.S. Department of Homeland Security.* https://www.dhs.gov/news/2024/04/12/department-homeland-security-announces-300-million-direct-funding-communities.

46   Vinicky, Amanda. 2023. "Brandon Johnson Joins Mayors of New York and Denver in Calling for Federal Support for Migrants While Pushing Back Against 'Reckless Approach' in Texas." *WTTW News.* https://news.wttw.com/2023/12/27/brandon-johnson-joins-mayors-new-york-and-denver-calling-federal-support-migrants-while.

47   Oversight Project (@OversighPR). 2023. X post. https://twitter.com/OversightPR/status/1724816264370311421.

48   Bowman, Rachel. 2024. "Denver City Council Approves Defund the Police Cuts - the Largest Ever in City's Budget - to Pay for Migrant Crisis." *Daily Mail.* https://www.dailymail.co.uk/news/article-13323941/Denver-city-council-approves-police-budget-cuts-migrant-crisis.html.

49   Rector, Robert. 2023. "The Net Fiscal Costs of Low-Skilled and Illegal Immigration for the U.S. Taxpayer." *U.S. Senate Budget Committee.* https://www.budget.senate.gov/imo/media/doc/rector_testimony_913.pdf.

50   "U.S. Debt Clock." usdebtclock.org.

51   8 U.S.C. § 1182.

52   8 U.S.C. § 1227.

53   2024. "Former CBP Chief on LOOPcast: 'What is Christian' About
     Biden Border Policies?" *Catholic Vote*. https://catholicvote.org/
     former-cbp-chief-on-loopcast-what-is-christian-about-biden-border-policies/.

54   "Candidate Biden Calls on Illegal Immigrants to Surge the Border." YouTube
     video. https://www.youtube.com/watch?v=rYwLYMPLYbo.

55   Vaughan, Jessica. 2024. "Biden Border Policies Are Working Fine — For
     the Cartels." *Center for Immigration Studies*. https://cis.org/Vaughan/
     Biden-Border-Policies-Are-Working-Fine-Cartels.

56   2023. "US-Mexico Border World's Deadliest Migration Land Route." *United
     Nations International Organization of Migration*. https://www.iom.int/news/
     us-mexico-border-worlds-deadliest-migration-land-route#:~:text=Gene-
     va%2FBerlin%2FSan%20Jos%C3%A9%20%E2%80%93,for%20migrants%20
     worldwide%20on%20record.

57   "Border Rescues and Mortality Data." *U.S. Customs and Border Protection*.
     https://www.cbp.gov/newsroom/stats/border-rescues-and-mortality-data.

58   "Border Rescues and Mortality Data." *U.S. Customs and Border Protection*.
     https://www.cbp.gov/newsroom/stats/border-rescues-and-mortality-data.
     Biden's policies have brought chaos not just to the border, but to every state in
     the U.S. Through the assistance of government-paid NGOs, nearly ten million
     inadmissible aliens have settled throughout the country with no advance
     notice to those states or localities. Schools have had to scramble to find addi-
     tional space, teachers, and resources to educate new foreign students, many
     of whom speak little to no English. Hospital waiting rooms and emergency
     rooms are overcrowded as the uninsured use hospitals for their primary care.
     A Yuma, Arizona, hospital reported that it had to provide over $26 million in
     uncompensated care to illegal aliens in one year. Hanauer, Mike. 2023. "To
     Keep Hospitals Open, We Need to Close Our Border." *Washington Times*.
     https://www.washingtontimes.com/news/2023/apr/10/to-keep-hospitals-
     open-we-need-to-close-our-border/. Meanwhile, Americans in these commu-
     nities receive less quality education, must delay their medical treatments, and
     pay more taxes for resources given to a growing illegal alien population.

59   2024. "Attorney General Miyares Challenges Biden Administration on Missing
     Migrant Children." *Office of the Attorney General of Virginia*. https://www.oag.
     state.va.us/media-center/news-releases/2697-february-29-2024-attorney-gen-
     eral-miyares-challenges-biden-administration-on-missing-migrant-children.

60   After receiving no response from Secretary Becerra, U.S. Representative
     Morgan Griffith (R-VA) introduced a bill requiring ORR to notify local
     schools and welfare agencies when placing unaccompanied children with
     sponsors. Unaccompanied Minor Placement Notification Act, 118th

Congress, 2d Session, https://www.congress.gov/bill/118th-congress/
house-bill/7854/text?s=1&r=1&q=%7B%22search%22%3A%22Unaccom-
panied+Minor+Placement+Notification+Act+%28H.R.+7854%29%22
%7D.

61 Staff. 2023. "Governor Ron DeSantis Signs Strongest Anti-Illegal Immigration
Legislation in the Country to Combat Biden's Border Crisis." https://www.
flgov.com/2023/05/10/governor-ron-desantis-signs-strongest-anti-illegal-im-
migration-legislation-in-the-country-to-combat-bidens-border-crisis/.

COVER CREDIT

1924us, run by Christian Watson and his wife Elle-May, is a small branding and creative studio focused on preserving timeless methods of creativity.

Christian Watson is an outspoken critic of pornography, abortion, and modern day trafficking. A former addict himself, he uses his platform to highlight projects and causes that further the betterment and preservation of a civil humanity.

He joined this project in the hopes that his skills could expand access to the knowledge within the cover. A father himself, he understands the necessity of looking after future generations and guiding them toward progress.

The artwork is meant to convey a triumphant child standing atop the Capitol building a striking visual that conveys our children as being the most important priority. With a faded flag gradient mixed in, the hope was to achieve a politically strong message while affirming appreciation for the country we belong to—even amidst difficult times.

EDITOR, KATY FAUST

Katy Faust is Founder and President of Them Before Us, a global children's rights nonprofit and the co-author of the book of the same title. She publishes and speaks widely on why marriage and family are matters of justice for children. Her articles have appeared in *Newsweek, USA Today, The Federalist, Public Discourse, WORLD Magazine, Washington Examiner, The American Mind,*

and *The American Conservative*. She is on the advisory board for the Alliance for Responsible Citizenship. Katy helped design the teen edition of CanaVox which studies sex, marriage, and relationships from a natural law perspective. She and her co-author detailed their philosophy of worldview transmission in *Raising Conservative Kids in a Woke City*. *Pro-Child Politics* is her third book. Katy and her husband are raising their four children in Seattle.

▀ EDITOR, EVAN MYERS

Evan Myers is a husband and father who works as an editor in Washington, D.C. He attended Furman University in Greenville, South Carolina, and is a proud native of Birmingham, Alabama.

▀ EDITOR, HOWE WHITMAN III

Howe Whitman III is Associate Editor at *National Affairs*. His writing has appeared in *First Things, The New Atlantis, The American Conservative, American Compass, Public Discourse*, and *Providence*. He has written about such topics as masculinity, college football, online vitalism, technocracy, and the American Puritans.